MORNINGS

WITH

Mom

A Daily Devotional

Barbara Lassman

Mornings with Mom
©2021 Barbara Lassman

ISBN: 978-1-09839-670-1

FOREWORD

In March of 2020, the Covid-19 pandemic brought the United States, along with the rest of the world, to a surreal standstill as national emergencies were declared and "stay at home" orders issued. What felt like an initial and irrational overreaction, or even a politically charged stratagem, became something very real as skyrocketing cases, hospitalizations, and deaths took center stage. By the end of March there were more than 200,000 documented cases in the United States and over 5,000 deaths. Within 18 months, those numbers would be dwarfed by nearly 200 million confirmed cases worldwide and 4.1 million deaths. Those numbers and mutating variants are still growing as of this publishing.

Shelter in place orders issued that March shut down businesses, closed offices, schools, daycares, churches, restaurants, clubs, canceled social events, entertainment productions, crippled social services, healthcare facilities, and mental health assistance, along with support groups everywhere. Covid-19 shut down virtually everything. The entire world came to an eerie halt and the vast majority of us were left at home, devoid of human contact, restricted to interaction with those living in our houses and apartments. Sometimes that felt fortunate, other times not so much! For those of us who live alone it was a lonely and isolated time. For all of us, it was a difficult time. The world had changed and would never be the same. Change causes fear, distress, anxiety, stress, resistance, and confusion. Those are the best words I can use to describe how I felt and am certain how we all felt to some extent. None of those feelings are good, none of those feelings are healthy, all those feelings typically manifest themselves as harmful behaviors. Alcohol and drug use was up 34% over the previous year, crime increased, domestic abuse swelled, depression abounded, relationships suffered, mental and physical health diminished, eating disorders were exacerbated, and general apathy and confusion set in. It was a PTSD type reaction that was very reminiscent of the days following the events of 9/11. That same hopeless, helpless, fearful feeling that no one was safe and there was no one to count on, no one to look to for guidance, no one to trust, and certainly no one to give us comfort, peace, and hope.

The Covid-19 pandemic was the same. There was no one we could trust, rely on, believe in, or look towards for guidance, direction, comfort, peace, or hope.

The politicians were pushing their own partisan agendas, the doctors were baffled, speculative at best, daily reversing course and guidance on safety protocols. Misinformation abounded and how to best manage the pandemic created a bitter polarization across the country. The news media was hyping the situation for ratings and the pharmaceutical companies were bickering over remedies while the vaccine makers rushed a skeptical product to market without anything close to a fully vetted trial or oversight process. Those we tend to rely on were floundering, searching for answers, while the rest of us watched our families and friends get sick, become hospitalized, and sometimes die. There was no one to trust, nothing concrete to hold on to, and nothing that made any of us think, "It's going to be ok. I'm going to be ok". The fight, flight, or freeze response kicks in during these situations. Some froze and were paralyzed, others took flight into themselves, burying their heads in the sand, ignoring reality, and a few fought. One of them would be my mom.

On a March morning, sitting at the kitchen table with a coffee, I got an email at 6:00 am …………………………

It was from my mom, and it started with a Bible verse from Nehemiah. *"This day is holy to our Lord, do not grieve, for the joy of the Lord is your strength"*. Kind of forgot about Him! I'm looking to our country's leaders, our doctors, our experts, the media, friends and family, anyone but God for my strength! Her one-page email included a few more Bible verses along with her interpretations of those versus and some insightful commentary. I replied with a "thank you for sending and have a great week" but didn't give much more thought to it. I was too worried about what was going on in the world!

Another one came the next day at 6:00 am. Same format, different versus, meaningful insights, same cup of coffee. Always relevant, positive, and uplifting. I noticed the distribution list. Mostly family members, but a few friends.

I got one the next day at 6:00 am and everyday thereafter. I noticed the distribution list getting larger. Apparently, mom had decided to put her trust in the Lord during this pandemic and had committed to religiously sending out her morning daily devotional. I didn't read them all the first few months, but repetition creates habit and after a while, I was waiting for my daily dose of sanity, of strength, and a reminder of where my faith and trust should lie.

My attitude changed, my outlook improved, my fear and anxiety began to disappear, and a peace returned. Someone to rely on. God and a persistent mother, whose insistence to stay the course never wavered. I told friends and neighbors and started forwarding the daily emails to them. She never gave up, despite not knowing who and how her daily emails were impacting others. She just kept sending them.

365 days later, an entire year without a missed morning email, I felt called to formally memorialize her devotionals in distributable print, making her Covid ministry available to the world through its publication. "Mornings with Mom" was born! Not just to speak the Word of God into others' lives, but to create a well-deserved legacy for a mom that would live on beyond her years. A tribute, not just to her, her tireless faith, commitment, and dedication, but most importantly to her God, my God, and our God.

We're all incredibly proud of mom, she has always been a steadfast Christian, strong in her faith, with a trust in the Lord that I sometimes have trouble understanding and worry that I will never achieve. Her commitment to God's Word, and ability to live according to it, has been an incredible example that warrants emulation. An ideal for all to aspire. Practice makes perfect, repetition creates habit, and dedication to scripture draws us closer to God. She may have been doing it for 60 years, but it's never too late for anyone to start.

We pray this devotional speaks to you the exact message God needs you to hear on the day you choose to read it. That it brings you comfort, peace, and joy as you pour a cup of coffee, take a few quiet morning minutes to be with the Lord, and helps you remember with Whom and where your trust should lie.

Mike Lassman

Table of Contents

All scripture is either from The Holy Bible, New International Version, NIV or The English Standard Version 2016, ESV

A MOMENT OF GRACE

DAY 1

God's grace is the free and unmerited favor of God as manifested in the salvation of sinners and the bestowal of blessing. Grace is the love of God shown to the unlovely; the peace of God given to the restless. Grace is love that cares and stoops and rescues.

To show us a moment of grace, I have chosen to focus on the word *"Selah"* which is used seventy-four times in the Bible. It is used seventy-one times in Psalms and three times in Habakkuk.

Selah gives us an opportunity to take a moment away from this crazy life we are living and consider the immense mysteries and wonders of God. It is just beyond our full understanding. It means to pause and reflect.

The first time the word *Selah* is used is in **Psalm 3:1-3 which says, *O Lord, how many are my foes. Many are rising against me; many are saying of my soul, there is no salvation for him in God. Selah***

Do you know people who are saying, "Where is God?" Are you secretly thinking the same thing? Where is God in any crisis? Well, He is right in the middle of it. He knows what He is doing. He desires that we turn toward Him rather than away from Him. Could it be that we are being separated from the things of this world, so that we can draw closer to Him? He is as close as we will allow Him to be. So today, spend a *Selah* moment with Him. Stop and reflect upon who He is and what He has done in your life.

It is so hard to be quiet and just sit still. Even when I am watching a great show on TV, I am up and down every commercial. I do not believe I would be a very good monk. I am wondering if I have missed a great many things the Lord was trying to tell me, because I cannot sit still. Maybe it isn't His fault I so often wonder where He is. Maybe it is mine.

"Selah!"

DAY 2

"Selah!" Take a moment to pause and reflect. Stop, look, and listen. The Lord has something very important to say. Maybe this is the day you will truly hear His voice. But you must stop, look, and listen.

The first *Selah* or the first stop in our Christian walk is to become a Christian. **Acts 16:31 says, *Believe in the Lord Jesus, and you will be saved, you and your household.*** Let's take a minute to thank God for our salvation.

The second *Selah* is **Psalm 3:3-4. *But you, O Lord are a shield about me, my glory, and the lifter of my head. I cried aloud to the Lord, and he answered me from his holy hill. Selah***

Today we definitely need a shield around us. He has promised as we cry out to Him that He will answer, and He will place the shield of faith around us.

Mark 11:24 says, *Whatever you ask in prayer, believe that you have received it, and it will be yours.*

Philippians 4:6-7 says, *Do not be anxious about anything, but in everything by prayer and supplication with thanksgiving let your requests be made known to God. And the peace of God, which surpasses all understanding, will guard your hearts and your minds in Christ Jesus.* (no anxiety plus peace)

1 Thessalonians 5:16-18 says, *Rejoice always, pray without ceasing, give thanks in all circumstances.* It seems there are some conditions to answered prayer. We must believe. We must give thanks even before we see the answer and when the circumstances aren't to our liking, we still must trust God and rejoice.

My Christian walk has been a steady but slow process. I think I was saved as a young child. I continued to be saved as a teenager. I was convicted as a young adult and today I am sold out. Was I saved as a child? "Yes", but salvation is not a one-time step. It is line upon line and precept upon precept. I am so glad!

"Selah!"

DAY 3

"Selah" pause and listen to what God has to say to you today. He does not speak collectively, but individually to each of us, because He loves us and wants a personal relationship with each of us.

Psalm 3:5-7 speaks of the enemies that have set themselves up against us. But God says in verse 8, ***Salvation belongs to the Lord; your blessing be on your people.*** *Selah*

What enemies are we fighting today? We might begin with the enemy of "fear". ***But God has not given us a spirit of fear but of power, love, and a sound mind.*** **(2 Timothy 1:7)**

So, salvation from fear belongs to the Lord. We do not have to fight it alone.

Then we have the enemy of "need", ***But God shall supply all our needs according to his riches.*** **(Philippians 4:19)**

So, salvation from need belongs to the Lord. We do not have to fight it alone.

What about the enemy of "isolation and separation"? Many times, we feel alone or lonely. But God says, ***I will never leave you nor forsake you.*** **(Deuteronomy 31:6.)**

Finally, we have the enemy at our gate whispering, "loss, loss". But God has said, ***Be strong and courageous. Do not fear or be in dread for it is the Lord your God who goes with you.*** **(Deuteronomy 31:6)**

Salvation from fear, need, isolation, separation, and loss belong to the Lord! Yea!

Over the years I have experienced all of the above and I am sure you have too. My question to myself is, "What have I done about it?" Have I been victorious, or have I slid under the covers moaning and groaning? Guilty on all accounts!

"Selah!"

DAY 4

So far, we have seen that salvation comes from God. *There is no other name by which we can be saved.* (Acts 4:12)

The one who hears, and answers prayers is God alone. He says if we will call upon Him, He will answer us. *Every good and every perfect gift is from above, coming down from the Father of lights, with whom there is no variation or shadow due to change.* (James 1:17)

God now attacks the root below the fruit. He asks us to look deeply into ourselves. He is willing to be our answer, but are we willing to admit there is a problem?

Psalm 4:2 says, O men how long shall my honor be turned into shame? How long will you love vain words and seek after lies? Selah

The question is, "How long?" How long will we seek after fleshly pleasures above a personal relationship with our Lord? How long will we be ruled by the ruler of this world? How long will we listen to the air waves instead of getting into the Word of God and finding out the truth, because it is the truth that will set us free.

I believe we are in the middle of a wakeup call from God. But He has promised, *I called to the Lord, who is worthy of praise, and have been saved from my enemies.* (2 Samuel 22:4) What or who is your enemy today? Are you calling on the Lord, or are you listening to the world and entering into fear and unbelief?

I am so thankful that God gives most of us time to grow up before He takes us home. If He had called me when I was young, I am not sure I would have made it. Looking back over my life, there were so many times I made the wrong choices; so many times, I stepped out of His will; so many times, I wished He would leave me alone and let me do my own thing. But I had a praying grandmother who was my hound dog to heaven. Today I am so grateful that she and God never gave up.

"Selah!"

DAY 5

Be angry and do not sin; ponder in your own hearts on your beds and be silent. Selah **(Psalm 4:4)**

Anger is a strong feeling of annoyance, displeasure, or hostility, which leads me to this question. Are you angry today? Are you angry because you feel God is unfair? Are you angry because your schedule has been disturbed? Are you angry because your finances are in jeopardy? Are you angry because God could have prevented the situation you are in, etc.? Are you angry?

Is there a chance God has a purpose in all of this? I am not saying God causes our trials, but that He can use these times to bring healing to our families, healing to our community and healing to our country.

Anger not only affects us but those around us. It affects our health. It affects our friendships. It affects our marriages. It affects our jobs. Anger is a losing battle.

It is time to stop, look, and listen to each other. It is time to call a friend we have offended. It is time to intercede for each other. It is time to look within ourselves, and then look outside ourselves to see what God has in store for us and others. It is time to stop being angry and ponder in our hearts the goodness of God and those around us. It is time to be silent.

For everything there is a season, and a time for every matter under heaven. **(Ecclesiastics 3:1)** Let's make this a season of forgiving!

Families are so different. Our family is full of originality. We have mullers, we have slackers, we have achievers, we have explorers, and we have tick booms. God has such a sense of humor. I am sure He was laughing the whole time He created us. He must have said, "Let's just see how they can learn to get along." Believe me it hasn't been easy, but we have done it. There is great love in our family, and we enjoy being together. God is good!

"Selah!"

DAY 6

If I have repaid my friend with evil or plundered my enemy without cause, let the enemy pursue my soul and overtake it, and let him trample my life to the ground and lay my glory in the dust. Selah (Psalm 4:4-5)

Ouch! This is not a good Selah! Maybe we should skip this one and move on to one that is more pleasant. However, this is the next place to pause and think! So here we go. Is there anyone you are angry with? Is there anyone you owe an apology to? Are you holding a grudge in your heart that keeps you from truly feeling free? The question then is, "Is it worth it?"

Matthew 5:23-24 says, *If you are offering your gift at the altar and there remember that your brother has something against you, leave your gift there before the altar and go. First be reconciled to your brother, and then come and offer your gift.*

James 4:16 says, *Where jealousy and selfish ambition exist, there will be disorder and every vile practice.*

1 John 4:11 says, If *God so loved us, we also ought to love one another.*

God is not speaking to the unbeliever, but to those who know Him. Let's take a moment and ask the Lord if there is any evil within us? Do we need to call someone and make amends? Do we need to repair a relationship or just strengthen those that are a little frayed? Let's do it today, so that our prayers will have a straight line to heaven.

I have always had a tick boom temper. The minute I have had my say I am over it. This is good for me, but it is bad for those around me. I am sure I have hurt many people without realizing it, because I explode and then walk on. I believe in generational curses, and I think I have handed this down to my youngest daughter and granddaughter. Lord forgive me!

"Selah!"

DAY 7

"Selah!" Pause and reflect. Take time to meditate on God's word.

Psalm 9:15-16 says, *The nations have sunk in the pit that they made; in the net that they hid, their own foot has been caught. The Lord has made himself known; he has executed judgment; the wicked are snared in the work of their own hands.* **Higgaijon.** *(no idea what that word means) Selah*

In the past couple of decades, we have taken God out of our nation and out of our lives. Today we are searching to bring Him back. We have realized our desperate need for Him. Does it always take a crisis to remember who we are and from whence we have come? But there is hope!

We as a nation are beginning to realize we cannot do it on our own. Alone we flounder, "But God!" Thankfully, His mercy endures forever.

1 Peter 2:9-10 says, *But you are a chosen race, a royal priesthood, a holy nation, a people for his own possession, that you may proclaim the excellencies of him who called you out of darkness into his marvelous light. Once you were not a people, but now you are God's people; once you had not received mercy, but now you have received mercy.*

With prayer and supplication, we are again becoming the people God intended us to be. Today we are not hardening our hearts but are listening to His still small voice and obeying.

Our youngest son and family went to the most wonderful church recently. It began at 10 and ended at 1:30. Can you even begin to imagine sitting that long in one place? But we do it all the time at ballgames. The worship was fantastic, the sermon was excellent, and the prayer afterwards was heavenly. My youngest granddaughter went forward for prayer and felt she would never be the same and she won't. At thirteen, she is such a strong Christian. Hallelujah!

"Selah!"

DAY 8

Psalm 9:19-20 says, *Arise, O Lord! Let not man prevail; let the nations be judged before you! Put them in fear, O Lord! Let the nations know that they are but men! Selah*

King Nebuchadnezzar said, *Is not this great Babylon, which I have built by my mighty power as a royal residence and for the glory of my majesty?* (Daniel 4:30)

Then he was driven from among men and ate grass like an ox, etc. *At the end of the days I, Nebuchadnezzar, lifted my eyes to heaven, and my reason returned to me, and I blessed the Most High, and praised and honored him who lives forever.* **(Daniel 4:34)**

When we begin to think we are higher than the Most High God, we too have a problem. It is like saying, "My way or the highway!" The Lord truly wants us to rely upon Him. He enjoys helping His people out. He wants to be a Father to us. He wants us to be His children. He loves us with an everlasting love.

Psalm 20:7 says, *Some trust in chariots and some in horses, but we trust in the name of the Lord our God.*

Proverbs 3:5-6 says, *Trust in the Lord with all your heart, and do not lean on your own understanding. In all your ways acknowledge him, and he will make straight your paths.*

Isaiah 26:4 says, *Trust in the Lord forever, for the Lord is an everlasting rock.*

We were looking for a place to build in Pagosa. We had spent an entire week searching and nothing seemed right. It was our last morning here. The realtor had one more plot of land to show us. We had decided maybe we weren't to move. She pulled up to this piece of land and I burst into tears. This was the property God had for us. But the price was too high. We gave her a figure and she just laughed. An hour later she called and said, "I can't believe it!" But God!

"Selah!"

DAY 9

This morning our Selah is found in **Psalm 20:19-20.** *Arise, O Lord! Let not man prevail; let the nations be judged before you! Put them in fear, O Lord! Let the nations know that they are but men! Selah*

I had no intention of repeating the same scripture, but I accidentally did. There must be a reason for it. So here goes!

We are beginning to realize we are but men! We can pray. We can believe, but it will be God who brings deliverance. As we humble ourselves before the mighty hand of God, He will exalt us. He will hear our prayers and answer.

Habakkuk 3:17-18 says, *Though the fig tree should not blossom, nor fruit be on the vines, the produce of the olive fails, and the fields yield no food, the flock be cut off from the fold and there be no herd in the stalls, yet I will rejoice in the Lord; I will take joy in the God of my salvation.*

Have we gotten to the place that we are taking joy in the God of our salvation even though we are uncertain of the future? Have we begun to learn that the joy of the Lord is truly our strength? Are we beginning to rejoice in the Lord always? Joy is not a feeling, but an act of faith that we choose to walk in. Maybe, if we had rejoiced just one more minute, something good would have happened.

Rejoice in hope, be patient in tribulation, be constant in prayer. **(Romans 12:12)**

Now is not the time to grow weary, but to rise up and rejoice in the Lord, and again I say rejoice!

Our youngest son recently moved to K.C. He was sure the Lord was in this move. But to date things have not turned out the way he expected. I am convinced that if he will rejoice just one more minute, something good will happen. I do not believe God puts a carrot in front of us just out of reach. He has a plan, but we need to rejoice in hope!

"Selah!"

DAY 10

It has been ten days since we began to look at the word *Selah*. In a nutshell these are some of the things we have questioned:

1. Where is our God?

2. Is He really our shield and our goodness?

3. What enemies are we fighting today? Could one be fear?

4. How long will we seek "things" instead of God?

5. Are we angry with God and each other?

6. How are we dealing with our anger or are we?

7. Is God still in America or has He left because of our unbelief?

8. Do we really believe we are but men/women and not God?

9. What will happen if we grow weary?

These are thought provoking questions. Maybe we should take a *Selah* moment and reflect on them.

Today we are looking at **Psalm 21:1-2, *O Lord, in your strength the king rejoices (we rejoice) and in your salvation how greatly he exults! You have given him (us) his heart's desire and have not withheld the request of his (our) lips.*** Selah

Lord, You have made us most blessed forever. You have made us glad with the joy of Your presence. Your steadfast love has created calm in our hearts. We remember Your steadfast love never ceases. Your mercies are new every day. We rely upon Your strength today. You have given us our heart's desire and have not withheld the request of our lips. We rejoice in Your salvation.

I wanted a car when I was getting ready to do my practice teaching. My father was a frugal man. He began to look. I had great expectation. The day I came home to find a car in the drive, and my parent's proudly standing there, I almost cried. The car was pea green and yellow. What college student wants a pea green car? But in all things, we give thanks to You! We rejoice in Your goodness!

"Selah!"

DAY 11

The question is, *Who shall stand in His holy place?*

The answer is, *He who has clean hands and a pure heart, who does not lift up his soul to what is false and does not swear deceitfully.*

Such is the generation of those who seek him, who seek the face of the God of Jacob! Selah (Psalm 24:3-6)

The key word here is "seek". It is defined as attempting or desiring to obtain or achieve something. It is to seek someone or something.

Matthew 6:33 says *But seek first the kingdom of God and his righteousness, and all these things will be added to you.*

This is a powerful promise for us today when our world is so unsettled, when our jobs are at risk, our health is in question, and we are feeling disjointed. He says, *Seek first the kingdom of God and...all these things will be added to you.*

Ask and it will be given to you; seek and you will find; knock and it will be opened to you. (Matthew 7:7)

So, brothers and sisters, seek first the kingdom of God and He will supply all your needs according to His riches in Christ Jesus. *"Selah!"*

We hadn't been married too long when my husband decided he didn't like engineering and wanted to go to Law School. We picked up and moved to Topeka, Kansas. He was going to school, and I needed to find a job. I had a degree in P.E. So, I applied and got a job in one of the local high schools. I don't know whether you have ever worked with high school girls, but it was a challenge to say the least. I sought a job, and I got an education. It was probably one of the hardest years of my life. But I learned a lot and was successful enough to be offered an even better job teaching the following year. When we ask we will receive. Help!

"Selah!"

DAY 12

Who is this King of glory? The Lord of hosts, he is the King of glory! Selah (Psalm 24:10)

It is time to praise the Lord, the King of glory, the Lord of hosts. But what does praise mean? Are there different kinds of praise? Today will be a teaching moment. There are eight names for praise.

1. Hallah - which means to boast, brag or rave about God even to the point of appearing foolish. *Because your love is better than life, my lips will glorify you. I will praise you as long as I live.* (Psalm 63:3-4)

2. Yadah – means to worship with extended hands. *Lift up your hands in the sanctuary and praise the Lord.* (Psalm 134:2)

3. Barak – is used to denote blessing. *The Lord gave and the Lord has taken away; may the name of the Lord be praised.* (Job 1:21)

4. Tehillah – means to sing or laud. *Sing to the Lord, for he has triumphed gloriously; the horse and his rider he has thrown into the sea.* (Exodus 15:1)

5. Zamar – means to pluck the strings of an instrument. *Speaking to one another with psalms, hymns, and songs from the Spirit. Sing and make music from your heart to the Lord.* (Ephesians 5:19)

6. Todah – means to shout or to address with a loud voice. *As soon as the people heard the sound of the trumpet, the people shouted a great shout, and the wall fell down flat.* (Joshua 6:20)

7. Shabach – also means to shout. *When I blow the trumpet, I and all who are with me, then blow the trumpets also on every side of all the camp and shout, "For the Lord and for Gideon."* (Judges 7:18)

8. Hallelujah – one who is excited about God. (Psalm 150)

When someone gives me a compliment, I feel good. When someone notices my new outfit, I feel good. But when God notices me, I feel good, and the reverse is true! God loves our praise!

"Selah!"

DAY 13

There are three Selah's in Psalm 32. They all have to do with forgiveness. We know that as a nation, we need to humble ourselves and ask forgiveness. As individuals I am sure we are daily doing the same. So, I am going to take the 3rd Selah and meditate on it this morning. We need encouragement. We need to know that God is on His throne. We need to know that He cares for us deeply, which He does.

Psalm 32:7 says, *You are a hiding place for me; you preserve me from trouble; you surround me with shouts of deliverance.* Selah

I love the fact that He is my hiding place. I picture myself in the closet with Him, deep within a stack of clothes, hidden from the world, sharing intimate secrets together. He is my hiding place!

Psalm 119:14 says, *You are my hiding place and my shield; I hope in your word.*

Psalm 119:105 says, *Your word is a lamp to my feet and a light to my path.*

Jesus said, *If you abide in my word, you are truly my disciples, and you will know the truth, and the truth will set you free.* (John 8:32)

My mother was always afraid. I don't know whether it had to do with the fact that her father died when she was five or something else. Every time the phone would ring one of us would have to answer it. She would begin to stutter and was unable to say a word. Her friends knew this and would begin to talk to her while she composed herself. It was a mystery to all of us. She hated being alone in the house when my father was gone. He traveled a lot with his job. My brother and I picked up some of her traits. The one I hate the most is being alone and afraid. I am doing better, but it is always just below the surface when I am by myself. At least I don't stutter. *You are my hiding place.*

"Selah!"

DAY 14

O Lord, make me know my end and what is the measure of my days; let me know how fleeting I am!...Surely all mankind stands as a mere breath! Selah (Psalm 39:4-6)

Today we stand in the truth of this scripture. As we watch TV, we see nothing but doom and gloom. No one knows the answer. But that is not true. There is One who measures our days. Our times are in His hands.

He says, *Teach us to number our days that we may get a heart of wisdom.* (Psalm 90:12)

It is a comfort to know that *"I know the plans I have for you, declares the Lord, plans for welfare and not for evil, to give you a future and a hope."* (Jeremiah 29:10)

He is not through with us yet. He knows us and He cares for each of us. Our time is in His hands.

He says, *"Before I formed you in the womb I knew you, and before you were born, I consecrated you."* (Jeremiah 1:5) He was speaking to Jeremiah, but He is also speaking to you and me. He knows us!

Who shall separate us from the love of Christ? Shall tribulation, or distress or persecution, or famine, or nakedness or danger, or sword...No, in all these things we are more than conquerors through him who loved us. For I am sure that neither death nor life, nor angels, nor rulers, nor things present nor things to come, nor powers, nor height nor depth, or anything else in creation, will be able to separate us from the love of God in Christ Jesus our Lord. (Romans 8:35-39)

My father was lying in the hospital dying. I had heard if you played scripture tapes from the Bible over someone, they would be healed. For a week I had sat by his bed and played the whole New Testament. There was no change. Then he began to sing, "Jesus Loves Me" and went into a coma. Shortly thereafter he died.

"Selah!"

DAY 15

Psalm 44:8 says, *In God we have boasted continually, and we will give thanks to* **your name forever.** *Selah*

In God we have boasted continually. I think we are behind in our praise. Too often, what we hear and what we speak is negative. It is time to look up instead of out. It is time to confess the wonders of God and His righteousness. It is time to take the Word and use it as a double-edged sword. The Psalms are full of God's praises. If we cannot think of anything to be thankful for, let's get into the Psalms.

Then Moses and the people of Israel sang this song to the Lord saying, "I will sing to the Lord, for he has triumphed gloriously; the horse and his rider he has thrown into the sea. The Lord is my strength and my song, and he has become my salvation; this is my God, and I will praise him, my father's God and I will exalt him." (Exodus 15:1-2)

Give thanks to the Lord, for his steadfast love endures forever. (2 Chronicles 20:21)

Finally, brothers (sisters) whatever is true, whatever is honorable, whatever is just, whatever is pure, whatever is lovely, whatever is commendable, if there is any excellence, if there is anything worthy of praise, think about these things. (Philippians 4:8)

I spoke to a friend and said, "How are you?" That was a big mistake. For the next few minutes, she told me everything that was wrong with her and everyone else. I did not leave that conversation edified. How could I have changed the tone of things? How could I have uplifted her? What could I have said that would have brought life? That is an assignment I am working on and asking you to do also. *If there is anything worthy of praise, think about these things.*

"Selah!"

DAY 16

Psalm 46:1-3 says, *God is our refuge and strength, a very present help in trouble. Therefore, we will not fear though the earth gives way, though the mountains be moved into the heart of the sea, though its waters roar and foam, though the mountains tremble at its swelling.* *Selah*

We are back to fear again. So, let's talk about it.

Job 3:25 says, *For the thing that I fear comes upon me, and what I dread befalls me.* So, what are we fearing, and who should we fear?

Fear not, for I am with you; be not dismayed for I am your God; I will strengthen you, I will help you, I will uphold you with my righteous right hand. **(Isaiah 41:10)**

Who should we really fear?

Only fear the Lord and serve him faithfully with all your heart. For consider what great things he has done for you. **(1 Samuel 12:24)** because…

The fear of the Lord is the beginning of knowledge. **(Proverbs 1:7)**

We need to adjust our thinking on fear and begin to fear the Lord. It is true that fear can torment us if we dwell on it; this is simply not from God. If we believe His word and act upon it, we have no reason to fear because fear can torment us. We need to be cautious, but we need to be filled with faith, not fear.

I was in high school. Some friends who lived across town asked me to go to the movie with them. They said their father would bring me home. After the show he picked them up. No way was he going to drive me clear across town. So, they left me standing by the theatre, in a scary part of Kansas City, in the middle of the night. I was petrified! My father finally showed up. There had to be angels all around me, even though at the time I did not know it. *God is our refuge and our strength, a very present help in time of trouble.*

"Selah!"

DAY 17

The Lord of hosts is with us; the God of Jacob is our fortress. Selah! (Psalm 46:7)

What is a fortress? It is a secure and strong place; a place of defense or security; intended to be impenetrable to enemies; a person or thing not susceptible to outside influences or disturbance; a place of protection. Wow! This is what God says He is to each of us. What more do we need? He is our fortress.

The Lord is my rock and my fortress and my deliverer, my God, my rock in whom I take refuge. (2 Samuel 22:2)

For you have been to me a fortress and a refuge in the day of my distress. (Psalm 59:16)

He alone is my rock and my salvation, my fortress; I shall not be greatly shaken. (Psalm 62:2)

I will say to the Lord, My refuge and my fortress, my God in whom I trust. (Psalm 91:2)

He is my steadfast love and my fortress, my stronghold and my deliverer. (Psalm 144:2)

David was a man after God's own heart. He believed God was his fortress and constantly confessed God's love, power, protection, mercy, etc.

I was a counselor at a summer camp in K.C. I had gone home for the weekend. My father brought me back. There was a shortcut through the woods, and so I got out of the car and began to walk. I hadn't gone far when I saw a man wandering around. I quickened my pace and prayed and prayed. Each step that I took I feared he had seen me. Finally, I reached the camp with an army encamped around me. *The Lord alone is my rock and my salvation, my fortress; I shall not be greatly shaken.*

"Selah!"

DAY 18

Be still and know that I am God. I will be exalted among the nations; I will be exalted in the earth! The Lord of host is with us; the God of Jacob is our fortress. Selah! (**Psalm 46:10-11**)

"Be still" is a command. How often do we take the time to be still and listen to the voice of God? When was the last time we quit begging and began to just listen with no ulterior motive? Listening is not easy. It is a skill that we must learn. It requires discipline and faith.

And know that I am God. We can say with Job that we have known about God, but do we really know Him? Do we trust Him with our families and our lives? Do we trust Him with our finances? Do we trust Him in uncertain times? Do we know God? The answer is *"Be Still!"*

Commit your way to the Lord; trust in him, and he will act...Be still before the Lord and wait patiently for him; fret not yourself. (**Psalm 37:5-7**) Are we committing our ways to the Lord and trusting Him, or are we worrying and praying, praying again, and then trying to do it on our own?

Oh, that my people would listen to me, that Israel would walk in my ways! I would soon subdue their enemies and turn my hand against their foes. (**Psalm 81:13-14**)

Listen to me, you who pursue righteousness, you who seek the Lord; look to the rock from which you were hewn, and to the quarry from which you were dug. (**Isaiah 51:1**)

I am not sure how to successfully listen to the Lord. I have tried all sorts of ways. I have laid on the floor with my nose in the rug. I have sat under a tree. I have shut myself in the bathroom. You name it. I have tried it. I have come to the conclusion that when God wants to speak to me, He will, and I will be still and listen!

"Selah!"

DAY 19

Clap your hands, all peoples! Shout to God with loud songs of joy! For the Lord, the Most High, is to be feared, a great king over all the earth. He subdues peoples under us, the pride of Jacob whom he loves. Selah (**Psalm 47:1-4**)

It is time to praise. It is time to fear God, which does not mean to be afraid of Him, but to reverently stand in awe of Him. It is a time to realize that He has everything under control. He has chosen us. We are His pride and joy. He loves us with an everlasting love. What more can we ask for?

Rejoice in the Lord always; again, I say rejoice. Let your reasonableness be known to everyone. The Lord is at hand; do not be anxious about anything but in everything by prayer and supplication with thanksgiving let your requests be made known to God. And the peace of God which surpasses all understanding, will guard your hearts and your minds in Christ Jesus. (**Philippians 4:4-6**)

He has placed within each of us His Holy Spirit who is here to lead us and to guide us into all truth. We have not been left alone but are surrounded by a great cloud of witnesses. We have His written word. We have the gifts of the Spirit to encourage us and to guide us. Most of all we have the Risen Lord who has given to each of us eternal life.

To him who is able to keep you from stumbling and to present you before his glorious presence without fault and with great joy – to the only God our Savior be glory, majesty, power and authority, through Jesus Christ our Lord, before all ages, now and forever more! Amen (**Jude 1:24**)

I remember the 1st time I raised my hands in church. I was sure everyone was watching, and I felt so conspicuous. Clapping is one thing. Raising your hands! Thinking back on it, what does it matter what people think? Who am I trying to impress? *Clap your hands, all people! Shout to God with loud songs of joy!*

"Selah!"

DAY 20

Great is the Lord and greatly to be praised in the city of our God...within her citadels God has made himself known as a fortress. God will establish the city forever. Selah (Psalm 48:1-3)

The Lord is my rock and my fortress and my deliverer, my God, my rock in whom I take refuge. (2 Samuel 22:2-3)

O my Strength, I will watch for you, for you, O God, are my fortress. (Psalm 59:9)

For you have been to me a fortress and a refuge in the day of my distress. O my Strength, I will sing praises to you, for you, O God, are my fortress, the God who shows me steadfast love. (Psalm 59:16-17)

He alone is my rock and my salvation, my fortress; I shall not be greatly shaken. (Psalm 62:2)

God has each of our lives under control. We may not see it nor believe it, but He is our fortress. As we walk closer and closer to Him, He reveals more of Himself to us. He has our best interest at heart. He has special plans for each of us if we will only trust and obey Him.

Though the fig tree should not blossom, nor fruit be on the vines, the produce of the olive fails, and the fields yield no food, the flock be cut off from the fold and there be no herd in the stalls, yet I will rejoice in the Lord; I will take joy in the God of my salvation. (Habakkuk 3:17-18)

Our oldest son has been an alcoholic. I say has been because I am believing it is over. I want to tell you, there is nothing worse than watching one of your children fight for his life over addiction. No one understands. No one really knows how to help. Some criticize, while others turn their backs. It is a lonely place to be in, not only for the addict but for the parents. *The Lord is my rock and my deliverer!*

"Selah!"

DAY 21

Psalm 49:13 says, *This is the path of those who have foolish confidence; yet after them people approve of their boasts.* Selah

All of life isn't in our hands. The news media is not our hope, because those who are reporting don't know what is going to happen. They don't know the beginning from the end. When we put our hope in them, our hope is misplaced. We walk in a spirit of fear, not in the confidence of our Lord. We walk in their confusion. Our boast must be in the Lord.

Let not the wise man boast in his wisdom, let not the mighty man boast in his might, let not the rich man boast in his riches but let him who boasts, boast in this, that he understands and knows me, that I am the Lord who practices steadfast love, justice, and righteousness in the earth. For in these things I delight, declares the Lord. **(Jeremiah 9:23-24)**

It is obvious our country is not walking in love for, *Love is patient and kind; love does not envy or boast; it is not arrogant or rude. It does not insist on its own way; it is not irritable or resentful.* **(1 Corinthians 13:4)**

As it is, you boast in your arrogance. All such boasting is evil. So, whoever knows the right thing to do and fails to do it, for him it is sin. **(James 4:16)**

Let the one who boasts, boast in the Lord. For it is not the one who commends himself who is approved, but the one whom the Lord commends. **(2 Corinthians 10:17-18)**

I used to have a real problem with pride. People were always telling me how good I was, and I believed them. Somewhere along the line, I began to realize my Christian walk was suffering and I wondered why. Pride hit me like a brick. I realized I thought more of myself then of the Lord. Now I see myself as a conduit with the Holy Spirit flowing through me. It is all Him and not me.

"Selah!"

DAY 22

I am sure we have all heard the statement, *"You can't take it with you!"* But sometimes I wonder if we really believe this. How tightly are we holding onto our possessions? Is God able to supply all of our needs according to His riches in Christ Jesus? The answer to that will show where our faith lies.

This is what happens to those who live for the moment, who only look out for themselves. Death herds them like sheep straight to hell; they disappear down the gullet of the grave. They waste away to nothing – nothing left but a marker in a cemetery. But me? God snatches me from the clutch of death, he reaches down and grabs me. Selah (Psalm 49:12-15)

Now this is a pretty heavy scripture without God! *For God so loved the world, that he gave his only Son, that whoever believes in him should not perish but have eternal life. For God did not send his Son into the world to condemn the world, but in order that the world might be saved through him. Whoever believes in him is not condemned, but whoever does not believe is condemned already, because he has not believed in the name of the only Son of God.* (John 3:16-17)

I have a question for you. "Do we believe God's promises?" The answer lies in our actions. So many times, I catch myself spouting scripture when I should be asking myself, "What do I really believe, and do I truly act upon it?" I am a reflection to others of what I believe. It is not what I say that matters, but what my life demonstrates. The proof is in the pudding.

I was thirty-three years old when a lady came into my life, and almost pushed me over the edge. I did not like her, but she was like the hound dog from heaven. She never gave up on me. To this day, I have her to thank as the instrument that God used to bring me to salvation. It is usually an unlikely source that leads us to the Lord. But aren't you glad there are people who are willing to go that extra mile! *For God so loved the world, that he gave his only Son.*

"Selah!"

DAY 23

The heavens declare his righteousness, for God himself is judge! Selah (**Psalm 50:6**)

God's righteousness represents His faithfulness and His goodness, His holiness, and His perfection.

From the rising of the sun to its setting God, is righteous. He never changes. His mercies are new every morning. Great is His faithfulness. Even the heavens declare His righteousness. He does not make mistakes. He has known from the foundation of the world what was, what is, and what will be. Nothing takes our Father by surprise. The beauty of it all is that He loves us with an everlasting love that does not change. When we are good or when we are bad, His love remains steadfast.

For he is good, for his steadfast love endures forever. (**2 Chronicles 5:13**)

His love is unwavering. His love is firmly fixed in place, and it encompasses you and me. Because He is faithful to His word, we can rest in His love. We have nothing to fear.

God is our refuge and strength, a very present help in trouble. Therefore, we will not fear though the earth gives way, though the mountains be moved into the heart of the sea. (**Psalm 46:1-2**)

God is not man, that he should lie, or a son of man, that he should change his mind. Has he said, and will he not do it? Or has he spoken, and will he not fulfill it? (**Numbers 23:19**)

Our oldest daughter went through a terrible divorce, believing that God would fix it. But He didn't. Ten years later after a bankruptcy and years of loneliness, she met the almost perfect man. God has blessed them abundantly above all that they could ask or think. He makes all things beautiful in His time!

"Selah!"

DAY 24

You love evil more than good and lying more than speaking what is right. Selah **(Psalm 52:3)**

Do we consider our words? Are we careful with our mouth or do we have oral diarrhea? Words are one thing that cannot be taken back. Once a word is spoken, it brings either life or death to the hearer. So, what are our words bringing to those around us?

The words of the wise heard in quiet are better than the shouting of a ruler among fools. **(Ecclesiastics 9:17)**

There are words that are everlasting, words that produce life and these are the words of the Lord. He says, ***Heaven and earth will pass away, but my words will not pass away.*** (Mark 13:31)

Jesus has made a profound promise to us when He said, ***If you abide in me, and my words abide in you, ask whatever you wish, and it will be done for you. By this my Father is glorified.*** **(John 15:4-8)**

The Father is glorified by our words. When we stand on His word, believe in His word, act upon His word, He is glorified. When was the last time you spoke His word with conviction and then acted on it? We have too many options in this world apart from His word. The early church would have shuttered at what is happening today. Let's get in the Word, speak the Word, and temper our words.

I tell you, on the day of judgment, people will give account for every careless word they speak, for by your words you will be justified, and by your words you will be condemned. **(Matthew 12:36-37)**

I honestly try to control my tongue, but it just seems to get away from me. Do you know what I mean? I walked into church last Sunday and *instantly* criticized something that I thought was wrong. Have you ever done that? *"Careless words!"*

"Selah!"

DAY 25

For strangers have risen against me, ruthless men seek my life; they do not set God before themselves. Selah (Psalm 54:3)

We are living in the world, but we are not of this world. All around us people are looking to things and solutions from this world, rather than to the Living God. When we say, "But God", they do not understand. Their ears are dull, and their hearts are hard. Therefore, they lash out against us. If they knew what we know, they would be at peace. Now is the time for us to begin interceding for the lost. Now is the time the lost may be more receptive to the gospel, but they will never know if we do not tell them.

How do we tell them? Do we beat them over the head with a Bible? Do we preach hell and damnation to them, or do we reach out to them with the love of God, not in words but in actions and deeds?

Actions truly do speak louder than words!

So, today as you go about your daily activities, begin to pray for your neighbor who doesn't go to church. Pray for your family members who have not yet come into the fold and those who may have shied away. Pray for our country, especially our President and the news media. Pray for an opportunity to share the love of Christ with someone today! Then watch and wait, because an opportunity will come, and we need to be prepared when it does.

You call me Teacher and Lord, and you are right, for so I am. If I then, your Lord and Teacher, have washed your feet, you also ought to wash one another's feet. For I have given you an example, that you should do just as I have done. (John 13)

I hate to say it, but I am not always a good neighbor. I remember when we first moved to town, a lady came over with a plate of cookies. I didn't know anyone and was so blessed by her gift. I wish I could say I have done the same.

"Selah!"

DAY 26

Oh, that I had wings like a dove! I would fly away and be at rest; yes, I would wander far away; I would lodge in the wilderness. Selah (Psalm 55:6)

Do you sometimes feel like running away, especially in times when things aren't going so well? To go anywhere would be better than staying one more day where you are at the moment. Stir crazy is a good phrase for how most of us feel when this happens. But there is hope on the horizon.

Come, my people, enter your chambers, and shut your doors behind you; hide yourselves for a little while until the fury has passed by. (Isaiah 26:20)

That is the invitation.

You are a hiding place for me; you preserve me from trouble; you surround me with shouts of deliverance. Selah (Psalm 32:7)

For he will hide me in his shelter in the day of trouble; he will conceal me under the cover of his tent; he will lift me high upon a rock. (Psalm 27:5)

In the midst of our hiding, we are still protected, loved, and cared for by the very God of the Universe! He has His hand upon each of us not as a matter of disciple but as a matter of love. He is aware of where we are and what we are going through. He is weeping with those who weep and rejoicing with those who rejoice. He has called us, and He is keeping us from the wiles of the enemy. He is drawing us unto Himself with cords of love that cannot be broken. He is listening to our hearts cry, and He cares.

Sometimes we just need a little alone time. A brisk walk in the mountains may be the very prescription we need to reevaluate and get a clear perspective of who we are. Things are not quite as bad as they seem when we breathe in the very breath of God. He is our hiding place!

"Selah!"

DAY 27

He redeems my soul in safety from the battle that I wage, for many are arrayed against me. God will give ear and humble them, he who is enthroned from of old, because they do not change and do not fear God. Selah (Psalm 55:18-19)

What battles are raging within you today? What things are warring against your flesh? What imaginations are tormenting your mind? We are in a continual spiritual battle and there is no time to sleep.

For though we walk in the flesh, we are not waging war according to the flesh. For the weapons of our warfare are not of the flesh but have divine power to destroy strongholds. We destroy arguments and every lofty opinion raised against the knowledge of God and take every thought captive to obey Christ. (2 Corinthians 10:3-5)

Not only is the battle raging in us, but all around us. We must choose to turn the other cheek when we are attacked with unwarranted anger. We must choose to love rather than retaliate, forgive rather than hold a grudge.

Blessed be the Lord, my rock, who trains my hands for war, and my fingers for battle; he is my steadfast love and my fortress, my stronghold, and my deliverer. (Psalm 144:1-2)

Though an army encamp against me, my heart shall not fear; though war arises against me, yet I will be confident. (James 4:7)

I was teaching a women's Bible Study. Half of these women were Catholic and the other half Lutheran. We came to the passage, *There is one mediator between God and mankind, the man Christ Jesus. (1 Timothy 2:4)* The next week there were no Catholics at Bible Study. It is funny how the Bible speaks differently to different people. *We destroy arguments and every lofty opinion raised against the knowledge of God.* Christ is our centerpiece!

"Selah!"

DAY 28

I cry out to God Most High, to God who fulfills his purpose for me. He will send from heaven and save me; he will put to shame him who tramples on me. Selah (**Psalm 57:2-3**)

I know the plans I have for you, declares the Lord, plans for welfare and not for evil, to give you a future and a hope. (**Jeremiah 29:11**)

This verse is one most of us know by heart, but do we take it to heart? Do you know that God loves you? He knows you by name. He knows your uprisings and your down sittings. He knows you! Did you ever really consider why?

For this purpose, I have raised you up, to show you my power, so that my name may be proclaimed in all the earth. (**Exodus 9:16**)

The Lord will fulfill his purpose for me; your steadfast love, O Lord, endures forever. (**Psalm 138:8**)

So why am I trying to figure it out? *Many are the plans in the mind of a man, but it is the purpose of the Lord that will stand.* (**Proverbs 19:21**)

And we know that for those who love God all things work together for good, for those who are called according to his purpose. (**Romans 8:28**)

There is a purpose for your life. Not only is there a purpose, but there is a reason you are on Planet Earth at this very moment. God does not make mistakes. As we seek His face, we will begin to realize what God has in mind for each of us. We each have different gifts and callings. What God has called me to do is probably not what He has called you to do. Often, we feel we are not doing enough, when we should realize we are doing just what God has called us to do. We are a body, not individual Lone Rangers. As each of us does the tasks He puts on our plate, we begin to function as a Body of Believers in power and might. Remember God will fulfill His purpose in you and in me despite our humanness.

"Selah!"

DAY 29

They dug a pit in my way, but they have fallen into it themselves. Selah **(Psalm 56:6)**

Have you ever been in a situation where you were the only Christian and those around you were trying to poke holes in what you believe? Have you been somewhere that people were making fun of Christians and you were afraid to stand up for what you believe? Or have you stood up for what you believe and had those around you shoot you down? I think we all have been in these situations at one time or another. The problem with most of us is that we insulate ourselves with Christians. I am guilty. I teach in a Christian school. I go to a Christian church. All my close friends are Christians.

Will my headstone read, *Truly, I say to you, wherever this gospel is proclaimed in the whole world, what she has done will also be told in memory of her.* **(Matthew 26:13)**

Jesus said, *Go into all the world and proclaim the gospel to the whole creation.* **(Mark 16:15)**

One thing Jesus did not say is that everyone will agree with you, love what you say, or follow you in total assent.

I have said these things to you that in me you may have peace. In the world, you will have tribulation. But take heart; I have overcome the world. **(John 16:33)**

The verse right before our Selah verse today says, *Be exalted, O God above the heavens! Let your glory be over all the earth!* **(Psalm 57:5)**

One of the hardest things for me to swallow is knowing that I have offended some of my family by my beliefs. I have tried to share Jesus with them, but I have come across as being judgmental. I have sometimes tried to bully or shame them into believing. Jesus said that we are to love one another as He has loved us.

"Selah!"

DAY 30

You, Lord God of hosts, are God of Israel. Rouse yourself to punish all the nations; spare none of those who treacherously plot evil. Selah (**Psalm 59:5**)

All the nations will say, "Why has the Lord done thus to this land? What caused the heat of this great anger?" Then the people will say, "It is because they abandoned the covenant of the Lord." (**Deuteronomy 29:24-25**)

Is there any chance this applies to the United States and other countries of the world? Have we abandoned God as a nation? Listening to the television, I can honestly say there has been very little said about God on the news or other media. Those in leadership rarely acknowledged the creator of the universe. We still have "In God We Trust" but do we? Ever since prayer was taken out of the schools, we have seen a gradual decline in faith in our country. Is God even still around?

These nations feared the Lord and also served their carved images. Their children did likewise and their children's children – as their fathers did, so they do to this day. (**2 Kings 17:41**)

If we were to take a survey in the United States, many people would indeed say they believe in God. But there is a difference in believing and really believing. Are we willing to stake our lives on the Lord Jesus Christ and the working of the Holy Spirit within us?

I still remember the day I realized the difference between believing and really believing. I was praying with a friend and felt the presence of the Holy Spirit strongly on me. I had never knowingly experienced the Holy Spirit before that moment. Later, I realized I had changed. I picked up my Bible and the words begin to jump out at me. Things I had never known before came alive. I truly was a new creation in Christ Jesus.

"Selah!"

DAY 31

That they may know that God rules over Jacob to the ends of the earth. Selah (**Psalm 59:13**)

If you read the verses preceding this they are really discouraging, but today I think we need to hear something positive. I am sure you will agree.

Let the heavens be glad, and let the earth rejoice, and let them say among the nations, "The Lord reigns!" (**1 Chronicles 16:31**)

It is so important to know God is still in control. At any moment He can change any situation. Sometimes He chooses to, and other times He chooses not to. The Lord reigns!

How beautiful upon the mountains are the feet of him who brings good news, who publishes peace, who brings good news of happiness, who publishes salvation, who says to Zion, "Your God reigns." (**Isaiah 57:10**)

Father, at this moment we need good news. We need to be encouraged. We need to know You are there. We need to know what to do and when to do it. We need peace and happiness in our lives. In other words, we need You!

Then I heard what seemed to be the voice of a great multitude, like the roar of many waters and like the sound of mighty peals of thunder, crying out, "Hallelujah! For the Lord our God the Almighty reigns. Let us rejoice and exult and give him the glory." (**Revelation 19:6-7**)

My mother-in-law was dying of Leukemia. I truly believed she was going to be healed. I had prayed, laid hands on her, had my friends pray, but she died. At the time, I was devastated. Where are you God? Looking back, had she lived, she would have been in for so many heartaches. I believe God in His mercy took her. As always, He knows what is best for each of us. The Lord our God reigns!

"Selah!"

DAY 32

O God, you have rejected us, broken our defenses; you have been angry; oh, restore us. You have made the land to quake; you have torn it open; repair its breaches, for it totters. You have made your people see hard things; you have given us wine to drink that made us stagger. You have set up a banner for those who fear you, that they may flee to it from the bow. Selah **(Psalm 60:1-4)**

This scripture is so applicable today. I think this describes our nation to a tee, but there is good news!

He brought me to His banqueting table and his banner over me is Love. **(Song of Solomon 2:4)**

A banner is a message or a sign. When the enemy sees it, he knows who he is contending with. The banner is the rod of God. It is the serpent on the pole. It is Jesus Christ on the cross.

Moses built an altar and called it, "The Lord is my Banner." He said, "Because hands were lifted up against the throne of the Lord." **(Exodus 17:15)**

Truly, hands have been lifted up against the throne of the Lord. But we are under God's banner. When the enemy comes in like a flood, the Lord will raise up a standard against him. We have nothing to fear except to fear the Lord our God. We need to rest in Him and in His promises because He has raised up a banner over us and that banner is His unfailing love for each one of us.

Jesus said, *"And I, when I am lifted up from the earth, will draw all people to myself."* **(John 12:32)**

I have a real beef with cell phones at the dinner table. I have an even bigger beef with cell phones in a restaurant. I do not believe when we sit down at God's banqueting table, there will be cell phones. He wants to talk with us and listen to us. When we have one ear to the phone, we miss out on so much of what is said.

"Selah!"

DAY 33

Let me dwell in your tent forever! Let me take refuge under the shelter of your wings! Selah **(Psalm 61:4)**

Let me take shelter under Your wings. What a comforting thought! Wings represent freedom, protection, refuge. They are a shield to those who hide under them. The Lord has provided us many ways to stay close to Him. Among them is hiding under His wings.

I love this scripture. *Keep me as the apple of Your eye; hide me in the shadow of Your wings.* **(Psalm 17:8)**

Hide me from the tempter. Hide me from things that could cause me to fall. Hide me from myself. I am hidden under the shadow of His wings.

How precious is your steadfast love, O God! The children of mankind take refuge in the shadow of your wings. **(Psalm 36:7)**

It is better to take refuge in the Lord than to trust in man. **(Psalm 118:8)**

A refuge is a shelter or protection from danger or distress; something to which one has recourse in difficulty. We are there right now. We need to know without a shadow of doubt what to do next. We are hearing all sorts of conflicting messages. All around us is confusion. But don't worry, be happy! We need to take shelter under Your wings, O Lord. We are helpless apart from You.

For you have been my help, and in the shadow of your wings I will sing for joy. My soul clings to you; your right hand upholds me. **(Psalm 63:7-8)**

My mother and I were coming home from Illinois, when suddenly we heard a thump, thump! Instantly I knew we had a flat tire. I hadn't changed a tire in years. But I got the jack and the spare out of the trunk. A man stopped and said, "The Lord told me to help you." I know this was an angel in disguise.

"Selah!"

DAY 34

They bless with their mouths, but inwardly they curse. Selah (Psalm 62:4)

We have all heard the saying, "Talking out of both sides of your mouth." We have all been guilty at one time or another. We are experiencing this through the news media in outrageous proportions. What do we believe and what is just a whisper in the wind?

Proverbs 18:21 says, *Death and life are in the power of the tongue, and those who love it will eat its fruits.*

I honestly believe what you confess you get. When we confess gloom and doom, we spread the seeds of this confession. When we confess hope, we encourage all of those around us.

By the blessing of the upright a city is exalted, but by the mouth of the wicked it is overthrown. **(Proverbs 11:11)**

Are we helping to bless our city and our churches, or are we overthrowing them? Are we lifting up those close to us, or adding to the negative vibes around us?

The heart of the righteous ponders how to answer, but the mouth of the wicked pours out evil things. **(Proverbs 15:18)**

We are all guilty of speaking before we think. Sometimes we are even guilty of spreading gossip because it makes us feel better about ourselves.

The good person out of the good treasure of his heart produces good, and the evil person out of his evil treasure produces evil, for out of the abundance of the heart his mouth speaks. **(Luke 6:45)**

My friend asks what I think of her new outfit. I rave about it. But I really think it is ugly and doesn't flatter her at all. What should I say? The truth or a lie?

"Selah!"

DAY 35

Trust in him at all times, O people; pour out your heart before him; God is a refuge for us. Selah (**Psalm 62:8**)

What does the word trust mean? It is a bold confidence, a sure security. Trust is what we do because of faith. It is believing God and His promises in all circumstances because He is a God who cares even when it feels like He doesn't.

I love this scripture. *Some trust in chariots and some in horses, but we trust in the name of the Lord our God.* (**Psalm 20:7**)

Today, instead of chariots and horses, what are we putting our trust in? Our answer will determine how we are doing in this life. If our hope is in the Lord, then we are sitting in our lawn chair sipping lemonade and eating bonbons.

Why? *You keep him in perfect peace whose mind is stayed on you, because he trusts in you.* (**Isaiah 26:3**)

What is your mind filled with? Is it filled with fear, insecurity, the unknown, or is it filled with trust in the living God, *Who is able to do far more abundantly than all that we ask or think according to the power at work within us?* (**Ephesians 3:20**)

Do you know that if you have followed every day, you have read 130 different scriptures and read the word *"Selah" many times*, which means to pause and to ponder. In other words, think about it.

Then He tells us to pour out our hearts to Him, for He is a good listener.

I live in the mountains. I am blessed beyond measure. Every morning when I get up, I look out and see God's wonderful world. In the winter I can view the snow-capped mountains. In the summer I watch the sun rise over them. I grew up in the city. I did not realize what I was missing. Now I truly understand the beauty of God's creation like never before. He is a Master Artist!

"Selah!"

DAY 36

All the earth worships you and sings praises to you; they sing praises to your name. Selah **(Psalm 66:4)**

I would venture to say most of us love God, but do not worship Him with our whole heart. Some definitions of worship are reverence, adoration, honor, homage to God, bowing down, venerate, respect and treasure. Worship means to love God so much that you don't question Him at all. It is the priority we place on who God is in our lives, and where He is on our priority list. David was a man after God's own heart. Here are some of the things he said:

Ascribe to the Lord glory due his name; worship the Lord in the splendor of holiness. **(Psalm 29:2)**

Oh come, let us worship and bow down; let us kneel before the Lord, our Maker! **(Psalm 96:6)**

Exalt the Lord our God, worship at his footstool! Holy is he! **(Psalm 99:5)**

Worthy are you, our Lord and God, to receive glory and honor and power, for you created all things and by your will they existed and were created. **(Revelation 4:11)**

In heaven, worship is the norm rather than the exception. Wouldn't it be easier to begin now rather than to shame faced stand before the One who lives forever and ever and realize how much we have missed on earth?

I grew up going to church on Sunday and Wednesday. It was a ritual at our house. I never gave it much thought. I just did it. My attitude about church was the same as my going. I just endured it until the Holy Spirit showed up in my life in a real and personal way. Now I go to church because I desire to know God and I want to fellowship with His people.

"Selah!"

DAY 37

There did we rejoice in him who rules by his might forever, whose eyes keep watch on the nations – let not the rebellious exalt themselves. Selah (Psalm 66:7)

Sometimes, I wonder if we understand who the ultimate ruler is? *"In the beginning God created."* He has a copyright to each of us because we are His creation. We were created by Him and for Him. Therefore, He has the right to do with each of us as He sees fit.

For by him all things were created, in heaven and on earth, visible and invisible whether thrones or dominions or rulers or authorities – all things were created through him and for him. (Colossians 1:16)

What does this mean in my life? First, He is my father. He takes care of me and supplies all my needs. He takes the time to listen to me and cares about what I care about. He has a plan for my life that will produce good and not evil. He has a future for me that is eternal. He will never leave me nor forsake me. He means what He says and says what He means. There is no shadow of turning with Him. He never changes. He is consistent in my life. Most importantly, He loves me with an everlasting love. What more could I ask of the Father?

For we are his workmanship, created in Christ Jesus for good works, which God prepared beforehand, that we should walk in them. (Ephesians 2:10)

O Lord, what is man that you regard him or the son of man that you think of him? (Psalm 144:3)

A friend and I were in Tulsa. I have absolutely no sense of direction. If you turn me around, I may head for home and get lost. I had just said, "I think we should go straight." As I said this it seemed a hand grabbed the steering wheel and turned us to the left. We both knew this was the hand of God. We began to rejoice!

"Selah!"

DAY 38

I will offer to you burnt offerings of fattened animals, with the smoke of sacrifices of rams; I will make an offering of bulls and goats. Selah! (Psalm 66:15)

What in the world does this have to do with us today? Nothing, because Jesus' blood is more than sufficient for all of those who call upon His name. However, we can offer our lives to Him. Below are some things we can offer Him.

Offer trust: *Offer right sacrifices and put your trust in the Lord.* (Psalm 4:5)

Offer thanksgiving: *Offer to God a sacrifice of thanksgiving.* (Psalm 50:14)

Offer joy: *I will offer in his tent sacrifices with shouts of joy.* (Psalm 27:6)

Offer our voices: *Let them offer sacrifices of thanksgiving and tell of his deeds in songs of joy.* (Psalm 107:22)

Offer ourselves: *Your people will offer themselves freely on the day of your power.* (Psalm 110:3)

Acknowledging His name: *Through him then let us continually offer up a sacrifice of praise to God, that is, the fruit of lips that acknowledge his name.* (Hebrews 13:15)

Offer gratefulness: *Therefore, let us be grateful for receiving a kingdom that cannot be shaken, and thus let us offer to God acceptable worship, with reverence and awe, for our God is a consuming fire.* (Hebrews 12:28)

Most of our friends before the mountains, were Catholic. I remember the number of times I gave up something for Lent. It was about as disastrous as dieting. Then I realized, when I began eating or whatever again, I did a double dip. I tried to sacrifice my tongue and had oral diarrhea. Can you relate? I don't think sacrifice is in my DNA.

"Selah!"

DAY 39

May God be gracious to us and bless us and make his face to shine upon us, Selah (Psalm 67:1)

We are blessed. We live in a free country. We have enough food to eat. We have nice homes. We have good vehicles. We have a good medical system. We have good schools. We have freedom of religion. There are many places we could live where this is not true. Do we really appreciate all that we have, or do we take it for granted?

Psalm 33:12 says, *Blessed is the nation whose God is the Lord.*

Psalm 94:12 says, *Blessed is the man whom you discipline, O Lord, and whom you teach out of your laws.*

Psalm 34:8 says, *Oh, taste and see that the Lord is good! Blessed is the man who takes refuge in him.*

Psalm 84:5 says, *Blessed are those whose strength is in you.*

Psalm 84:12 says, *Blessed is the one who trusts in you.*

Psalm 112:1 says, *Blessed is the man who fears the Lord, who greatly delights in his commandments! His offspring will be mighty in the land, the generation of the upright will be blessed.*

There are conditions to blessing even in the spiritual realm.

When I was growing up, I used to hear, "If you will eat your spinach, I will give you..." It is like, "If you will, I will." My grandmother used to say this little rhyme to me all the time. "I knew a little girl who had a little curl right in the middle of her forehead. And when she was good, she was very, very good. And when she was bad, she was horrid." That was me! There are conditions to blessings.

"Selah!"

DAY 40

Let the nations be glad and sing for joy, for you judge the peoples with equity and guide the nations upon earth. Selah (Psalm 67:4)

We live in a world that seems to think everything in life belongs to us and the decisions we make are ours to make. We have become independent of everything and everyone. We are used to doing it, "Our way!"

Psalm 86:9-10 says, *All the nations you have made shall come and worship before you, O Lord, and shall glorify your name. For you are great and do wondrous things; you alone are God.*

"You alone are God." How many little gods have we put in front of God? How many things have seemed more important? How many times have we ignored the nudging of the Holy Spirit to go ahead and do our own thing?

The Lord has made known his salvation; he has revealed his righteousness in the sight of the nations. (Psalm 98:2)

In the United States we cannot say we did not know. Our nation was founded on "In God We Trust". We cannot say we have not heard the promises of God, because we have. The problem is maybe we have refused to listen.

Then you will call on me and come and pray to me, and I will hear you. You will seek me and find me, when you seek me with all your heart. I will be found by you, declares the Lord, and I will restore your fortunes and gather you from the nations. (Jeremiah 29:12-14) Selah"

I think sometimes seeking God is like an Easter egg hunt. The eggs are hidden all around us. All we must do is to find them and put them into our basket. But we give up too soon? Have we found the pearl of great price?

"Selah!"

DAY 41

O God, when you went out before your people, when you marched through the wilderness, Selah **(Psalm 68:7)**

God will go out before His people. He has promised to be with us and never leave us even when we are in the wilderness. His banner over us is love and that never changes. So, take a deep breath and know everything is under control.

Ezra 8:22 says, *The hand of our God is for good on all who seek him, and the power of his wrath is against all who forsake him.*

We are in His hands. We have nothing to fear. But those who refuse to come to His banqueting table stand under His wrath. Scary!

But my eyes are toward you, O God, my Lord; in you I seek refuge; leave me not defenseless! **(Psalm 141:8)**

In response He says, **"*For I am with you to save you," declares the Lord.* (Jeremiah 30:11)**

Each day as we grow stronger in the Lord our faith increases and our trust in Him is better established. When any battle is over, we should be able to look back and see how our lives have changed for the better. Nothing happens that takes Him by surprise and in all things, we are more than conquerors through Christ.

Behold, this is our God; we have waited for him that he might save us. This is the Lord; we have waited for him; let us be glad and rejoice in his salvation. (Isaiah 25:9)

They who wait for the Lord shall renew their strength; they shall mount up with wings like eagles; they shall run and not be weary; they shall walk and not faint. (Isaiah 40:31) My idea of waiting is two minutes. I like instant pudding. I want instant results. I like microwaves. Should I go on? Praying and waiting are hard!

"Selah!"

DAY 42

Blessed be the Lord, who daily bears us up; God is our salvation. Selah (**Psalm 68:19**)

God daily, not occasionally or when He feels like it, but daily bears us up. What does this mean to you and me? Not only is He our salvation, but He is daily active in each of our lives. He cares about us and is aware of where we are and what is going on in each of our lives. He cares with an undying love for each of us individually. That is mind boggling to me. I have trouble just caring for those around me. But God cares!

2 Corinthians 9:8 says, *And God is able to make all grace abound to you, so that having all sufficiency in all things at all times, you may abound in every good work. He has distributed freely; he has given to the poor; his righteousness endures forever.*

So, what does the Lord desire of each of us?

Blessed is the one who listens to me, watching daily at my gates, waiting beside my door. For whoever finds me finds life and obtains favor from the Lord. (**Proverbs 8:34-35**)

Yet they seek me daily and delight to know my ways. (**Isaiah 58:2**)

I will bless the Lord at all times; his praise shall continually be in my mouth. My soul makes its boast in the Lord; let the humble hear and be glad. (**Psalm 34:1**)

All God asks of us is that we love Him; desire to follow Him; praise Him for who He is and walk in right standing with Him and with our fellowmen.

My youngest son wanted a blue Honda moped. He and I prayed that he would find one. The next day one of his friends told him he was selling his blue Honda moped. Prayers like these answered, make believers out of us and our children.

"Selah!"

DAY 43

O kingdoms of the earth, sing to God; sing praises to the Lord, Selah (**Psalm 68:32**)

Have we forgotten how to sing? If the only book of the Bible we read is Psalms, it is full of commands to sing. God must think that singing is important, or He would not have asked us to do it. When you are listening to a song that you really like, what happens? You begin to tap your foot, sing along and to feel uplifted. So, God's command to sing is for your own good, as is everything else He asks you to do.

Exodus 15:21 says, *Sing to the Lord, for he has triumphed gloriously.*

2 Samuel 22:50 says, *For this I will praise you, O Lord among the nations, and sing praises to your name.*

1 Chronicles 16:23 says, *Sing to the Lord, all the earth! Tell of his salvation from day to day.*

Isaiah 12:5 says, *Sing praises to the Lord, for he has done gloriously; let this be made known in all the earth.*

Zephaniah 3:14 says, *Sing aloud, O daughter of Zion, shout, O Israel! Rejoice and exult with all your heart, O daughter of Jerusalem.*

1 Corinthians 14:15 says, *I will sing praise with my spirit, but I will sing with my mind also.*

Our oldest grandson loves to sing. He has written many songs which have been sung, not only by him, but by other entertainers. My prayer is that one day he will begin to write and sing songs to the Lord. He has so much talent, which is God given. *Sing praises to the Lord, for he has done gloriously; let this be made known in all the earth.*

"Selah!"

DAY 44

When the earth totters, and all its inhabitants, it is I who keep steady its pillars. Selah (Psalm 75:3)

When I think of totter, I picture someone stumbling around in a feeble or unsteady way, maybe because of an earthquake. God is saying when this happens, He is there to steady things.

Psalm 60:1-2 says, *O God, you have rejected us, broken our defenses; you have been angry; oh, restore us. You have made the land to quake; you have torn it open; repair its breaches for it totters.*

I feel we have been tottering like a teeter-totter, back and forth, tossed about by every wave of the sea. Do this! Do that! Who do we listen to and what do we do? Confusion has set in. There is only One who truly knows the answers, and at the moment, He is not speaking, or is it we are not listening?

Joel 3:16 says, *The Lord roars from Zion, and utters his voice from Jerusalem, and the heavens and the earthquake. But the Lord is a refuge to his people, a stronghold to the people of Israel.*

Do we have to wait until the Lord roars or are we able to hear His still small voice? Regardless of what others do, we need to know what God wants us to do and be obedient to His voice. We need not totter just because the world around us is unstable. Our stability comes from the Lord.

I was just coming in from a prayer meeting, and as I opened the garage door, I hear a voice say as clear as day, "Don't kick against the goad!" I had no idea what a goad was. I quickly went inside and looked it up. Paul was on the road to Damascus when Jesus turned his life upside down. He was about to do the same with mine.

"Selah!"

DAY 45

Then he broke the flashing arrows, the shield, the sword, and the weapons of war. Selah (**Psalm 76:3**)

We are in a battle even if we do not realize it. There is an enemy out there that is trying to destroy us. We may think it is China or some other country but, the battle is not with flesh and blood, but with powers and principalities, rulers of darkness. Our battle is not physical, but it is spiritual, and we cannot fight it alone.

Exodus 14:14 says, *The Lord will fight for you, and you have only to be silent.*

Deuteronomy 1:30 says, *The Lord your God who goes before you will himself fight for you.*

2 Chronicles 20:17 says, *You will not need to fight in this battle. Stand firm, hold your position, and see the salvation of the Lord on your behalf…do not be afraid and do not be dismayed.*

We have a commander-in-chief. His name is Jesus, and He has given us strict orders. He tells us to be silent. I think we are losing the battle so often with our mouth. We are confessing negative, negative, negative. Then He tells us He will go before us. He does not tell us to begin the battle and then call Him when we see we are losing. We are to stand firm and hold our position. So, what is your position? *Fight the good fight of faith. Take hold of the eternal life to which you were called.* (**1 Timothy 6:12**)

We are in a battle. We need to choose which side we are on.

Our oldest son's daughter battled for years for her father. When she was in high school, she used to send him scriptures. She stuck Lamentations 3:1-33 in his Bible one day. Later he found the scripture and realized God was speaking to him. He was to write a book, "Allowing God to Destroy What's Destroying You!" Because of her obedience, he was obedient and wrote, "Killing Mr. Hyde".

"Selah!"

DAY 46

When God arose to establish judgment, to save all the humble of the earth. Selah (**Psalm 76:9**)

Do we truly know what it means to be humble? The dictionary defines it as meek, deferential, respectful, submissive, unassertive, modest, patient. Humility does not get frustrated with the imperfections of others. It is tolerant of self. Humility recognizes its own limitations and knows none of us are perfect. Finally, humility is teachable. What a list of dos and don'ts! I will never say I am humble again. There is only One who truly knows what humility means and His name is Jesus.

Psalm 18:27 says, *For you save a humble people, but the haughty eyes you bring down.*

Proverbs 11:2 says, *When pride comes, then comes disgrace, but with the humble is wisdom.*

Isaiah 66:2 says, *But this is the one to whom I will look: he who is humble and contrite in spirit and trembles at my word.*

Do you suppose we will begin to hear from God when we stop trying to do things on our own; when we take the time to listen and then act upon what we hear? It seems then we will begin to see answers. Are we teachable?

James 4:6 says, *God opposes the proud but gives grace to the humble.*

James 4:10 says, *Humble yourselves before the Lord, and he will exalt you.*

Teaching school is a humbling experience. Young students especially are so honest. If you want to know what they are thinking, just ask them. Sometimes it is better not to ask. They are open and transparent. I am wondering if they could teach us a lesson or two.

"Selah!"

DAY 47

When I remember God, I moan; when I meditate, my spirit faints. Selah (Psalm 77:3)

Psalm 63:5 says, *My mouth will praise you with joyful lips, when I remember you upon my bed, and mediate on you in the watches of the night.*

I was excited when I read the *Selah* for today because it was exactly what I wanted to say this morning. I just finished a book that tried to prove that Jesus was just a man. All the way through the book I thought that at the end the man would come to realize who Jesus really is. But he did not. To some this would have been a faith tester, but for me it just reinforced who Jesus is. During the night I began at the beginning of the alphabet and praised God for who He is with every single letter beginning with Almighty and ending with Zealous.

Psalm 119:148 says, *My eyes are awake before the watches of the night, that I may meditate on your promise.*

I will ponder all your work and meditate on your mighty deeds. Your way, O God is holy. What God is great like our God? (Psalm 77:12-13)

I am good at asking God for things, but do I ever ponder? Do I mediate on Him and His goodness? Do I pause and reflect on the cross and the price that Christ paid for me? Have I ever prayed without asking for something?

There is no greater blessing then to meditate on who God is and what He has done for each of us. As I remember the birth of my first child, I was in awe of each little finger and toe, just as I am sure God was when He breathed the breath of life into man. He looked man over and said, "Perfect!" just as I looked my daughter over and said, "Perfect!" Four times I experienced the perfection of birth and praised God.

"Selah!"

DAY 48

Has God forgotten to be gracious? Has he in anger shut up his compassion? Selah (**Psalm 77:9**)

The question is, "Has God turned off his compassion?" It would certainly seem so as our world is in such turmoil. Never in my lifetime have I seen so much confusion and frustration. Maybe the question should be, "Why not?" As a nation how have we been living? How has the world been responding to the Living Lord? God has the power and the right to punish us. He has the power to wipe us off the face of the earth and start all over, but He will not.

The steadfast love of the Lord never ceases; his mercies never come to an end; they are new every morning; great is your faithfulness. (**Lamentations 3:22-23**)

For the Lord will not cast off forever, but, though he cause grief, he will have compassion according to the abundance of his steadfast love. (**Lamentations 3:31**)

The greatest proof of His steadfast love is the cross. Until we truly understand what the cross meant to Him, we will never truly understand compassion. When we do not understand compassion, we cannot show it to others.

He has urged us, ***Do not be conformed to this world, but be transformed by the renewal of your mind, that by testing you may discern what is the will of God, what is good and acceptable and perfect.*** (**Romans 12:2**)

Return to the Lord your God, for he is gracious and merciful, slow to anger, and abounding in steadfast love; and he relents over disaster. (**Joel 2:13**)

We are not of this world. We are sojourners waiting for the next train to heaven. We have an assignment here, but when it is complete, we will be taken one way or another into our eternal home. I sure hope I go up in a cloud to meet the Lord in the air. But either way it will be heavenly!

"Selah!"

DAY 49

You with your arm redeemed your people, the children of Jacob and Joseph. Selah! (Psalm 77:15)

Remember the song, "I've been redeemed by the blood of the lamb"? It is true we have been redeemed and we are free. We are on our way to heaven shouting, "Victory!"

But some of us have stopped remembering. *They did not remember his power or the day when he redeemed them from the foe.* (Psalm 78:42). It is time to "*Selah*" and stop to remember what God has done for us through Jesus Christ our Lord.

I have blotted out your transgressions like a cloud and your sins like mist; return to me, for I have redeemed you. (Isaiah 44:22)

Isaiah 43:1 says, *Fear not, for I have redeemed you; I have called you by name, you are mine.* So, I can sing, "I am my Beloved's, and He is mine and His banner over me is love."

And, I can say, *Let the redeemed of the Lord say so, whom he has redeemed from trouble.* (Psalm 107:2) Trouble may be in our path, but we can step aside and not let it overtake us. "*Selah!*"

You have led in your steadfast love the people whom you have redeemed; you have guided them by your strength to your holy abode. (Exodus 15:13)

Break forth together into singing, you waste places of Jerusalem, for the Lord has comforted his people; he has redeemed Jerusalem. (Isaiah 52:9)

Have you ever been praising God as you were driving and looked out your side window and seen the guy next to you shaking his head? Do you agree with him as he muttered, "Another crazy driver!" or do you wonder if he is the crazy one?

"Selah!"

DAY 50

In distress you called, and I delivered you; I answered you in the secret place of thunder; I tested you at the waters of Meribah. Selah (**Psalm 81:7**)

Does God test us? Is this Biblical? The answer is yes. As a schoolteacher, I know the importance of testing. We will never know what a student knows until he or she is tested. It is the same way with God. But the test is more for us than Him.

For you, O God, have tested us; you have tried us as silver is tried. (**Psalm 66:10**)

O Lord of hosts who tests the righteous, who sees the heart and the mind. (**Jeremiah 20:12**)

Nowhere does it say God is testing the unsaved. He is testing the righteous. Look at Job.

There the Lord made for them a statute and a rule, and there he tested them saying, "If you will diligently listen to the voice of the Lord your God, and do that which is right in his eyes, and give ear to his commandments and keep all his statutes, I will put none of the diseases on you that I put on the Egyptians, for I am the Lord, your healer." (**Exodus 15:25-26**)

An interesting scripture in **Proverbs 27:21** says, *A man is tested by his praise.*

In this you rejoice, though now for a little while, if necessary, you have been grieved by various trials, so that the tested genuineness of your faith – more precious than gold that perishes though it is tested by fire – may be found to result in praise and glory and honor at the revelation of Jesus Christ. (**1 Peter 1:6-7**)

Our dog was dying. We thought the vet would have to put her to sleep. I kept thinking about how God cares for the birds of the air. With this in mind, I prayed for the Lord to heal our dog. I waited. I prayed again. I waited and I waited. One morning she jumped on the bed, perfectly whole. God even cares about our pets!

"Selah!"

DAY 51

How long will you judge unjustly and show partiality to the wicked? Selah **(Psalm 82:2)**

God will only put up with wickedness for so long and then He will judge. Just watching the news can open our eyes to things that God does not like. I cringe when someone says, "God" in any way other than to praise Him. This is a small evil, but is it? We are told not to take the Lord's name in vain. The Bible is our standard.

A worthless person, a wicked man, goes about with crooked speech, winks with his eyes, signals with his feet, points with his finger, with perverted heart devises evil, continually sowing discord; therefore, calamity will come upon him suddenly; in a moment he will be broken beyond healing. **(Proverbs 6:12-15).** Now that is one scary scripture.

A child covers his eyes and says, "You can't see me!" He truly believes that he is invisible, but is he? It is the same way with sin.

For God will bring every deed into judgment, with every secret thing, whether good or evil. (Ecclesiastes 12:4)

Isaiah 5:20 says, *Woe to those who call evil good and good evil, who put darkness for light and light for darkness, who put bitter for sweet and sweet for bitter.*

There is a way that seems right to a man, but its end is the way of death. **(Proverbs 14:12)**

It is so difficult not to compromise when we all want to be liked and accepted. It is so difficult to stand for God and His righteousness when everything around speaks the opposite. It is so difficult to raise a Christian family in this day and age. Everywhere we go we run headlong into the world and its ways. But God!

"Selah!"

DAY 52

Blessed are those who dwell in your house, ever singing your praise! Selah **(Psalm 84:4)**

There is joy in knowing Jesus. Being a Christian is the most joyous experience and lifestyle we can live. One of the signs that we are Christians is that we exhibit love and joy. Our lives are a reflection of the peace within us. We are a peculiar people.

Hebrews 12:2 says, *Let us run with endurance the race that is set before us looking to Jesus, the founder and perfecter of our faith, who for the joy that was set before him endured the cross.*

Jesus endured the cross with joy because He knew the end of the story. We also know the end of the story. Not only did Jesus have joy but also the disciples had joy when they discovered He was no longer in the tomb. Thus, we began our Christian walk.

Romans 14:17 says, *For the kingdom of God is not a matter of eating and drinking but of righteousness and peace and joy in the Holy Spirit.*

And the disciples were filled with joy and with the Holy Spirit. **(Acts 13:52)**

Count it all joy, my brothers when you meet trials of various kinds for you know that the testing of your faith, produces steadfastness. And let steadfastness have its full effect, that you may be perfect and complete, lacking nothing. **(James 2:4)**

Jesus said, *I have no greater joy than to hear that my children are walking in truth.* **(3 John 1:4)** Today let's walk in true joy.

Does this mean from the moment of our salvation, we can expect to feel joy? Great thought but we need an attitude adjustment for this to happen. The joy is there but it is a choice. Remember Jesus, <u>O</u>thers, <u>Y</u>ou! "Joy". An old acronym.

"Selah!"

DAY 53

O Lord God of hosts, hear my prayer; give ear, O God of Jacob! Selah (Psalm 84:8)

Have you ever asked yourself, "Does God really hear my prayer? Does He care about this one little piece of sand or star in the sky?" The answer to this question is, "Yes!" Not a single prayer goes unnoticed by our loving and knowing Father.

Rejoice always, pray without ceasing, give thanks in all circumstances; for this is the will of God in Christ Jesus for you. (1 Thessalonians 5:17)

He is telling us that we can talk with Him all the time. He is always there ready to listen. But how do I know that what I am praying is God's will? How do I know what to pray when I cannot see a solution? What if what I am praying is not according to His will?

The answer is, *Likewise the Spirit helps us in our weakness. For we do not know what to pray for as we ought, but the Spirit himself intercedes for us with groanings too deep for words.* (Romans 8:26)

The Lord's prayer is a good starting point. **(Luke 11:1)** In it we find all our needs met. We pray for daily bread. He says He will supply all our needs. We pray for forgiveness. When we confess our sins, He is faithful to forgive us our sins and cleanse us of all unrighteousness. We pray not to be tempted beyond what we can handle, and He has promised us a way out. Prayer is our way of communicating with our Father and more importantly, His way of communicating with us. So, pour out your heart to the Lord and be assured He is listening. *Selah!*

Sometimes we just need to be really honest with the Father and say, "Help me. I am clueless. I need Your wisdom and I bow down to Your answer." You will be surprised at the outcome of this totally yielded prayer.

"Selah!"

DAY 54

You forgave the iniquity of your people; you covered all their sin. Selah (Psalm 85:2)

Matthew 1:21 says, *She will bear a son, you shall call his name Jesus, for he will save his people from their sins.*

The good news is that Christ did not cover our sins, but He has come to remove them. As far as the East is from the West, He will remember them no more. It is as if they never were. If we could only grasp this, we would quit beating ourselves up over past failures! When confessed, sins are no more!

1 Corinthians 15:3 says, *Christ died for our sins in accordance with the Scriptures.* Was His death useless? If we are still holding onto past sins, then it was. Selah!

Acts 10:43 says, <u>*Everyone*</u> *who believes in him receives forgiveness of sins through his name.* **That means you!**

He has delivered us from the domain of darkness and transferred us to the king-dom of His beloved Son, in whom we have redemption the forgiveness of sins. **(Colossians 1:13-14)**

We no longer live in darkness, but we live in the light of his Son, Jesus Christ. We are new creations in Him. We are saved, sanctified, and set apart unto Him.

Hebrews 10:12-14 says, *But when Christ had offered for all time a single sacrifice for sins, He sat down at the right hand of God, waiting from that time until His enemies should be made a footstool for His feet. For by a single offering, He has perfected for all time those who are being sanctified.*

Sometimes I think God gets tired of our "forgive me" prayers. How many times do we have to say I am sorry? If we believe He forgives. Then that settles it!

"Selah!"

DAY 55

Glorious things of you are spoken, O City of God. Selah (Psalm 87:3)

What glorious things are coming out of our mouths?

James 3:8 tells us that, *No human being can tame the tongue…With it we bless our Lord and Father, and with it we curse people, who are made in the likeness of God.*

Matthew 12:37 says, *For by your words you will be justified, and by your words you will be condemned.*

Have you taken a word check lately? Are your words affirming or do they bring discouragement? Are they many or are they few? Do they edify or do they tear down?

Ecclesiastes 6:11 says, *The more words, the more vanity.*

Ecclesiastes 9:17 says, *The words of the wise heard in quiet are better than the shouting of a ruler among fools.*

Finally, **Ecclesiastes 12:11 says,** *The words of the wise are like goads.*

Today, I ask myself, "What glorious things are coming out of my mouth? Are they edifying and uplifting? Do they bring others closer to Christ? Are they life changing, or do they bring death?"

Have you noticed that sometimes when you speak truth you make people angry? Conviction is a funny thing. It hardly ever begins with a word of praise, but it is so necessary in each of our lives. Sometimes, when we become angry with someone's words, we need to put the thought on a shelf and let it rest a while. Later, we may come back and realize that person was right. Maybe not!

"Selah!"

DAY 56

The Lord records as He registers the peoples, "This one was born there." Selah (Psalm 87:6)

God has a record of your life. I cannot imagine how big His filing cabinet must be. In reading life after death accounts, people consistently say that their life flashed before them. Even though they saw the worst things they had done, there was a huge sense of God's love covering them. Right there we should learn a lesson.

Romans 14:12 says, *Each of us will give an account of himself to God.* There is nothing hidden from God, but He still loves us unconditionally. That is mind boggling.

Hebrews 4:13 says, *No creature is hidden from his sight, but all are naked and exposed to the eyes of him to whom we must give account.* We may be saved and sanctified, but we still have to own up to our errors and our lifestyles. This isn't so that He can punish us, but so that we can realize how much He loves us and how deep and wide His forgiveness is towards us.

Not only will the people of God be judged, but also those who have chosen to reject Him. Look at **1 Peter 4:5,** *But they will give account to Him who is ready to judge the living and the dead.* There is a judgment coming, but we have nothing to worry about because we are His and He is ours. What a relief!

If the only thing we understand about the cross is forgiveness, then that is enough to shout, Alleluia!

When we were little, we used to play hide and seek. We were always sure our hiding place was the best, and we would not be found. It seems to me this is true also in our Christian walk. We think we are hiding things from God because we do not immediately see consequences, but we eventually will be found.

"Selah!"

DAY 57

Psalm 88:6-7 says, *You have put me in the depths of the pit, in the regions dark and deep. Your wrath lies heavy upon me, and you overwhelm me with all your waves. Selah*

Have you ever felt like you were in a pit and there seemed to be no way out? I am sure we all have at times. Well right now there seems to be no beginning and no ending to the dilemmas we are facing. It is a pit! The world is clueless, and we are in the midst of all this chaos. Does God really know what is going on? Does He have a plan in all of this? Are we just pawns on the playing field? The answer is definitely, "Yes! Yes! and No!"

Jonah knew exactly what we are going through when he was in the belly of the big fish. He could see no way out and the seaweed was choking him. In the midst of this he said, *In my distress I called to the Lord, and he answered me. From deep in the realm of the dead I called for help, and you listened to my cry.* **(Jonah 2:1- 2)**

Jonah had rejected the call of God. He had tried to run from the Lord. His only redeeming quality was that he was honest with the sailors and saved them when he said, *Pick me up and throw me into the sea, and it will become calm. I know that it is my fault that this great storm has come upon you.* **(Jonah 1:12)**

It took Jonah three days to finally see the light both literally and figuratively. *What I have vowed I will make good. I will say, "Salvation comes from the Lord." And the Lord commanded the fish, and it vomited Jonah onto dry land.* **(Jonah 2:9-10)**

Many will put their trust in the Lord because of our confession and our lifestyles in the midst of what from all outward appearances seems like a disaster. People are watching to see how we will react. Is our God really who we say He is? The proof is in the pudding. Let's be a light to those around us. Let's be upbeat and positive.

"Selah!"

DAY 58

Do you work wonders for the dead? Do the departed rise up to praise you? Selah **(Psalm 88:7)**

What do we know about heaven from the word of God? Well, first we know our Father lives in heaven. **(Matthew 6:9)** Then we know He has a kingdom. **(Matthew 6:10)** We know we will receive rewards in heaven which will cause us to leap for joy. **(Luke 6:23)** We know our names are written in heaven. **(Luke 10:20)** We know that heaven rejoices when one sinner repents. **(Luke 15:7)** We know there will be treasures in heaven. **(Luke 18:22)**

We know that a person cannot receive even one thing unless it is given from heaven. **(John 3:27)** Jesus is the bread that came down from heaven. **(John 6:42)** Remember manna also came from heaven. We know that the Holy Spirit fills us with his Spirit, and He is in heaven. **(Acts 2:2-4)**

We know that heaven is God's throne, and the earth is His footstool. **(Acts 7:49)** We know that we shall bear the image of the heavenly man. **(1 Corinthians 15:49)** We know we will be united with Christ in heaven. **(Ephesians 1:10)**

We know that at the name of Jesus every knee will bow, in heaven and on earth and under the earth. **(Philippians 2:10)** We know our citizenship is in heaven. **(Philippians 3:20)**

We know we have a great high priest in heaven, named Jesus. **(Hebrews 4:14)** We know Jesus is coming back with a shout from heaven. **(1 Thessalonians 4:16)**

But in keeping with his promises we are looking forward to a new heaven and a new earth, where righteousness dwells. **(2 Peter 3:13)**

There are hundreds of "Life After Death" books on the market. If it were just one or two, we might question. But with so many people sharing their personal experiences, we must pause and wonder, "Could this be true?"

"Selah!"

DAY 59

I will establish your offspring forever and build your throne for all generations. Selah (Psalm 89:4)

And if it is evil in your eyes to serve the Lord, choose this day whom you will serve, whether the gods your fathers served in the region beyond the River, or the gods of the Amorites in whose land you dwell. But as for me and my house, we will serve the Lord. (Joshua 24:15)

As parents we have a huge responsibility, *to Train up a child in the way he should go; even when he is old, he will not depart from it.* **(Proverbs 22:6)** Today many parents are giving mixed signals to their children. We are saying we believe, but our actions are crying out, "NOT!" In the midst of this, our children are confused and really don't know what to believe. These should not be my friends.

Isaiah 59:21 says, *My Spirit that is upon you and my words that I have put in your mouth, shall not depart out of your mouth, or out of the mouth of your off-spring, or out of the mouth of your children's offspring, says the Lord, from this time forth and forever.*

It is so much more difficult today with all the social media. Our children are exposed to things we never dreamed of. Therefore, we need to be more vigilant then ever in our homes to display true Christianity. We model what our children will become and that is really scary. But how? By loving them!

Love is patient and kind; love does not envy or boast; it is not arrogant or rude. It does not insist on its own way; it is not irritable or resentful; it does not rejoice at wrongdoing but rejoices with truth. Love bears all things, believes all things, hopes all things, endures all things. (1 Corinthians 13)

We are in an endurance race. The only way we can win is to follow the great commandment. *"Love one another even as I have loved you."*

"Selah!"

DAY 60

Like the moon it shall be established forever, a faithful witness in the skies. Selah (**Psalm 89:37**)

I have read and reread this whole chapter several times. I think this verse is referring to the Word of God. I think the verse is saying that God's word remains forever even as the moon and the stars in the sky. With this thought in mind, here goes my thought for the day.

My question is this, "Is the Word of God unchangeable?" Does God mean what He says, and does He say what He means? Before our walk can become stable, we need to establish what we believe about the Word of God. Otherwise, we are tossed about by every whim of doctrine.

And the Lord said to Moses, "Is the Lord's hand shortened? Now you shall see whether my word will come true for you or not." (**Numbers 11:23**)

God does not mind our asking. He wants to show us the faithfulness of His word. We only have to ask.

He says, *I will not violate my covenant or alter the word that went forth from my lips."* (Psalm 89:34)

In other words, He is saying, He will not change His mind. What He has spoken He will stand behind. He says, *I the Lord do not change.* (Malachi 3:6)

I am wondering today if we really believed that the Word of the Lord was forever, and that we could not only believe it but speak it, would our lives be different? Would we walk in power such as Peter and Paul? Would people seek us out wanting to know about our Lord? Would the word "But" be erased from our vocabulary? I don't know, but I do understand the enormous responsibility afforded us when we do speak the Word. We must be sure it is His Word and not ours. *For the word of God is living and active, sharper than any two-edged sword.* (Hebrews 4:12)

"Selah!"

DAY 61

Like the heavens praise your wonders, O Lord, your faithfulness in the assembly of the holy ones! For who in the skies can be compared to the Lord? Who among the heavenly beings is like the Lord, a God greatly to be feared in the counsel of the holy ones, and awesome above all who are around him. Selah (Psalm 89:5-7)

We drove to Durango this afternoon and as we were driving the clouds became bigger and more massive. They were pure white and majestic. The mountains were capped with snow, even though the terrain was green. It would have been difficult not to acknowledge the splendor of God's creation. Right in front of us were multitudes of colors expressing the creativity of our God. If we can praise the wonders here on earth, I can hardly imagine what the wonders of heaven will be like. Remember when we use to see figures in the cloud? I still do!

Yours, Lord, is the greatness and the power and the glory and the majesty and the splendor, for everything in heaven and earth is yours. Yours, Lord, is the kingdom; you are exalted as head over all. (1 Chronicles 29:11)

It becomes easy to praise when we look up and out and see what the Lord has done. When we breathe in the scent of the roses and catch a glimpse of a herd of elk grazing in the low land.

When I consider your heavens, the work of your fingers, the moon, and the stars, which you have set in place, what is mankind that you are mindful of them, human beings that you care for them? (Psalm 8:3-4)

And he passed in front of Moses, proclaiming, "The Lord, the Lord, the compassionate and gracious God, slow to anger, abounding in love and faithfulness." (Exodus 34:6)

He is not only faithful to those on the earth but in the assembly of the holy ones.

Who is like you, Lord God almighty? You, Lord, are mighty, and your faithfulness surrounds you. (Psalm 89:8) What a mighty God we serve!

"Selah!"

DAY 62

You have cut short the days of his youth; you have covered him with shame. Selah (**Psalm 89:45**)

Remember not the sins of my youth or my transgressions; according to your steadfast love remember me, for the sake of your goodness, O Lord! (**Psalm 25:7**)

It is a time to remember what has been, what is and what is to come. It is a time to reflect on our Nation and on our personal lives. There is nothing wrong with looking back and reflecting on what used to be, but we do not live in the past, but in the now.

We need to ask ourselves what we have learned from the past? What things would we have done differently if given another opportunity, and what things would we repeat because they were good?

We need to let go of those things that have held us back and look forward to what is ahead. How can we be part of the solution rather than part of the problem? How can we better serve those around us in the future? How can we encourage those that are discouraged? How can we help those in need? What difference can we make in the lives of others? Are we aware of the things going on around us or are we living in a bubble?

Today is truly the first day of the rest of our lives. Yesterday is gone and tomorrow has not yet come. What are we doing today? When we come to this day next year, will we have a totally different perspective than we have today? Will God be pleased?

For I will be merciful toward their iniquities, and I will remember their sins no more. (**Hebrews 8:12**)

"Selah!"

DAY 63

What man can live and never see death? Who can deliver his soul from the power of Sheol? Selah (**Psalm 89:48**)

Jesus said, *"I am the resurrection and the life. Whoever believes in me, though he dies, yet shall he live, and everyone who lives and believes in me shall never die. Do you believe this?"* (**John 11:25**)

Jesus question then is the same today. Do you believe this? The answer to this question is the most important answer you will ever give because it determines life from death. "Yes Lord, I believe!"

And just as it is appointed for man to die once, and after that comes judgment, so Christ, having been offered once to bear the sins of many, will appear a second time, not to deal with sin but to save those who are eagerly waiting for him. (**Hebrews 9:27-28**)

As we settle what we believe, then we can eagerly await the final reward. No longer do we need to walk in fear, but we can walk in faith.

For if you live according to the flesh you will die, but if by the Spirit you put to death the deeds of the body, you will live. For all who are led by the Spirit of God are sons of God. For you did not receive the spirit of slavery to fall back into fear, but you have received the Spirit of adoption as sons, by whom we cry, "Abba! Father!" (**Romans 8:13-15**)

I was thinking about my father this morning and realized that I did not need to continually beg him to be my father. He just was! It is the same way with Father God. When we are His, we are His. We do not need to continually beg Him but just accept the fact and walk in it. This revelation sets us free to be the people God wants us to be. Perfect love casts out all fear and Father God is perfect love.

So, take a deep breath and whisper "Father". He hears and He answers.

"Selah!"

DAY 64

They make their tongue sharp as a serpent, and under their lips is the venom of asps. Selah (Psalm 140:3)

Luke 6:45 says, *The good person out of the good treasure of his heart produces good, and the evil person out of his evil treasure produces evil, for out of the abundance of the heart his mouth speaks.*

Consider how important our words are to those around us and to ourselves. **Proverbs 18:21 says,** *Death and life are in the power of the tongue and those who love it will eat its fruits.*

Psalm 39:1 says, *I will guard my ways, that I may not sin with my tongue; I will guard my mouth with a muzzle.* I picture a dog with a muzzle on, which prevents him from biting people. (like our words do sometimes)

Psalm 141:3 says, *Set a guard, O Lord, over my mouth; keep watch over the door of my lips!* In other words, muzzle my mouth.

Even though we are speaking of the mouth, it is really a heart issue. We speak what is in our heart and our heart is tempered by the things we put in it. What are we allowing into our hearts? Are they filled with the goodness of God or with worldly matters?

Matthew 15:11 says, *It is not what goes into the mouth that defiles a person, but what comes out of the mouth; this defiles a person.*

Let the words of my mouth and the meditation of my heart be acceptable in your sight, O Lord, my rock, and my redeemer. (Psalm 19:14)

The answer to my dilemma is my rock and my redeemer. He is able to do abundantly more than I ask or think! He can tame my tongue.

"Selah!"

DAY 65

Grant not, O Lord, the desires of the wicked; do not further their evil plot, or they will be exalted! Selah **(Psalm 140:8)**

For everyone who does wicked things hates the light and does not come to the light, lest his works should be exposed. But whoever does what is true comes to the light, so that it may be clearly seen that his works have been carried out in God. **(John 3: 20-21)**

I am sure you know that most crime does not happen during the day but at night. Most sin is committed under cover. Even Christian sin is hidden from the eyes of the believers and we Christians do sin. The secret is to stay in the light.

But the Lord is faithful. He will establish you and guard you against the evil one. **(2 Thessalonians 3:2-3)**

Matthew 6:13 as part of the Lord's prayer says And lead us not into temptation but deliver us from evil. Jesus is talking to believers. We are not immune from sin.

But Jesus says, *"Watch and pray that you may not enter into temptation. The spirit indeed is willing, but the flesh is weak."* **(Matthew 26:41)**

Even Paul who walked as closely to the Lord as anyone said, *Wretched man that I am! Who will deliver me from this body of death?* **(Romans 7:24)**

But we have hope! *No temptation has overtaken you that is not common to man. God is faithful, and he will not let you be tempted beyond your ability, but with the temptation he will also provide the way of escape, that you may be able to endure.* **(1 Corinthians 10:13)**

There is a way of escape. His name is Jesus.

"Selah!"

DAY 66

We live in an arrogant society. I will do it my way. I know what is best. Do not tell me what to do or where to go. Even our children seem bent on having it their own way. This week a person was murdered for asking someone to wear a face mask. Arrogance is a sin. There is a difference between arrogance and confidence. I am confident in my God and His ability. I know He is able to do exceedingly, abundantly more than I ask or think. This is not arrogance.

The dictionary defines arrogance as "Exaggerating or disposed to exaggerate one's own worth or importance often by an overbearing manner, haughty, pretentious, proud, scornful." You get the picture.

2 Timothy 3:1-5 says, *In the last days there will come times of difficulty. For people will be lovers of self, lovers of money, proud, arrogant, abusive, disobedient to their parents, ungrateful, unholy, heartless, unappeasable, slanderous, without self-control, brutal, not loving good, treacherous, reckless, swollen with conceit, lovers of pleasure rather than lovers of God, having the appearance of godliness, but denying its power. Avoid such people.*

2 Samuel 22:28 says, *You save a humble people, but your eyes are on the haughty to bring them down.*

Psalm 25:9 says, *He leads the humble in what is right, and teaches the humble his way.*

God opposes the proud but gives grace to the humble...Humble yourselves before the Lord, and he will exalt you. **(James 4:6-10)**

Do you think at times we need to eat a little humble pie?

"Selah!"

DAY 67

I remember the days of old; I meditate on all that you have done; I ponder the work of your hands. I stretch out my hands to you; my soul thirsts for you like a parched land. Selah (**Psalm 143:5-6**)

This is the last "Selah!" in the Psalms. There are three more which we will look at but since this is the last one in Psalms, I think it is probably the most important. He says, "I ponder the work of your hands."

Ponder means to consider something deeply and thoroughly; meditate, mull over, reflect upon, give thought to. It literally means to weigh something. Often, I am guilty of reading God's word but not pondering over it; taking the time to really digest what He is saying. Guilty!

Psalm 64:9 says, *Then all mankind fears; they tell what God has brought about and ponder what he has done. Take a minute to ponder what God has done in your life.*

I will ponder all your work and meditate on your mighty deeds. (**Psalm 77:12**)

Ponder the path of your feet; then all your ways will be sure. Do not swerve to the right or to the left; turn your foot away from evil. (**Proverbs 4:26-27**)

So far, we have spent 67 days thinking and pondering on God's word. We have searched a multitude of topics and hopefully have taken the time to ponder on the things we have read. It is interesting that the word "ponder" is only used five times in Psalms, two times in Proverbs and one time in Isaiah. Yet the richness of the scripture only happens when we take the time to ponder what we are reading. Prayerfully, I hope today you will truly spend time pondering at least one scripture and come away with new revelation since this is what the word "Selah!" truly means.

DAY 68

O Lord, I have heard the report of you, and your work, O Lord, do I fear. In the midst of the years revive it; in the midst of the years make it known; in wrath remember mercy. God came from Teman, and the Holy One from Mount Paran. Selah (Habakkuk 3:1-3)

Mercy means to show compassion or forgiveness toward someone whom it is within one's power to punish or harm. In order to truly understand God's mercy, we must understand His great love for us even when we do not deserve it. When God instructed Moses to build a tabernacle, He included in it a mercy seat made of pure gold. He said, "There I will meet with you, and from above the mercy seat... I will speak to you." (Exodus 25:17) It is in God's mercy that He speaks to us.

Lamentations 3:22-23 says, *The steadfast love of the Lord never ceases; his mercies never come to an end; they are new every morning; great is your faithfulness.*

As for you, O Lord, you will not restrain your mercy from me; your steadfast love and your faithfulness will ever preserve me! (Psalm 40:11)

God's steadfast love is always tempered by His mercy. If it were not so, we would all be destroyed by God's holiness.

Psalm 145:9 says, *The Lord is good to all, and his mercy is over all that he has made.*

From the moment God breathed the breath of life into Adam, He was exhibiting His mercy. He already had a plan for redemption in place, knowing that man would fall.

He saved us, not because of works done by us in righteousness, but according to his own mercy. (Titus 3:5)

"Selah!"

DAY 69

You stripped the sheath from your bow, calling for many arrows. Selah (Habakkuk 3:9)

Does God ever get angry? Sometimes I think we think He just covers His eyes at the sin in the world and plays like it never happened. But that is not true.

Now therefore go, and I will be with your mouth and teach you what you shall speak. But he said, "Oh, my Lord, please send someone else." Then the anger of the Lord was kindled against Moses. (Exodus 4:12-14)

Why was God angry? When God tells us to do something, He also equips us to do it and expects us to trust Him. He does not call the equipped but those who need to rely upon Him.

And the people complained in the hearing of the Lord about their misfortunes, and when the Lord heard it, his anger was kindled. (Numbers 11:1)

God had brought the people out of Egypt, parted the red sea, given them water to drink, sent manna and quail, protected them all along the way and they did not appreciate what He had done for them, instead they complained.

God gets angry when we do not appreciate all that He has done for us. He has provided for all of our needs and even many of our wants. We need to take the time to thank Him for all he has done for us and for providing for our future. We are His inheritance. We are not orphans in the Kingdom of God but sons and daughters of the Most High!

Why then were you not afraid to speak against my servant Moses? And the anger of the Lord was kindled against them, and he departed. (Numbers 12:8-9)

God is angry when we speak against his anointed. You are part of the anointed.

"Selah!"

DAY 70

You crushed the head of the house of the wicked, laying him bare from thigh to neck. Selah (Habakkuk 3:13)

What a note to end this series on! There are 73 "Selahs" in the word and we have covered them all. If nothing else, I hope we are more conscious of pausing and contemplating what God is saying. I hope we are learning not to take God's word for granted. I hope out of this time together you have drawn closer to God. Let's look at a few things that God calls wicked.

Exodus 23:1 says, You shall not spread a false report. You shall not join hands with a wicked man to be a malicious witness. In other words, God does not like gossip.

1 Samuel 1:9 says, He will guard the feet of his faithful ones, but the wicked shall be cut off in darkness, for not by might shall a man prevail. God wants us to rely upon Him. He wants us to trust His will.

Proverbs 4:14 says, Do not enter the path of the wicked, and do not walk in the way of the evil. We are told to pick our friends carefully.

John 3:20 says, For everyone who does wicked things hates the light and does not come to the light, lest his works should be exposed. Anything that we do should not be done in darkness. We should not be afraid to have our lives as an open book. God wants the world to see us and proudly say, "These are My kids!"

God loves us!

"Selah!"

THE HOLY SPIRIT AND YOU

DAY 71

And behold, I am sending the promise of my Father upon you. But stay in the city until you are clothed with power from on high. (**Luke 24:49**)

When our youngest son was about 5 years old, he came home from Sunday School one Sunday and said, "I am afraid of the Holy Ghost. I don't like ghosts." Now at the time I thought this was funny, but in reflecting, I believe many of us are afraid of the Holy Spirit. We are afraid of those things we do not understand. Hopefully, as we begin to study why the Holy Spirit came to dwell among us, we will become more comfortable and begin to long for His presence in our lives in new and deeper ways.

He has always been around since the beginning of time. *In Genesis 1:1-2 it says, In the beginning, God created the heavens and the earth. The earth was without form and void, and darkness was over the face of the deep. And the Spirit of God hovered over the face of the waters.*

Hover means to move to and from near a place. I like to think of the Holy Spirit hovering over us as we go about our day-to-day activities. The Spirit has promised He will never leave us nor forsake us. He is hovering over us!

Who is the Spirit of the Lord? *Isaiah 11:2 says, And the Spirit of the Lord shall rest upon him, (Jesus) the Spirit of wisdom and understanding, the Spirit of counsel and might, the Spirit of knowledge and the fear of the Lord.*

Romans 8:26-27 says, *Likewise the Spirit helps us in our weakness. For we do not know what to pray for as we ought, but the Spirit himself intercedes for us with groanings too deep for words. And he who searches hearts knows what is in the mind of the Spirit, because the Spirit intercedes for the saints according to the will of God.*

When we are totally stumped trying to pray for someone, we have nothing to fear because the Spirit will help us pray according to the will of God. He is our helper.

"Come Holy Spirit, Come!"

DAY 72

The Holy Spirit is part of the Trinity. He has always been and will always be. He is an integral part of the whole Bible. He was in the beginning and His job description has never changed.

When Moses was instructed by God to build the tabernacle God called Bezalel to be his craftsman. *And I have filled him with the Spirit of God, with ability and intelligence, with knowledge and all craftsmanship, to devise artistic designs, etc.* **(Exodus 31:3)** Bezalel knew how to build the tabernacle, because the Spirit was directing him. The Spirit anointed builders.

Then in **Numbers 11:25**, God transferred some of his power from Moses to the seventy elders. *Then the Lord came down in the cloud and spoke to him and took some of the Spirit that was on him and put it on the seventy elders. And soon the Spirit rested on them, they prophesied.* The Spirit anointed leaders.

The Lord raised up Othniel...The Spirit of the Lord was upon him, and he judged Israel. **(Judges 3:10)** The Spirit anointed judges.

Then Samuel took the horn of oil and anointed him in the midst of his brothers. And the Spirit of the Lord rushed upon David from that day forward. **(1 Samuel 16:13)** The Spirit anointed kings.

In **2 Chronicles 15:1**, *The Spirit of the Lord came upon Azariah the son of Oded, and he went out to meet Asa and said to him, "Hear me, Asa and all Judah and Benjamin. The Lord is with you while you are with him. If you seek him, he will be found by you, but if you forsake him, he will forsake you."* The Spirit anointed messengers.

Psalm 143:10 says, *Teach me to do your will, for you are my God! Let your good Spirit lead me on level ground!* The Spirit is a teacher.

If the Spirit anointed all of these men of God, I wonder what He can do in each of our lives, if we will allow Him? Don't ever underestimate His power in your life.

"Come Holy Spirit, Come!"

DAY 73

Let's look at just a few more passages in the Old Testament before we head to the New Testament.

And I will put my Spirit within you and cause you to walk in my statutes and be careful to obey my rules. (**Ezekiel 36:27**) The Spirit helps us walk in His ways.

The hand of the Lord was upon me, and he brought me out in the Spirit of the Lord and set me down in the middle of the valley; it was full of bones. (**Ezekiel 37:1**) The Spirit will show us truths in His word.

And I will not hide my face anymore from them, when I pour out my Spirit upon the house of Israel, declares the Lord God. (**Ezekiel 39:29**)

But as for me, I am filled with power, with the Spirit of the Lord, and with justice and might, to declare to Jacob his transgression and to Israel his sin. (**Micah 3:8**) The Spirit will convict of sin.

I am with you, declares the Lord of hosts, according to the covenant that I made with you when you came out of Egypt. My Spirit remains in your midst. Fear not. (**Haggai 2:5**) The Spirit of God was with the people all through the Old Testament.

Then he said to me, "This is the word of the Lord to Zerubbabel: Not by might, nor by power, but by my Spirit, says the Lord of hosts." (**Zechariah 4:6**) The Spirit does for us what we cannot do for ourselves.

In the Old Testament the Spirit came upon certain people for certain tasks, but in the New Testament the Spirit entered into all those who believed. We have the power to do what God has called us to do because the Holy Spirit dwells in us.

And it shall come to pass afterwards, that I will pour out my Spirit on all flesh; your sons and your daughters shall prophesy, your old men shall dream dreams, and your young men shall see visions. Even on the male and female servants in those days I will pour out my Spirit. (**Joel 2:28-29**) We are living in those days.

We are living in the most exciting times since creation.

"Come Holy Spirit, Come!"

DAY 74

We have seen some of the ways the Holy Spirit operated in the Old Testament. But does He do the same in the New? We saw that He inspired builders and appointed judges and kings. He sent out messengers and teachers. He showed people how to walk in His ways. He revealed truth and convicted people of their sins. However, as we saw His Spirit was on certain people, not everyone.

Now we come to the New Testament.

And behold, I am sending the promise of my Father upon you. But stay in the city until you are clothed with power from on high. (**Luke 24:49**) He was specifically speaking to the 11 disciples, but 120 people took Him at His word. They waited, they prayed, they watched, and they expected.

Now we might say these were special people, not the ordinary run of the mill. Were they? Are we?

But you are a chosen people, a royal priesthood, a holy nation, God's special possession, that you may declare the praises of him who called you out of darkness into his wonderful light. (**1 Peter 2:9**)

He is speaking of you and me. We are now those who are the called, filled with His Holy Spirit, equipped to do His will. We are His workmanship created in Christ Jesus.

Since He has given each of us an assignment, we need the Holy Spirit operating in our lives in a real and personal way to fulfill our calling.

You, however, are not in the realm of the flesh but are in the realm of the Spirit, if indeed the Spirit of God lives in you. And if anyone does not have the Spirit of Christ, they do not belong to Christ. But if Christ is in you, then even though your body is subject to death because of sin, the spirit gives life because of righteousness. (**Romans 8:9-10**)

When we ask Jesus Christ to dwell in us, the Spirit of God comes in to make His home in us and we are led by Him. What a relief! We don't have to go it alone.

"Come Holy Spirit, Come!"

DAY 75

Let's begin at the beginning of the Holy Spirit's indwelling in believers.

"Peace be with you! As the Father has sent me, I am sending you." And with that he breathed on them and said, "Receive the Holy Spirit. If you forgive anyone's sins, their sins are forgiven; if you do not forgive them, they are not forgiven." **(John 20: 21-23)**

Jesus was about to return to His Father. He did not want to leave those on earth defenseless. As the disciples were together, Jesus came and stood among them. He again showed them His hands and side. These people were no different from you and me. Show me one more time and I will believe. How many times have I said or thought that? Oh, me of little faith!

At that moment they received the Holy Spirit. But I have noticed that they and we are constantly needing a recharge. A little dab will not do us! The Holy Spirit is with us to fill us and fill us and refill us. We need to be continually open to Him. Understand though, when we receive Jesus Christ into our hearts, we receive the Holy Spirt in His fullness. Praise God!

Proof of this is in **Acts 1:4-5** *Do not leave Jerusalem, but wait for the gift my Father promised, which you have heard me speak about. For John baptized with water, but in a few days you will be baptized with the Holy Spirit.*

The disciples had received the Holy Spirit when Jesus breathed on them. But He was saying, "Wait there is more." The Holy Spirit wants to be an active part of each of our lives. He wants to live His life through us. He is just waiting for us to consent. I do not believe the Holy Spirit will do anything in our lives apart from our willingness to allow Him to do so. Salvation is a gift we must receive. God does not force Himself on us. He does not force His love on us. He does not force us to obey. He waits yearning for our consent. He has given us free will. Hmmm! Think on that a minute.

"Holy Spirit you are welcome in this place. Omnipotent Father of mercy and grace. You are welcome in this place."

"Come Holy Spirit, Come!"

DAY 76

We have confessed with our mouth and believed in our heart that Jesus is the Christ, the Son of the Living God. The Spirit of God has now come to dwell in us. Is this all there is to it? We are saved, sanctified, and set apart but to what? We are to now walk in the Spirit.

Those who live in accordance with the Spirit have their minds set on what the Spirit desires. The mind governed by the flesh is death, but the mind governed by the Spirit is life and peace. (**Romans 8:5-6**)

Therefore, there is now no condemnation for those who are in Christ Jesus, because through Christ the law of the Spirit who gives life has set you free from the law of sin and death. (**Romans 8:1-2**)

What a freeing thought. We can now walk unafraid knowing that as we walk, the Spirit of God inside us will lead us and guide us into all truth. When our minds are stayed on Him, we will hear His still small voice directing our steps. *This is the way walk in it.*

For those who are led by the Spirit of God are children of God. The Spirit you received does not make you slaves, so that you live in fear again; rather the Spirit you received brought about your adoption to sonship. And by him we cry, "Abba, Father." The Spirit himself testifies with our spirit that we are God's children. (**Romans 8:14-16**)

"Does God take care of His own?" The answer is a resounding, "Yes!" Many children do not understand some of the rules and regulations that their parents put down. They think they are unreasonable until they too become a parent. In the same way God is looking out for each of us. He cares for us. Sometimes we do not understand the way He leads us, but if we will follow, eventually we will see. Have you ever noticed that the more difficult a situation, the harder it is to resolve, the more you learn in the end? God is looking for end results, not moment by moment victories. Learn to trust Him and His ways!

"Come Holy Spirit, Come!"

DAY 77

Is the Holy Spirit any different in the New Testament than He was in the Old Testament? I don't think so. He says, *"I am the Lord. I change not."* So, what is different in the New Testament? Something wonderful! He does not come upon certain people, but He is within all who believe. He doesn't care whether we are rich or poor. He doesn't care about the color of our skin. He doesn't care if we are young or old. He wants to indwell each of us and become our Helper. I can use all the help I can get.

If you love me, you will keep my commandments. And I will ask the Father, and he will give you another Helper, to be with you forever, even the Spirit of truth, whom the world cannot receive because it neither sees him nor knows him. You know him, for he dwells with you and will be in you. (John 14:16-17)

Remember Jesus is at the right hand of the Father making intercession for us. He is not dwelling with us but with the Father. However, He has not left us as orphans but has sent His Holy Spirit to live in us. We are covered!

These things I have spoken to you while I am still with you. But the Helper, the Holy Spirit, whom the Father will send in my name, He will teach you all things and bring to your remembrance all that I have said to you. (John 14:26)

Nevertheless, I tell you the truth: it is to your advantage that I go away, for if I do not go away, the Helper will not come to you. But if I go, I will send him to you. And when he comes, he will convict the world concerning sin and righteousness and judgement: concerning sin, because they do not believe in me; concerning righteousness, because I go to the Father, and you will see me no longer; concerning judgment, because the ruler of this world is judged. (John 16:7-11)

We have a Helper who is only waiting for us to ask for His help! Let's do it and see how much better our lives become under His supreme rule.

"Come Holy Spirit, Come!"

DAY 78

He is our Paraclete. This means called to come along side. He is our advocate, intercessor, pleader, comforter, aider, consoler, defender, helper, etc.

He is our deposit, seal, and earnest. *And it is God who establishes us with you in Christ, and has anointed us, and who has also put his seal on us and given us his Spirit in our hearts as a guarantee.* (1 Corinthians 1:21-22)

He who has prepared us for this very thing is God, who has given us the Spirit as a guarantee. (2 Corinthians 5:5)

In him you also, when you heard the word of truth, the gospel of your salvation, and believe in him, were sealed with the promised Holy Spirit, who is the guarantee of our inheritance until we acquire possession of it, to the praise of his glory. (Ephesians 1:13-14)

What does this mean to you and me? A big, huge sigh! When we receive the Holy Spirit, we are sealed. Our salvation is guaranteed. We are on our way to heaven shouting, "Victory!"

Does this mean we can relax and do our own thing? I don't think so. But it does mean if we walk with Him and talk with Him and obey Him, we have absolutely nothing to worry about. We can spend our days basking in His presence with the full knowledge that one day we will spend eternity with Him. We are saved, sealed, and packaged to enter into the fullness of life with Him.

Then the question becomes, "Why aren't we?" Could unbelief be part of the problem? Could the cares of this world be another part of the problem? Could unforgiveness be part of the problem? Add a few of your own reasons. I think we can find many. "Trust and obey. There is no other way to be happy in Jesus than to trust and obey." I love that song and need to sing it more often.

The Paraclete is with us. He wants to come along side of us and be involved in every part of our lives. The choice is ours.

"Come Holy Spirit, Come!"

DAY 79

But I say, walk by the Spirit, and you will not gratify the desires of the flesh.
(Galatians 5:16)

What a powerful promise. If we walk by the Spirit, we will not gratify the desires
of the flesh. It seems I am always trying to gratify the desires of the flesh. Just one
more donut, just one word in my defense, just this one TV show. It's not too bad.
Think of some of the things you struggle with. There is an answer to our problem.
Walk by the Spirit.

For the desires of the flesh are against the Spirit, and the desires of the Spirit are
against the flesh, for these are opposed to each other, to keep you from doing the
things you want to do. **(Galatians 5:16)**

It is New Year's Day. You decide to make a few resolutions. Good idea but almost
always impossible to keep. There we go again fighting the flesh.

Now the works of the flesh are evident: sexual immorality, impurity, sensuality,
idolatry, sorcery, enmity, strife, jealousy, fits of anger, rivalries, dissensions, divi-
sions, envy, drunkenness, orgies and things like these. **(V19-20)**

About half of these I can mark off as not a problem, but then I come to jealousy,
anger, rivalries, dissension, division, envy. Ok Lord, quit meddling. So again, what
is the answer? Walk by the Spirit.

But the fruit of the Spirit is love, joy, peace, patience, kindness, goodness, faith-
fulness, gentleness, self-control: against such things there is no law. **(V 22)**

And those who belong to Christ Jesus have crucified the flesh with its passions
and desires. **(V24)**

I have noticed that the longer I walk with the Lord, the more of these things are
dropping off. I do not struggle like I did when I first began to walk. I am in the
Word more. I pray more. I listen more. I accept more. I give more. I believe more.

"Come Holy Spirit, Come!"

DAY 80

The Holy Spirit is our counselor. **Isaiah 11:2 says** *He is the Spirit of counsel and might.*

Thinking about the fruit of the Spirit, I realize that I need a Counselor to help me walk in the Spirit. I cannot do it by myself. Sometimes I feel unlovely, unkind, uncaring but I have a go-between, the Holy Spirit to counsel me and point me in the right direction.

And I will ask the Father, and he will give you another Helper (Counselor) to be with you forever, even the Spirit of truth. (**John 14:16**) We have not been left defenseless. We have an advocate in the Holy Spirit. He is here to lead us and guide us into all truth.

Nevertheless, I tell you the truth: it is to your advantage that I go away for if I do not go away the Helper (Counselor) will not come to you. But if I go, I will send him to you. And when he comes, he will convict the world concerning sin and righteousness and judgment; concerning sin, because they do not believe in me; concerning righteousness, because I go to the Father, and you will see me no longer; concerning judgment, because the ruler of this world is judged. (**John 14:7-11**)

Do you know other people are not our problem? We do not need to point fingers. We do not need to judge. We do not need to condemn. We have the Counselor who is willing and able to pass judgment in a way that will not destroy but build up the Body of Christ. He is able to turn the heartless into those with a heart full of praise. He is able to convict the convicts and soften the hearts of those who are full of hate. He is able to show mercy, love and grace in a way that brings healing to the nations.

For we know him who said, "Vengeance is mine; I will repay." And again, "The Lord will judge his people." (**Hebrews 10:30**)

"Come Holy Spirit, Come!"

DAY 81

What no eye has seen, nor ear heard, nor the heart of man imagined, what God has prepared for those who love him…these things God has revealed to us through the Spirit. **(1 Corinthians 2:9-10) (All scriptures today are from 1 Corinthians 2.)**

God speaks to us through the Holy Spirit. When we hear a whisper, a thought, or a word it is coming from the Holy Spirit. He is the part of the Trinity that is dwelling with us today. He is our Paraclete.

For the Spirit searches everything, even the depths of God. **(V10)** What He hears from the Father or the Son, He relates to us. He always has an ear to the Father.

For who knows a person's thoughts except the spirit of that person, who is in him? So also no one comprehends the thoughts of God except the Spirit of God. **(V11)** This is a very comforting verse for me because I know that only God knows our thoughts. Satan cannot get into our heads except by suggestions that we react to. He does not know what we are thinking unless we verbalize it. For this reason, when we are in a battle with him, we need to speak scripture out loud. He has no idea what we are saying when it is only a thought. Jesus said, "It is written" each time the Devil tempted Him. He did not think it, but He spoke it.

Now we have received not the spirit of the world, but the Spirit who is from God, that we might understand the things freely given us by God. And we impart this in words not taught by human wisdom but taught by the Spirit, interpreting spiritual truths to those who are spiritual. **(V12-13)**

The natural person does not accept the things of the Spirit of God, for they are folly to him, and he is not able to understand them because they are spiritually discerned. **(V14)** Have you ever wondered why non-believers don't get it?

For who has understood the mind of the Lord so as to instruct him? But we have the mind of Christ. **(V15)**

"Come Holy Spirit, Come!"

DAY 82

"I am sending you." And when he had said this, he breathed on them and said to them, "Receive the Holy Spirit. If you forgive the sins of any, they are forgiven then; if you withhold forgiveness from any, it is withheld." (**John 20:22**)

The Holy Spirit is called the Ruach or the breath of God. *Then the Lord God formed the man of dust from the ground and breathed into his nostrils the breath of life and the man became a living creature.* (**Genesis 2:7**) I am wondering if the breath of the Holy Spirit left man when he sinned and was banned from the Garden of Eden? Is the breath of life what we are missing until we ask Jesus Christ to become our Lord and Master? What do you think?

But it is the spirit in man, the breath of the Almighty that makes him understand. It is not the old who are wise, nor the aged who understand what is right. (**Job 32:8-9**) No it is the Spirit of God which gives wisdom and understanding to each of us. So, we need to receive the Holy Spirit.

The Spirit of God has made me, and the breath of the Almighty gives me life. (**Job 33:4**) When the Lord God breathed into man's nostrils was this the breath of the Holy Spirit? Remember in the Old Testament the Holy Spirit came upon certain people. He was not within all mankind.

By the word of the Lord the heavens were made, and by the breath of his mouth all their host. (**Psalm 33:6**) Jesus is the Word. The Holy Spirit is the breath of God. The Trinity has always worked together.

Thus says God, the Lord, who created the heavens and stretched them out, who spread out the earth and what comes from it, who gives breath to the people on it and spirit to those who walk in it. (**Isaiah 42:5**)

I am praying that the Holy Spirit will again breathe on us that we may live.

"Come Holy Spirit, Come!"

DAY 83

Jesus answered, "Truly, truly, I say to you, unless one is born of water and the Spirit, he cannot enter the kingdom of God. That which is born of flesh is flesh, and that which is born of the Spirit is spirit. Do not marvel that I said to you, You must be born again." (John 3:5-7)

Jesus is saying we must be born of water and the Spirit. I had never really thought about this scripture until recently. He is saying water and the Spirit. Do you suppose the water is baptism?

Whoever believes and is baptized will be saved, but whoever does not believe will be condemned. (Mark 16:16) Isn't it fun to read the Word and suddenly see something that you have never seen before. Each day in the Word is a new experience if we will allow ourselves to get out of the box. About the time I think I know something; the Word throws a curve in my theology.

Jesus is saying we must be born of water and the Spirit. In the Old Testament people were saved by the blood of bulls and goats, but in the New Testament we are saved by the blood of Jesus Christ, once and for all.

And while staying with them he ordered them not to depart from Jerusalem, but to wait for the promise of the Father, which, he said, "you heard from me; for John baptized with water, but you will be baptized with the Holy Spirit not many days from now." (Acts 1:4-5) In obedience to the Son of God, we are to be baptized with the Holy Spirit. Baptism is a symbol of our commitment to God.

I remember going down into the water and coming up feeling clean all over. I remember being baptized in the Holy Spirit and immediately feeling a new lease on life, a new understanding of the Word of God, a strong urge to follow Him with my whole heart. My first love has never left me. There have been times when I have strayed, but the Holy Spirit has always been there to nudge me back into the presence of God. Remember when we are saved, we receive the Holy Spirit.

"Come Holy Spirit, Come!"

DAY 84

Truly, I say to you, all sins will be forgiven the children of man, and whatever blasphemies they utter, but whoever blasphemes against the Holy Spirit never has forgiveness but is guilty of an eternal sin. (Mark 3:28-29)

I am not sure I know what this means. What are ways that we might blaspheme the Holy Spirit? When I was growing up, we never spoke of the Holy Spirit. We always talked about Jesus. I did not know anything about the Holy Spirit. It wasn't that I was opposed to the Holy Spirit, but I was just ignorant concerning Him and His purpose in my life. I knew we were baptized in the name of the Father and the Son and the Holy Spirit but that is where my understanding ended.

Sometimes, I think we have completely ignored Him, but He is the part of the Trinity that has been sent to earth during this dispensation. The Father is in heaven and Jesus is seated at His right hand making intercession for us. So, what is the Holy Spirit doing in my life?

Do you suppose the following scripture could not only apply to Jesus but to each of us?

The Spirit of the Lord is upon me, because he has anointed me to proclaim good news to the poor. He has sent me to proclaim liberty to the captives and recovering of sight to the blind, to set at liberty those who are oppressed, to proclaim the year of the Lord's favor. (Luke 4:18-19)

We know that every part of this scripture is Biblical for believers today. But do we realize that to accomplish these feats we need the Holy Spirit?

It is the Spirit who gives life; the flesh is no help at all. (John 6:63)

For those who live according to the flesh set their minds on the things of the flesh but those who live according to the Spirit set their minds on the things of the Spirit. (Romans 8:5)

We are Spirit-filled saints. Help us Lord to rely more and more on your Spirit, the Spirit of Truth and less and less on our own understanding.

"Come Holy Spirit, Come!"

DAY 85

For all who are led by the Spirit of God are sons of God. For you did not receive the spirit of slavery to fall back into fear, but you have received the Spirit of adoption as sons, by whom we cry, "Abba! Father!" The Spirit himself bears witness with our spirit that we are children of God. (Romans 8:15-16)

We are children of God! Now this is something to shout about. We have been saved, sanctified, set apart unto God. We are His kids. He loves us. He wants the very best for us. One day He wants us to join Him in heaven. He has prepared a place for us. We are not orphans. We are children of the King of Kings, the Lord of Lords. We are royalty.

The mark of a true Christian is to *Let love be genuine. Abhor what is evil; hold fast to what is good. Love one another with brotherly affection.* Out-do one another in showing honor. Do not be slothful in zeal, be fervent in spirit, serve the Lord. Rejoice in hope, be patient in tribulation, be constant in prayer. Contribute to the needs of the saints and seek to show hospitality…etc. **(Romans 12:9-13)**

But how can we do all of these things? Through the power of the Holy Spirit. We have not been left defenseless. The Holy Spirit is here to lead us and guide us in all things. No longer do we have to do it "My way" but in the power of the Holy Spirit. His ways are so much better than ours.

For the kingdom of God is not a matter of eating and drinking but of righteousness and peace and joy in the Holy Spirit. (Romans 14:17)

No wonder Satan has caused so much division concerning the Holy Spirit. He knows that when we walk in the Spirit, we walk in power. He does not want us to tap into the Holy Spirit because he knows when we do, he is defeated. So put on the whole armor of God and stand fast.

"Holy Spirit you are welcome in this place! Omnipotent Father of mercy and grace. You are welcome in this place."

"Come Holy Spirit, Come!

DAY 86

May the God of hope fill you with all joy and peace in believing, so that by the power of the Holy Spirit you may abound in hope. (**Romans 15:12**)

Was the Holy Spirit given only to the Jews or was the Spirit poured out to all believers? Good question? Was the power of the Holy Spirit given only once to each believer or can we be constantly refilled? I am like the gas tank in my car. I continually need a refilling because I run out of gas. I am so thankful that the Holy Spirit realizes my need and is constantly filling me up.

I like this really old song. "Fill my cup Lord. I lift it up Lord. Come and quench the thirsting of my soul. Bread of heaven fill me 'til I want no more. Fill my cup. Fill it up and make me whole." I am thirsty!

For I will not venture to speak of anything except what Christ has accomplished through me to bring the Gentiles to obedience-by word and deed, by the power of signs and wonders, by the power of the Spirit of God. (**Romans 15:18-19**)

The Holy Spirit was meant for every believer. In fact without the Holy Spirit we are not saved. We should be yearning for more and more of Him every day. We need all of the help we can get to live in this world and yet not be of it.

What no eye has seen, nor ear heard, nor the heart of man imagined, what God has prepared for those who love him - these things God has revealed to us through the Spirit. For the Spirit searches everything, even the depths of God. (**1 Corinthians 2:9-10**)

The Spirit has been sent to us these last days as our Paraclete. He is the breath that we breathe. He is the joy that we feel. He is the expression of the Father in each of our lives. Let Him come in and fill you up. He is waiting and willing.

"Come Holy Spirit, Come!"

DAY 87

If the Spirit of him who raised Jesus from the dead dwells in you, he who raised Christ Jesus from the dead will also give life to your mortal bodies through his Spirit who dwells in you. **(Romans 8:11)**

In the Old Testament the Holy Spirit came upon certain people as we have said, but in the New Testament He is in all believers. The new covenant is so much better than the old for each of us because we have access to the Spirit all the time. We do not have to hope He shows up to help us. He is readily available if we will ask.

You, however, are not in the flesh but in the Spirit, if in fact the Spirit of God dwells in you. **(Romans 8:9)**

In him you also are being built together into a dwelling place for God by the Spirit. **(Ephesians 2:22)** We are His dwelling place.

So, the question is, "Do we have to keep our temple spick 'n span for the Holy Spirit?"

Do you not know that your body is a temple of the Holy Spirit within you, whom you have from God? You are not your own, for you were bought with a price. So, glorify God in your body. **(1 Corinthians 6:19-20)**

It looks like we need to get out the Windex. I would not think of having guests in my home if I had not cleaned it up. In the same manner we need a clean temple for the Holy Spirit.

Galatians 5:19 tells us what needs cleaned out of our lives. *Now the works of the flesh are evident: sexual immorality, impurity, sensuality, idolatry, sorcery, enmity, strife, jealousy, fits of anger, rivalries, dissensions, divisions, envy, drunkenness, orgies and things like these.*

No problem my temple is clean except for…

"Come Holy Spirit, Come!"

DAY 88

But when the Helper comes, whom I will send to you from the Father, the Spirit of truth, who proceeds from the Father, he will bear witness about me. **(John 15:26)**

The Holy Spirit is not only the Father's helper, but He is also our Helper. I need all the help I can get. There is so much that I do not know. There are so many times I am not sure which direction to go. Sometimes even mundane things like what should I wear? What should I say? I don't have to look far for the answer. He is inside me only waiting for me to ask.

Hear, O Lord, and be merciful to me! O Lord, be my helper! **(Psalm 30:10)** His reply is, "Here I am!"

John 14:26 says, *But the Helper, the Holy Spirit, whom the Father will send in my name, he will teach you all things and bring to your remembrance all that I have said to you.*

Have you ever tried to remember a name, or an event and it would not pop up in your mind? I do it all the time. Then I ask the Holy Spirit to bring it to my remembrance and suddenly out of nowhere the answer will come. What a mighty God we serve. He will even help us with the little things, the seemly unimportant things.

He has said, "I will never leave you nor forsake you." So, we can confidently say, "The Lord is my helper; I will not fear; what can man do to me?" **(Hebrews13:5-6)**

Perfect love casts out all fear because fear has torment. When we rely on the Holy Spirit and try not to do things our way, we will find that fear goes, and faith takes hold of our lives.

Behold, God is my helper; the Lord is the upholder of my life. **(Psalm 54:4)**

Today make a conscious decision to let go and let God.

"Come Holy Spirit, Come!"

DAY 89

Likewise, the Spirit helps us in our weakness. For we do not know what to pray for as we ought, but the Spirit himself intercedes for us with groaning too deep for words. (**Romans 8:26**)

So often I want to pray for someone or something, but I really do not know what to pray. I want to pray according to the will of God, but I am not sure what His will is in the situation. Have you ever been there in your prayer life? Well, we have an advocate in the Holy Spirit. In those moments, He will do the praying for us if we will yield to Him.

And he who searches hearts knows what is the mind of the Spirit, because the Spirit intercedes for the saints according to the will of God. (**V27**)

What a relief to know that I don't have to worry if my prayer is according to God's will. It will be if the Spirit is doing the interceding for me. I know I want what God wants and I know that He hears my feeble cry. However, He is not only listening to me, but He is listening to the Spirit within me crying out. He listens and He answers the pray of the Holy Spirit because He already knows it is according to His will.

And we know that for those who love God all things work together for good, for those who are called according to his purpose. (**V 28**)

When we accept Jesus Christ as our Lord and Savior we are called. We were called even before we answered the call, but our reply seals our relationship with Him. Knowing this, all things work together for our good. Does He really mean all things? Sometimes the worst times in our lives become the milestones for His greatest glory and ultimately ours. Think of a time you were in a trial. Was God there? Obviously, you got through it because you are still here. What then shall we say to these things? If God is for us, who can be against us? (V 31)

Spend some time reflecting on impossible situations that you survived with the help of the Holy Spirit.

"Come Holy Spirit, Come!"

DAY 90

Before I begin the next three days I want to say, you will either agree, disagree or be totally clueless. Please hang in there and ask the Lord to show you what He means. Following these we will be doing the Fruit of the Spirit which is not controversial.

Jesus said to them again, "Peace be with you. As the Father has sent me, even so I am sending you." And when he had said this, he breathed on them and said to them, "Receive the Holy Spirit." (John 20:21-22)

And while staying with them he ordered them not to depart from Jerusalem, but to wait for the promise of the Father, which, he said, "you heard from me; for John baptized with water, but you will be baptized with the Holy Spirit not many days from now. (Acts 1:1-5)

But you will receive power when the Holy Spirit has come upon you, and you will be my witnesses in Jerusalem and in all Judea and Samaria, and to the end of the earth. (Acts 1:8)

When the day of Pentecost arrived, they were all together in one place. And suddenly there came from heaven a sound like a mighty rushing wind, and it filled the entire house where they were sitting. And divided tongues as of fire appeared to them and rested on each one of them. And they were all filled with the Holy Spirit and began to speak in other tongues as the Spirit gave them utterance. (Acts 2:1-4)

Jesus had breathed on the disciples and said, "Receive the Holy Spirit." The question is, did they have the Holy Spirit? According to the word they did. Then why were they to wait? They had received the Holy Spirit, but now He was saying, *"But you will receive power when the Holy Spirit has come upon you."* I know lots of Christians who have very little power. I wonder, are they missing something? Is there a difference between a breath and baptism? Remember the disciples ran when Jesus was on the cross. But they never ran after Pentecost.

And they were all filled with the Holy Spirit and began to speak in other tongues. All meant everyone, not just the disciples.

"Come Holy Spirit. Come!"

DAY 91

Peter was commissioned by God to go to Caesarea to Cornelius's home. He was a gentile as were all of those in his house.

While Peter was still saying these things, the Holy Spirit fell on all who heard the word. And the believers from among the circumcised who had come with Peter were amazed because the gift of the Holy Spirit was poured out even on the Gentiles. For they were hearing them speaking in tongues and extolling God. Then Peter declared, "Can anyone withhold water for baptizing these people, who have received the Holy Spirit just as we have?" (Acts 10:44-47)

On the Day of Pentecost, the only people baptized in the Holy Spirit with the evidence of speaking in tongues were Jews. Now the Lord had instructed Peter to go to the Gentiles and offer them the same gift. But Jews had nothing to do with Gentiles. This was a very difficult thing for Peter to do, but he was obedient.

The Lord confirmed his instructions to Peter when all of those at Cornelius's home began to speak in tongues. This must have been quite a shock to Peter and the men who had come with him. God loved the Gentiles just as much as He loved the Jews. Unheard of, but true!

In His love He knows we need more than a breath. We need the power of the Holy Spirit in order to walk this walk and talk this talk. Never in the history of this world have we needed a touch from the Holy Spirit more than we do right now. In order to reach to the ends of the earth, we need supernatural wisdom and the boldness to speak it and live it.

I am so thankful that I have been accepted in the Beloved even though I am not a Jew. I am so thankful that I have all the rights and privileges and have received all the gifts Christ has to offer me as unworthy as I am.

So, before you throw away the baby with the bathwater, please be open-minded and ask the Lord what gifts He would like to give you and open your heart to receive them.

"Come Holy Spirit, Come!"

DAY 92

Paul passed through the inland country and came to Ephesus. There he found some disciples. And he said to them, "Did you receive the Holy Spirit when you believed?" And they said, "No, we have not even heard that there is a Holy Spirit." And he said, "Into what then were you baptized?" They said, "Into John's baptism." …And when Paul had laid his hands on them, the Holy Spirit came on them, and they began speaking in tongues and prophesying. There were about twelve men in all. (Acts 19:1-7)

When I was 33 years old, I met a woman who asked me the same question and I answered, "I have never heard about this experience." As I watched her life, I began to realize she had something I did not have. God gives us the desires of our hearts and my desire was to have everything Jesus had to offer. So, I asked her to pray for me. Several days later I was in the shower singing a worship song and suddenly, I began to sing in another language. This experience totally changed my life. It was like my eyes were open and scripture came alive. I seemed to know when others needed prayer and I prayed for them in my special prayer language. I trusted the Holy Spirit to pray through me the things needed. Since that day I have prayed often in tongues and felt the presence of the Lord so strongly in my life. That is why I want so badly to give this gift to others knowing that it will do to them even more than it has done for me.

In 1 Corinthians 12 and 14 we find instructions for the use of this gift. I do not believe Paul would have written this portion of scripture unless there were many with this gift and some were abusing it. We have not only seen three specific times that it happened in the New Testament but also instructions for its use. I wonder if we should ponder the importance of it. It was for the Jews and the Gentiles. It was for the believers of that day, and I believe the believers of today.

I think there is a difference in the prayer language and speaking in tongues in the church which is one of the 9 gifts of the Spirit. To another various kinds of tongues, to another the interpretation of tongues. **(1 Corinthians 12:10)**

The important thing in each of our lives is that we yield to the Holy Spirit.

"Come Holy Spirit, Come!"

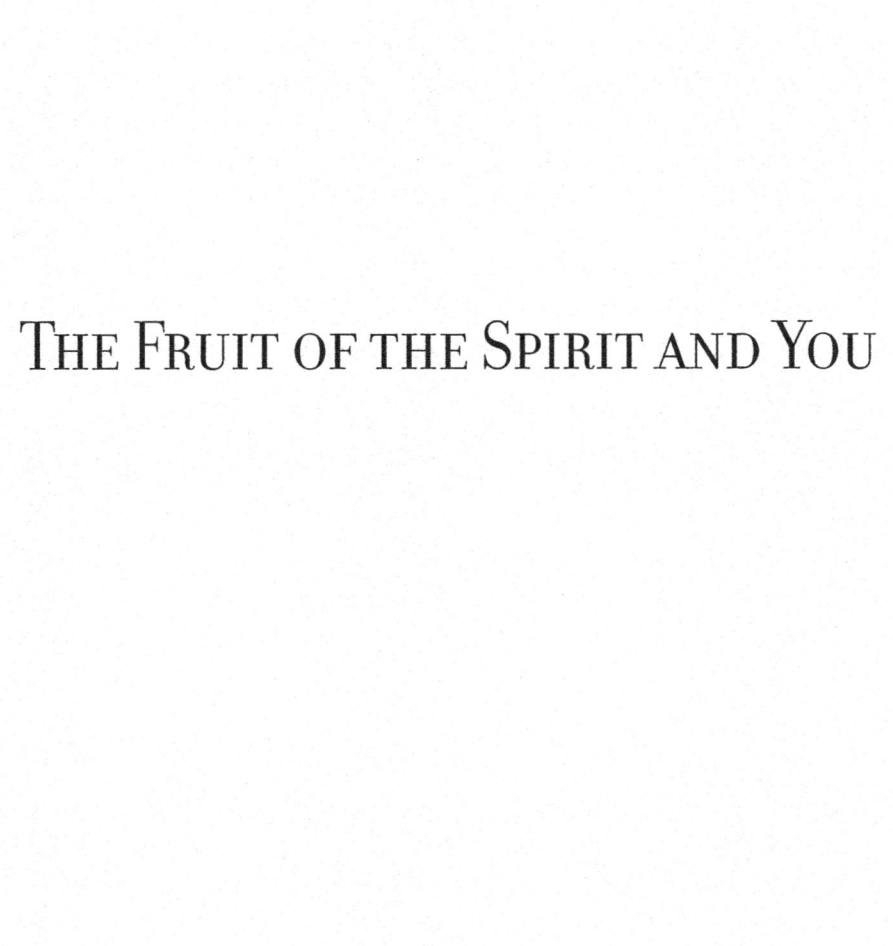

THE FRUIT OF THE SPIRIT AND YOU

DAY 93

But the fruit of the Spirit is love, joy, peace, patience, kindness, goodness, faithfulness, gentleness, self-control, against such things there is no law. (Galatians 5:22)

As we walk in the Spirit, the fruit of the Spirit should become more and more evident in our lives. Day one in this walk we are not mature Christians, nor do we display mature fruit. But little by little we are changed into the image of Christ. It is not a one-time change, but a gradual change reflecting more and more of His likeness.

For you were called to freedom, brothers (sisters). Only do not use your freedom as an opportunity for the flesh, but through love serve one another. For the whole law is fulfilled in one word: You shall love your neighbor as yourself. (Galatians 5:13-14)

But I say, walk by the Spirit, and you will not gratify the desires of the flesh. (Galatians 5:16)

I love the following verse in Micah, and it pretty well summarizes the fruit of the Spirit. *He has told you, O man, what is good; and what does the Lord require of you but to do justice, and to love kindness, and to walk humbly with your God.* (Micah 6:8) Humility is the secret to success.

Psalm 136:1 tells us to *Give thanks to the Lord, for he is good, for his steadfast love endures forever.*

I cannot whip up love or any of the fruit of the Spirit, but I receive love from God as I receive every other gift. It is His love flowing through me to others. Any other kind of love is a counterfeit. We are told to walk in Agape Love which is from God.

Paul says, *Be watchful, stand firm in the faith, act like men (women), be strong. Let all that you do be done in love.* (1 Corinthians 16:13)

As we begin looking at the Fruit of the Spirit, remember everything we say or do should be tempered in love for love covers a multitude of sins.

"But the greatest of these is love!"

DAY 94

But the fruit of the Spirit is love, joy, peace, patience, kindness, goodness, faith-fulness, gentleness, self-control; against such things there is no law. (Galatians 5:22-23)

Jesus said to Simon Peter, "Simon, son of John, do you love me more than these?" He said to him, "Yes, Lord, you know that I love you." He said to him, "Feed my lambs." He said to him a second time, "Simon, son of John, do you love me?" He said to him, "Tend my sheep." He said to him the third time "Simon, son of John, do you love me?" Peter was grieved because he said to him the third time, "Do you love me?" and he said to him, "Lord, you know everything; you know that I love you." Jesus said to him, "Feed my sheep." (John 21:15-17)

Three times Peter had denied Christ. Three times Christ ask Peter to reaffirm his love for him. I sometimes wonder how many times I need to reaffirm my love for Christ. How many times have I denied Him? How many times have I been remiss in doing things that He has asked me to do? How many times have I failed to show love to others? I feel Christ is asking me, "Do you love me more than these?"

I began to wonder what "these things" are that are more important to me than Christ? Is my family more important? Is my job more important? Are my friends more important? Are material things more important? Continue the list with me...

Before I can give love, I must possess love. In order to possess love, I must have love abiding in me. Therefore, I must have the Spirit actively moving in my life.

A new commandment I give to you, that you love one another; just as I have loved you, you also are to love one another. By this all people will know that you are my disciples if you have love for one another. (John 13:34-35)

The very first fruit of the Spirit that we are to strive for and earnestly desire is love.

This is my commandment, that you love one another as I have loved you. Greater love has no one than this, that someone lay down his life for his friends. (John 15:12-13)

I think this is more than *Do unto others as you would have them do unto you.* I think this is the willingness to sacrifice with open hands, extending love where love is not deserved; yielding to the voice of the Father; thinking about others with no thought for yourself.

Peter, do you love me more than these? Then feed my lambs and my sheep.

"But the greatest of these is love!"

DAY 95

But the fruit of the Spirit is love, joy, peace, patience, kindness, goodness, faithfulness, gentleness, self-control; against such things there is no law. **(Galatians 5:22-23)**

You have heard that it was said, you shall love your neighbor and hate your enemy. But I say to you, love your enemies and pray for those who persecute you, so that you may be sons of your Father who is in heaven. **(Matthew 5:43)**

Now Matthew is meddling. He says to love your enemies. Love those who persecute you. But that's not fair. They do not deserve my love. What if they have done something really horrible to me? What if they killed my best friend? What if... But the word tells us to love them. To me this is where the gospel really gets tough. We can say we love, but do we still harbor grudges and hatred in our hearts?

Which commandment is the most important of all? Jesus answered, "The most important is, Hear, O Israel: The Lord our God, the Lord is one. And you shall love the Lord your God with all your heart and with all your soul and with all your mind and with all your strength. The second is this: You shall love your neighbor as yourself. There is no commandment greater than these." **(Mark 12:29-31)**

But my neighbor's dog barks all night long. My neighbor's yard hasn't been mowed in a month. My neighbor is always leaning over the fence gossiping. My neighbor comes in drunk and wakes up the whole neighborhood. My neighbor...

Therefore, be imitators of God as beloved children. And walk in love, as Christ loved us and gave himself up for us, a fragrant offering and sacrifice to God. **(Ephesians 5:1-2)**

Carefully studying the above scriptures, there doesn't seem to be a loophole or an excuse for not loving everyone. But God, I can't! You are right in your own strength or in my own strength we cannot love. But in the power of the Holy Spirit all things are possible.

Forgiving each other; as the Lord has forgiven you, so you also must forgive. And above all these, put on love which binds everything together in perfect harmony. **(Colossians 3:13-14)**

But the fruit of the Spirit is love, joy, peace, patience, kindness, goodness, faithfulness, gentleness, self-control; against such things there is no law. **(Galatians 5:22-23)**

"But the greatest of these is love!"

DAY 96

But the fruit of the Spirit is love, joy, peace, patience, kindness, goodness, faithfulness, gentleness, self-control; against such there is no law. (Galatians 5:22-23)

Speaking the truth in love. (Ephesians 4:15) Have you ever tried to tell a friend something that she or he needed to hear, but you knew if you did you would offend that person? So, what did you do? Speak it anyway or just hold your tongue? I think we need to discern the difference between criticizing and speaking something that will edify, uplift, and help another. Then we must bathe our words in prayer. But sometimes things need to be said.

We need to remember that *A joyful heart is good medicine, but a crushed spirit dries up the bones.* (Proverbs 17:22)

Death and life are in the power of the tongue, and those who love it will eat its fruits. (Proverbs 18:21)

The words of a man's mouth are deep waters; the fountain of wisdom is a bubbling brook. (Proverbs 18:4)

So, we must admonish each other to be truthful, but be sure what we say to each other is truly from the heart of God and not a personal opinion flavored with jealousy or strife.

And it is my prayer that your love may abound more and more, with knowledge and discernment, so that you may approve what is excellent, and so be pure and blameless. (Philippians 1:9)

My desire is that you always be honest with me, but temper what you say in love. I need to hear your wisdom. I need to listen to your opinions, but I do not need your criticism. There is enough of that going around for all of us. *A friend loves at all times.* (Proverbs 17:17)

"But the greatest of these is love!"

DAY 97

But the fruit of the Spirit is love, joy, peace, patience, kindness, goodness, faithfulness, gentleness, self-control; against such things there is no law. (Galatians 5:22-23)

Love is patient and kind; love does not envy or boast; it is not arrogant or rude. It does not insist on its own way; it is not irritable or resentful; it does not rejoice at wrongdoing but rejoices with the truth. Love bears all things, hopes all things, endures all things. Love never ends. (1 Corinthians 13:1-8)

Love is patient uncomplaining, tolerant, long-suffering, even-tempered, calm, serene, understanding, etc.

Love is compassionate, understanding, etc.

Love is not envious, begrudging, coveting, resentful, discontent, jealous, spiteful,

Love does not boast, brag, swagger, gloat, show off, self-praise, exaggerate, overstate, etc.

Love is not arrogant, haughty, conceited, self-important, opinionated, full of oneself, overbearing, pompous, snobby, smug, uppity, etc.

Love is not rude, ill-mannered, impolite, discourteous, impertinent, insolent, disrespectful, ungracious, brash, derogatory, abusive, etc.

Love is not resentful, irritated, exasperated, displeased, dissatisfied, spiteful, bitter, envious, etc.

Have you ever stopped to think what this scripture is really saying? I know definitions can be boring, but I want you to take a moment today and analyze each of these definitions. Do you ever slip into one of these? I do and cringe.

We're not perfect but we are getting there.

"But the greatest of these is love!"

DAY 98

But the fruit of the Spirit is love, joy, peace, patience, kindness, goodness, faithfulness, gentleness, self-control; against such things there is no law. **(Galatians 5:22-23)**

Do you remember the old song, "What the World needs now is love, sweet love." I think we need to resurrect that song. Our world is in a mess with wars, rumors of war, unrest, fighting within and without, etc. You name it!

We will end our look at love with **(1 John 4)** *Beloved, let us love one another, for love is from God, and whoever loves has been born of God and knows God. Anyone who does not love does not know God, because God is love.* **V. 7-8**

These are a powerful couple of verses. If we don't love, we don't know God. Love is more of an action than an expression. By that I mean we "do" love. We walk out love. We express love by what we do more than what we say.

Beloved, if God so loved us, we also ought to love one another. **(V 11)** Our response to God's love should be to love others just as He has loved us. But sometimes I cannot or won't love another person. Maybe I need a little dose of the Holy Spirit who is the author of love.

No one has ever seen God; if we love one another, God abides in us and his love is perfected in us. **(V 12)** So how do we know that we have the Spirit living within us? We love one another unconditionally.

God is love, and whoever abides in love abides in God and God abides in him. **(V 16)** What does it mean to abide? (obey, follow, stand by, stick to, go along with, acknowledge, respect) Those definitions are ones I would like to see in a friend or in myself with a friend.

There is no fear in love, but perfect love casts out fear. For fear has to do with punishment, and whoever fears has not been perfected in love. **(V 18)** You may have to think about my next statement, but I think lots of us are afraid to love because we may get hurt. We may be vulnerable. We may be rejected. We may look foolish. Add a few…

And this commandment we have from him; whoever loves God must also love his brother. **(V 21)** The bottom line is if we say we love God, we must also love others. (Period)

"But the greatest of these is Love!"

DAY 99

But the fruit of the Spirit is love, joy, peace, patience, kindness, goodness, faith-fulness, gentleness, self-control; against such things there is no law. (Galatians 5:22-23)

I realized something as I was praying this morning. In order to minister in the gifts of the Spirit one must be filled with the fruit of the Spirit. Otherwise, we will abuse the gifts. Just a thought.

Today we will begin looking at joy. **Nehemiah 8:10 says,** *The joy of the Lord is your strength.* **Proverbs 17:22 says,** *A joyful heart is good medicine.* So instead of filling drug prescriptions maybe we need to begin to find joy in the Lord, in others and in ourselves. There is really a therapeutic value to a good laugh.

Psalm 16:11 says, *You make known to me the path of life; in your presence there is fullness of joy; at your right hand are pleasures forevermore.* And who is sitting at the right hand of the Father but Jesus. I used to have a picture of Jesus laughing. I am sure some of you have seen it or have it. I loved that picture. It showed a side of Jesus that we often forget about. He was full of joy.

Psalm 30:5 says, *Weeping may tarry for the night, but joy comes with the morn-ing.* My mother was dying, and I had gone to church. My husband was with her when she died. I felt so guilty about not being there. Then the Lord gave me this scripture. He reassured me that she was now in the presence of the Lord and full of joy. There is great joy in heaven!

Psalm 47:1 says, *Clap your hands, all peoples! Shout to God with loud songs of joy!* David knew how to praise the Lord. Not only did he feel joy inside, but he expressed it outwardly. He even danced before the Lord and God was pleased. So today let's spend a few minutes being joyful before the Lord.

"But the greatest of these is love!"

DAY 100

But the fruit of the Spirit is love, joy, peace, patience, kindness, goodness, faithfulness, gentleness, self-control; against such things there is no law. (Galatians 5:22-23)

Psalm 51:12 says, *Restore to me the joy of your salvation, and uphold me with a willing spirit.* Have you ever felt like you needed a good makeover? It always feels good to go to the beauty shop or to have a pedicure. It seems to restore something within us. We look in the mirror and see a new person. Well joy can and will do the same thing. Sometimes we need a spiritual makeover. But how do we get it? First turn on some really good gospel music. Grab a cup of coffee and go sit on your deck watching a sunrise. Begin thanking God for all the things He has done for you and through you. Bask in His presence and see if joy doesn't just bubble up inside you. That is restoration!

Then *Shout for joy to God, all the earth; sing the glory of his name; give to him glorious praise! Say to God, How awesome are your deeds! So great is your power that your enemies come cringing to you.* (Psalm 66:1-3)

Then take an attitude check. Do you feel the joy of the Lord singing through you? Do you sense His presence surrounding you? Has the enemy fled in terror? Yes!

For you, O Lord, have made me glad by your work; at the works of your hands, I sing for joy. (Psalm 92:4)

The Psalms are full of the praises of God. When you are having a downer and we all do, turn to David and the Psalms.

He will yet fill your mouth with laughter and your lips with shouting. (Job 8:21)

"But the greatest of these is love!"

DAY 101

But the fruit of the Spirit is love, joy, peace, patience, kindness, goodness, faithfulness, gentleness, self-control; against such things there is no law. **(Galatians 5:22-23)**

Deceit is in the heart of those who devise evil, but those who plan peace have joy. **(Proverbs 12:20)**

Have you ever considered choosing joy? Most of us just let our feelings run rampant. We ask each other, "How are you feeling today?" Then we go off on a tirade telling all our troubles.

I call heaven and earth to witness against you today, that I have set before you life and death, blessing and curse. Therefore, choose life that you and your offspring may live. **(Deuteronomy 30:19)**

Joy is a choice as are all the other fruits of the Spirit. We were not meant to grovel through life in a pit of anger and depression. God wants us to find joy in life.

I will turn their mourning into joy; I will comfort them and give them gladness for sorrow. **(Jeremiah 31:13)** The Lord wants a joyful people. What a witness joy is to the world around us.

Though the fig tree should not blossom, nor fruit be on the vines, the produce of the olive fails and the fields yield no food, the flock be cut off from the fold and there be no herd in the stalls, yet I will rejoice in the Lord; I will take joy in the God of my salvation. God the Lord is my strength. **(Habakkuk 3:17-19)**

It is time for an attitude check. Am I someone people like to be around? Do I edify and uplift others? Is my attitude one of gratitude? *Is the joy of the Lord my strength?*

"But the greatest of these is Love!"

DAY 102

But the fruit of the Spirit is love, joy, peace, patience, kindness, goodness, faithfulness, gentleness, self-control; against such things there is no law. (Galatians 5:22-23) *"The joy of the Lord is our strength."*

Just so, I tell you, there will be more joy in heaven over one sinner who repents than over ninety-nine righteous persons who need no repentance. (Luke 15:7)

When we begin to judge others for their sins, we need to reconsider what the Lord says about sinners. There is joy in heaven over one sinner who repents. As the thief on the cross turned to Christ in his dying moments, heaven began to rejoice. Can you imagine the party they threw for his salvation? Can you imagine the party they threw for your salvation? The question is: Are we joyful when we see the thief on the cross, who deserved to die, repent, or are we saying, that's not fair?

He has delivered us from the domain of darkness and transferred us to the kingdom of his beloved Son, in whom we have redemption, the forgiveness of sins. (**Colossians 1:13-14**) Now that is something to be joyful about!

I sometimes wonder if we are more like the Prodigal's brother. *Son, you are always with me, and all that is mine is yours. It was fitting to celebrate and be glad, for this your brother was dead, and is alive; he was lost, and is found.* (Luke 15:31-32) There was joy in that household!

Therefore, since we are surrounded by so great a cloud of witnesses, let us also lay aside every weight, and sin which clings so closely, and let us run with endurance the race that is set before us, looking to Jesus, the founder and perfecter of our faith, who for the joy that was set before him endured the cross, despising the shame, and is seated at the right hand of the throne of God. (Hebrews 12:1-2) Let's be imitators of Christ!

"But the greatest of these is love!"

DAY 103

But the fruit of the Spirit is love, joy, peace, patience, kindness, goodness, faithfulness, gentleness, self-control; against such things there is no law. (Galatians 5:22-23)

Count it all joy, my brothers (sisters), when you meet trials of various kinds, for you know that the testing of your faith produces steadfastness. And let steadfastness have its full effect, that you may be perfect and complete, lacking nothing. (James 1:2-4)

Now you are beginning to meddle. Joy is great when we are feeling joyful, and the world is right. But I don't know about joy when everything is falling apart. I don't know about joy when I am in the middle of a trial. I don't know about joy when I see death and destruction. Let's look at the scripture again. There is a reward for testing and trials. They produce steadfastness.

In this you rejoice, though now for a little while, if necessary, you have been grieved by various trials, so that the tested genuineness of your faith-more precious than gold that perishes though it is tested by fire-may be found to result in praise and glory and honor at the revelation of Jesus Christ. (1 Peter 1:6-7)

If we come through trials on the other side filled with joy, we have passed the test. We have showed the Father we are faithful through good and bad.

Though you do not now see him, you believe in him and rejoice with joy that is inexpressible and filled with glory, obtaining the outcome of your faith, the salvation of your souls. (1 Peter 1:8-9)

Can we look upon trials as a time of joy? This is a hard one and not easily achieved. But when we can see the good in all things, we can feel joy.

"But the greatest of these is love!"

DAY 104

But the fruit of the Spirit is love, joy, peace, patience, kindness, goodness, faithfulness, gentleness, self-control; against such things there is no law. (Galatians 5:22-23)

For to us a child is born, to us a son is given; and the government shall be upon his shoulder, and his name shall be called Wonderful Counselor, Mighty God, Everlasting Father, Prince of Peace. (Isaiah 9:6)

Jesus is called the Prince of Peace. Jesus and the disciples were in a boat. Jesus was asleep when a great storm arose. *And he awoke and rebuked the wind and said to the sea, "Peace! Be still!" And the wind ceased, and there was a great calm.* (Mark 4:39)

Every storm in our lives can be calmed when we look toward the peace of Jesus. Does this mean the storm will immediately go away? No! But this does mean He will be with us in the midst of it. We can take His hand and rely upon His peace to carry us through.

In peace I will both lie down and sleep; for you alone, O Lord, make me dwell in safety. (Psalm 4:8)

Peace is the third fruit of the Spirit. I wonder if there is an order to the fruit of the Spirit. If so, love is the first fruit, followed by joy and then peace. When we trust and obey, the fruit of the Spirit will be evident in our lives, and we will have peace.

Great peace have those who love your law; nothing can make them stumble. (Psalm 119:165)

Therefore, since we have been justified by faith, we have peace with God through our Lord Jesus Christ. (Romans 5:1) Peace is a gift from God.

"But the greatest of these is Love!"

DAY 105

But the fruit of the Spirit is love, joy, peace, patience, kindness, goodness, faithfulness, gentleness, self-control; against such things there is no law. (**Galatians 5:22-23**)

Peace be with you. As the Father has sent me, even so I am sending you. (**John 20:21**) (Jesus)

Grace to you and peace from God our Father and the Lord Jesus Christ. (**Romans 1:7**) (Paul)

May grace and peace be multiplied to you. (**1 Peter 1:2**) (Peter)

Grace, mercy, and peace will be with us, from God the Father and from Jesus Christ the Father's Son, in truth and love. (**2 John 1:3**) (John)

May mercy, peace, and love be multiplied to you. (**Jude 1:2**) (Jude)

Jesus gave peace to the disciples and in turn they are giving us that peace. The beginning of almost every epistle in the New Testament begins with an exhortation to live in peace. Obviously, it is very important to God that we live in peace, or it would not have been mentioned so many times. But by looking at our world today, I fail to see that we are obeying His command to live in peace. There are wars and rumors of war everywhere. In the United States there are riots and unrest. Within our families there are quarrels and fights. What has happened to our peace?

Have nothing to do with foolish, ignorant controversies; you know that they breed quarrels. And the Lord's servant must not be quarrelsome but kind to everyone, able to teach, patiently enduring evil, correcting his opponents with gentleness. (**2 Timothy 2:23-24**)

He gives us the peace that passes all human understanding. Let us receive it!

"But the greatest of these is love!"

DAY 106

But the fruit of the Spirit is love, joy, peace, patience, kindness, goodness, faithfulness, gentleness, self-control; against such things there is no law. **(Galatians 5:22-23)**

Whoever desires to love life and see good days, let him keep his tongue from evil and his lips from speaking deceit; let him turn away from evil and do good; let him seek peace and pursue it. **(1 Peter 3:10-11)**

We are told to seek peace, but how do we do that? Is it possible to live in peace as we look around at the confused world we inhabit?

Finally, brothers (sisters), whatever is true, whatever is honorable, whatever is just, whatever is pure, whatever is lovely, whatever is commendable, if there is any excellence, if there is anything worthy of praise, think about these things... practice these things, and the God of peace will be with you. **(Philippians 4:8-9)**

When I was trying to learn how to play the violin, I had to practice, practice, practice and my poor parents had to listen to the squeaks and squawks. But practice makes perfect, which is also true when we think about mastering peace. Practice, practice, practice! It won't be perfect the first time.

May the Lord give strength to his people! May the Lord bless his people with peace. **(Psalm 29:11)** Remember we cannot do it on our own. We need the power of the Holy Spirit moving in our lives and peace will come.

And let the peace of Christ rule in your hearts, to which indeed you were called in one body. And be thankful. **(Colossians 3:15)** Let it happen. Allow peace to flow.

Because... *The fruit of the Spirit is love, joy, peace, patience, kindness, goodness, faithfulness, gentleness, self-control; against such things there is no law.*

"But the greatest of these is love!"

DAY 107

But the fruit of the Spirit is love, joy, peace, patience, kindness, goodness, faith-fulness, gentleness, self-control; against such things there is no law. (Galatians 5:22-23)

Mark 9:49 tells us to, *Be at peace with one another.* **Proverbs 12:20 says,** *Deceit is in the heart of those who devise evil, but those who plan peace have joy.*

Is peace a choice? I think so. Sometimes it required a few deep breathes and a moment of whispered prayer. Have you ever planned to confront someone in anger? We all have. But have you ever planned to confront them in peace?

For to set the mind on the flesh is death, but to set the mind on the Spirit is life and peace. (Romans 8:6)

Romans 14:18 says, *So then let us pursue what makes for peace and for mutual upbuilding.* What does it mean to pursue? (go after, run after, chase, hunt, stalk) To pursue is an action. So, let's go for it!

We need to be *Eager to maintain the unity of the Spirit in the bond of peace.* **(Ephesians 4:3)**

I wonder how many things that we disagree on are worth the fight? We are so polarized in the United States now. Are all the issues we are upset about really that important? If God is in control of our universe, our nation, our town, and our lives, do we have a reason to disagree? If He is in charge let Him be. Be an instrument of peace.

A harvest of righteousness is sown in peace by those who make peace. (James 3:18)

"But the greatest of these is love!"

DAY 108

But the fruit of the Spirit is love, joy, peace, patience, kindness, goodness, faithfulness, gentleness, self-control; against such things there is no law. (Galatians 5:22-23)

You keep him in perfect peace whose mind is stayed on you, because he trusts in you. (Isaiah 26:3) Someone has said that life is 10% what happens to you and 90% how you handle it. One of the strongest witnesses we can give the world, especially those around us is peace in the midst of turmoil. "Trust the Lord, live obediently no matter what your circumstances, and keep you hope fixed on God's ultimate promise of deliverance." (Introduction to the Book of 1 Peter)

Do not be anxious about anything, but in everything by prayer and supplication with thanksgiving let your requests be made known to God. And the peace of God, which surpasses all understanding, will guard your hearts and your minds in Christ Jesus. (Philippians 4:6-7)

Peace and trust go hand in hand. We cannot have peace without trusting that *God is able to do far more abundantly than all that we ask or think, according to the power at work within us.* (Ephesians 3:20) Where does the power come from that is within us but from the Holy Spirit?

Peace like all the fruits of the Spirit is an act of our will. We must choose to be peaceful even when everything around us is screaming anger and dissension. Peace speaks louder than words.

Strive for peace with everyone, and for the holiness without which no one will see the Lord. (Hebrews 12:14) *Be at peace among yourselves.* (1 Thessalonians 5:13)

Now may the Lord of peace himself give you peace at all times in every way. (2 Thessalonians 3:16)

"But the greatest of these is love!"

DAY 109

But the fruit of the Spirit is love, joy, peace, patience, kindness, goodness, faithfulness, gentleness, self-control; against such things there is no law. (Galatians 5:22-23)

Because you have kept my word about patient endurance, I will keep you from the hour of trial that is coming on the whole world, to try those who dwell on the earth. I am coming soon. Hold fast what you have, so that no one may seize your crown. (Revelation 3:10-11)

The Christian walk is a walk of patience. So many times, we ask God, "Why?" and receive no answer. Other times we determine to change, but the change doesn't come as we had hoped. Sometimes we even wonder if God is real or a figment of our imagination. Now if you have never wondered about the reality of God, I want to meet you.

Jesus said to him, "Have you believed because you have seen me? Blessed are those who have not seen and yet have believed." (John 20:29) There is a saying, "Seeing is believing" but Jesus is asking us to believe without seeing. This is called patient endurance.

Therefore, since we are surrounded by so great a cloud of witnesses, let us also lay aside every weight, and sin which clings so closely, and let us run with endurance (patience) the race that is set before us, looking to Jesus, the founder and perfecter of our faith, who for the joy that was set before him endured the cross, despising the shame, and is seated at the right hand of the throne of God." (Hebrews 12:1-2)

How much have I had to endure for Christ? I have not been burned at the stake, or thrown into a lion's den, or sawed in half? Could my endurance or patience be my day to day walk among many who do not believe? Could my patience be loving the unlovely? Could my patience be holding my tongue and listening to other, really listening?

"But the greatest of these is love!"

DAY 110

But the fruit of the Spirit is love, joy, peace, patience, kindness, goodness, faithfulness, gentleness, self-control; against such things there is no law. (Galatians 5:22-23)

Be still before the Lord and wait patiently for him. (Psalm 37:7) Patience is hard for us today. We are so use to instant everything. We are impatient at the stop light, the grocery store, the post office, etc. We have lost the art of waiting.

But they who wait for the Lord shall renew their strength; they shall mount up with wings like eagles; they shall run and not be weary; they shall walk and not faint. (Isaiah 40:31) Teach me Lord to wait!

The farmer is the best example of waiting patiently. He tills the soil, plants the seed, waters, and waits. One day he sees a tiny green sprout and knows that before long the wait will be over. Why can't we be like that in everyday life?

The Lord passed before him (Moses) and proclaimed, "The Lord, the Lord, a God merciful and gracious, slow to anger, and abounding in steadfast love and faithfulness." (Exodus 34:6)

The Lord is not slow to fulfill his promise as some count slowness, but is patient toward you, not wishing that any should perish, but that all should reach repentance. (2 Peter 3:9) Our best example of patience is the Lord Himself. He does not give up on us even though we sometimes give up on others. He is always waiting for His child to come home. His patience is everlasting!

But I received mercy for this reason, that in me, as the foremost, Jesus Christ might display his perfect patience as an example to those who were to believe in him for eternal life. (1 Timothy 1:15-16) Jesus never gives up, so neither should we.

"But the greatest of these is love!"

DAY 111

But the fruit of the Spirit is love, joy, peace, patience, kindness, goodness, faithfulness, gentleness, self-control; against such things there is no law. (Galatians 5:22-23)

What does patience mean? Forbearance, tolerance, restraint, endurance, lenience, perseverance, persistence, staying power, determination.

I, therefore, a prisoner for the Lord, urge you to walk in a manner worthy of the calling to which you have been called, with all humility and gentleness, with patience, bearing with one another in love, eager to maintain the unity of the Spirit in the bond of peace. (Ephesians 4:1)

We are told to be eager to maintain the unity of the Spirit in the bond of peace. This means we are to be patient with each other. We are to walk in unity. But how can we do this when we are so polarized? Never in my life have I seen such division in the church. Never have I seen Christians so unwilling to think about others before they think about themselves. Never have I seen Christians so unwilling to compromise for the sake of others. Where are we headed with this attitude? Certainly, we are not maintaining the unity of the Spirit in the bond of peace. During these troubling times we are to endure with love.

From the day we heard, we have not ceased to pray for you, asking that you may be filled with the knowledge of his will in all spiritual wisdom and understanding, so as to walk in a manner worthy of the Lord, fully pleasing to him: bearing fruit in every good work and increasing in the knowledge of God; being strengthened with all power, according to his glorious might, for all endurance and patience with joy. (Colossians 1:9-11)

It is time for us to pray for unity in the body and may it begin with me.

"But the greatest of these is love!"

DAY 112

But the fruit of the Spirit is love, joy, peace, patience, kindness, goodness, faithfulness, gentleness, self-control; against such things there is no law. (Galatians 5:22-23)

Be still before the Lord and wait patiently for him. (Psalm 37:7)

For most of us patience is not one of our long suits. How do we acquire patience? I've tried many things people suggested but none is a lasting solution. I am wondering if age helps? Maybe. Waiting on others is one thing but waiting on the Lord is another. How often do we take time to wait on the Lord? As I wait and try to listen my mind begins to roam, and I must keep redirecting it toward Him. Lord help!

I waited patiently for the Lord; he inclined to me and heard my cry. He drew me up from the pit of destruction, out of the miry bog, and set my feet upon a rock, making my steps secure. He put a new song in my mouth, a song of praise to our God. (Psalm 40:1-3) David knew how to wait patiently on the Lord. If he could, so can we. But it takes patience and practice!

And thus Abraham, having patiently waited, obtained the promise. (Hebrews 6:15)

Do you suppose we are not waiting patiently on the Lord, but asking and then trying to do what we have asked for ourselves? I believe this Christian walk is a walk of patience.

Now to him who is able to do far more abundantly than all that we ask or think. (Ephesians 3:20) Patience! Patience!

I know you are enduring patiently and bearing up for my name's sake, and you have not grown weary. (Revelation 2:3) Let us not grow weary in patiently waiting on the Lord. He will come through if we wait.

"But the greatest of these is love!"

DAY 113

But the fruit of the Spirit is love, joy, peace, patience, kindness, goodness, faithfulness, gentleness, self-control; against such things there is no law. (Galatians 5:22-23)

He has told you, O man, what is good; and what does the Lord require of you but to do justice, and to love kindness, and to walk humbly with your God. (Micah 6:8) That is all the Lord requires of us plus believing that Jesus is the Christ, the Son of the Living God. Sounds simple until we begin to look at what that really means.

Kindness: concern, caring, consideration, thoughtfulness, selflessness, compassion, sympathy, understanding, benevolence, generosity, tolerance, etc. Now it is a horse of a different color.

Whoever pursues righteousness and kindness will find life, righteousness, and honor. (Proverbs 21:21) Like all of the other fruit of the Spirit, kindness is given to us by the Holy Spirit and pursued by us. It is a two-way transaction. He gives and we must act on the gift.

The woman who fears the Lord, opens her mouth with wisdom, and the teaching of kindness is on her tongue. (Proverbs 31:26) I wonder who taught her to be kind. *Train up a child in the way he should go; even when he is old, he will not depart from it.* (Proverbs 22:6) So kindness is learned. Kindness is displayed by our lives. Kindness is a gift and an action.

Thus says the Lord of hosts, Render true judgments, show kindness and mercy to one another. (Zechariah 7:9) Kindness comes in many forms. It may be a phone call, a word of encouragement, a thoughtful act or deed, a listening ear, a plate of cookies, helping someone across the street. Kindness does not have to be monetary and usually isn't. It is just thinking of others more than yourself. You know the rule. It requires vulnerability.

"But the greatest of these is love!"

DAY 114

But the fruit of the Spirit is love, joy, peace, patience, kindness, goodness, faithfulness, gentleness, self-control; against such things there is no law. (Galatians 5:22-23)

Every time Jesus prayed for someone, He felt compassion or kindness for that person. *When he saw the crowds, he had compassion for them, because they were harassed and helpless, like sheep without a shepherd.* (Matthew 9:36) *When he went ashore, he saw a great crowd, and he had compassion on them and healed their sick.* (Matthew 14:14) *I have compassion on the crowd, because they have been with me now three days and have nothing to eat.* (Mark 8:2) To the widow whose son had died, *And when the Lord saw her, he had compassion on her and said to her. "Do not weep."* (Luke 7:13) And Jesus raised him from the dead. Everything that Jesus did was out of a heart of compassion and kindness.

Sometimes I think we should check our motives. Do they match up with Jesus?

But love your enemies, and do good, and lend, expecting nothing in return, and your reward will be great, and you will be sons of the Most High, for he is kind to the ungrateful and the evil. Be merciful, even as your father is merciful. (Luke 6:35-36)

There were no strings attached to the Fathers actions. It is so easy to be kind to our friends, to those who will return our kindness, to those who are grateful for the kindness we bestow. But how hard it is to do for others when they do not even acknowledge our gift? I think these are the ones the Father really wants us to reach out to. They are those most in need of our kindness.

As a father shows compassion to his children, so the Lord shows compassion (kindness) to those who fear him. (Psalm 103:13)

"But the greatest of these is love!"

DAY 115

But the fruit of the Spirit is love, joy, peace, patience, kindness, goodness, faithfulness, gentleness, self-control; against such things there is no law. **(Galatians 5:22-23)**

Since I have written this scripture at the beginning of each of these thoughts, are you beginning to skip over it? When Jesus said a thing more than once or twice it meant it really was important. I hope you will take a moment to read Galatians 5:22-23 with your heart. We so need this passage today!

Note then the kindness and the severity of God: severity toward those who have fallen, but God's kindness to you, provided you continue in his kindness. **(Romans 11:22)** His kindness is part of His nature, and we are made in His image. So, we too should show kindness to everyone. Not just those we like but those who rub us the wrong way.

Or do you presume on the riches of his kindness and forbearance and patience, not knowing that God's kindness is meant to lead you to repentance. **(Romans 2:4)** I think this scripture might be a double-edged sword. God's kindness leads us to repentance and our kindness to others leads them to repentance. *Selah!* Pause and reflect on this one.

He who withholds kindness from a friend forsakes the fear of the Almighty. **(Job 6:14)**

I led them with cords of kindness, with bands of love, and I became to them as one who eases the yoke on their jaws, and I bent down to them and fed them. **(Hosea 11:4)** This is just a small part of God's kindness and His love towards us.

But God, being rich in mercy, because of the great love with which he loved us... that in the coming ages he might show the immeasurable riches of his grace in kindness toward us in Christ Jesus. **(Ephesians 2: 4 & 7)**

"But the greatest of these is love!"

DAY 116

But the fruit of the Spirit is love, joy, peace, patience, kindness, goodness, faith-fulness, gentleness, self-control; against such things there is no law. (Galatians 5:22-23)

Put on then, as God's chosen ones, holy and beloved, compassionate hearts, kind-ness, humility, meekness, and patience, bearing with one another and, if one has a complaint against another, forgiving each other; as the Lord has forgiven you, so you also must forgive. (Colossians 3:12-13)

Paul says to "put on" kindness. When I get up in the morning I put on my clothes, but do I also put on kindness? Maybe we need to get up each morning and not only get dressed but put on the fruit of the Spirit. Have you ever done that? Is kindness a daily act of obedience?

But when the goodness and loving kindness of God our Savior appeared, he saved us, not because of works done by us in righteousness, but according to his own mercy. (Titus 3:4-5)

Could this be a key to kindness? When I least deserve for others to be kind to me, they choose to follow the Lord's leading and pour out abundant kindness on me. I wonder what would happen in our homes, our lives, our nation if we decided to put on kindness instead of criticism? It might be worth trying!

Because: *The Lord is righteous in all his ways and kind in all his works.* (Psalm 145:17) We are told to follow in His steps.

Be kind to one another, tenderhearted, forgiving one another, as God in Christ forgave you. (Ephesians 4: 31)

Today purposely render an act of kindness to someone who really doesn't deserve it and see what changes in that person and in you.

"But the greatest of these is love!"

DAY 117

But the fruit of the Spirit is love, joy, peace, patience, kindness, goodness, faithfulness, gentleness, self-control; against such things there is no law. (Galatians 5:22-23)

And the Lord's servant must not be quarrelsome but kind to everyone, able to teach, patiently enduring evil, correcting his opponents with gentleness. (2 Timothy 2:24)

The word quarrel is a by-product of our culture at the moment. We are so polarized on almost everything. What has happened to "peace on earth goodwill to men"? We need a spoonful of kindness.

"In overflowing anger for a moment, I hid my face from you, but with everlasting love I will have compassion (kindness) on you," says the Lord your Redeemer. (Isaiah 54:8) Come Lord Jesus!

For the Lord will not cast off forever, but, though he cause grief, he will have compassion (kindness) according to the abundance of his steadfast love. (Lamentations 3:32)

Our hope is in the Lord and Him only. It is His kindness that will sustain us in these times of unrest. He has not left us, nor will He forsake us.

The steadfast love of the Lord never ceases; his mercies never come to an end; they are new every morning; great is your faithfulness. (Lamentations 3:22-23)

So do not lose heart. *Trust in the Lord with all of your heart, and do not lean on your own understanding. In all your ways acknowledge him, and he will make straight your paths.* (Proverbs 3:5) *Cloth* yourself with kindness!

"But the greatest of these is love!"

DAY 118

But the fruit of the Spirit is love, joy, peace, patience, kindness, goodness, faith-fulness, gentleness, self-control; against such things there is no law. (Galatians 5:22-23)

God is the personification of every single fruit of the Spirit. Just wrap your mind around that for a moment. He is love, joy, peace, patience, kindness, goodness, faithfulness, gentleness, and self-control. He is not asking us to be or do anything He is not or will not do Himself. What a mighty God we serve!

Moses said, "Please show me your glory". And he said, "I will make all my goodness pass before you and will proclaim before you my name, The Lord." (Exodus 33:19)

Goodness: virtue, morality, integrity, honesty, truth, trustworthiness, fairness, impartiality, consideration, worthiness, tenderness, patience, understanding, love

Let your priests, O Lord God, be clothed with salvation, and let your saints rejoice in your goodness. (2 Chronicles 6:41) If it were not for the goodness of God we would be destroyed. We live because of His goodness.

Psalm 23:6 says, *Surely goodness and mercy shall follow me all the days of my life, and I shall dwell in the house of the Lord forever.* His goodness and His mercy are with me all the days of my life and at the end of my life He has promised me life everlasting.

So, I can pray, *Remember not the sins of my youth or my transgressions; according to your steadfast love remember me, for the sake of your goodness, O Lord.* (Psalm 25:7)

As far as the east is from the west, so far does he remove our transgressions from us. As a father shows compassion to his children, so the Lord shows compassion to those who fear him. (Psalm 103:12-13) His goodness endures forever!

"But the greatest of these is love!"

DAY 119

But the fruit of the Spirit is love, joy, peace, patience, kindness, goodness, faithfulness, gentleness, self-control; against such things there is no law. **(Galatians 5:22-23)**

Oh, how abundant is your goodness, which you have stored up for those who fear you. **(Psalm 31:19)** Just think about this for a minute. The Lord has stored up goodness for those who fear Him. Not only is He giving us goodness now, but He has a reserve of goodness stored up for us. If we could only grasp the goodness of God, we would relax and let Him be God.

This reminds me of an old song we use to sing. "For the Lord He is good and His mercy endureth forever. For the Lord He is good and forever His mercy endured."

In your goodness, O God, you provided for the needy. **(Psalm 66:10)** *My God will supply every need of yours according to his riches in glory in Christ Jesus.* **(Philippians 4:19)** He will make provision for His people because of His goodness.

They shall come and sing aloud on the height of Zion, and they shall be radiant over the goodness of the Lord. **(Jeremiah 31:12)** When was the last time you stopped to thank the Lord for His goodness to you and to those around you? Do we take His goodness for granted?

Afterward the children of Israel shall return and seek the Lord their God, and David their king, and they shall come in fear to the Lord and to his goodness in the latter days. **(Hosea 3:5)** I think we are in those latter days. But have we become so comfortable that we have lost the fear of the Lord and His goodness towards us?

For how great is his goodness, and how great his beauty? **(Zechariah 9:17)** Today let's take a few minutes to reflect on His goodness and to thank Him for it.

"But the greatest of these is love!"

DAY 120

But the fruit of the Spirit is love, joy, peace, patience, kindness, goodness, faithfulness, gentleness, self-control; against such things there is no law. (Galatians 5:22-23)

They shall pour forth the fame of your abundant goodness and shall sing aloud of your righteousness. (Psalm 145:7)

It is interesting that everything I have found in scripture is about God's goodness. I began to think we are to be like Him. So regardless of whether goodness is about Him or about us, it should be the same. We are made in His image and His likeness.

But when the goodness and loving kindness of God our Savior appeared, he saved us, not because of works done by us in righteousness but according to his own mercy. (Titus 3:4)

We should be so thankful that God is good because it is out of His goodness that He has saved us. He could have scrapped the whole universe and began again as He did in Noah's day. But instead, He has not given up on us, still hoping that some will be saved.

The Lord looks down from heaven on the children of man, to see if there are any who understand, who seek after God. (Psalm 14:2) *I say to the Lord, "You are my Lord; I have no good apart from You."* (Psalm 16:2) That is my confession today!

Good and upright is the Lord; therefore, he instructs sinners in the way. He leads the humble in what is right and teaches the humble his way. All the paths of the Lord are steadfast love and faithfulness, for those who keep his covenant and his testimonies. (Psalm 25:8-10)

Oh, taste and see that the Lord is good! Blessed is the man who takes refuge in him! (Psalm 34:8)

"But the greatest of these is love!"

DAY 121

But the fruit of the Spirit is love, joy, peace, patience, kindness, goodness, faithfulness, gentleness, self-control; against such things there is no law. (Galatians 5:22-23)

Trust in the Lord and do good; dwell in the land and befriend faithfulness. Delight yourself in the Lord, and he will give you the desires of your heart. (Psalm 37:3-4)

To trust means to cling to with all your might. I can picture being in a storm with the wind raging, the house shaking, the roof blowing off, hanging onto a doorpost with all my might. That is the kind of trust the Lord wants us to have in Him. *Every good gift and every perfect gift is from above, coming down from the Father of lights, with whom there is no variation or shadow due to change.* (James 1:17)

Now what does trust have to do with good? Everything! If we truly believe that God loves us and only wishes for our good, then we will cling to Him in all situations believing that He knows what is best for us.

Answer me, O Lord, for your steadfast love is good; according to your abundant mercy, turn to me. (Psalm 69:16) When someone is drowning and a lifeguard tries to rescue him, many times the person fights rather than yielding to the rescuer. When I truly begin to understand the goodness of God, I will quit fighting and cling to Him in total trust.

For the Lord God is a sun and shield; the Lord bestows favor and honor. No good thing does he withhold from those who walk uprightly. O Lord of hosts, blessed is the one who trusts in you! (Psalm 84:11-12)

For you, O Lord, are good and forgiving, abounding in steadfast love to all who call upon you. (Psalm 86:5) David knew the goodness of God.

"But the greatest of these is love!"

DAY 122

But the fruit of the Spirit is love, joy, peace, patience, kindness, goodness, faithfulness, gentleness, self-control; against such things there is no law. **(Galatians 5:22-23)**

Oh, give thanks to the Lord for he is good, for his steadfast love endures forever! Let the redeemed of the Lord say so. **(Psalm 107:1-2)**

Have you ever tasted something that was so good that you begged for the recipe? When people look at me, I want them to say, "You are so good. I want to know why, or I want the recipe." Our lives are a living epistle of something. I want mine to reflect the goodness of God.

For he satisfies the longing soul, and the hungry soul he fills with good things. **(Psalm 107:9)**

You are good and do good; teach me your statutes. **(Psalm 119:68)** Is goodness something that we can learn or are we born with it? I kind of think it is both. Some of us by nature seem good, while others of us are always struggling in our own power to reflect goodness. The problem with "self-helps" is that they never last. They are like a New Year's resolution. Until we give God all our uglies we will struggle with them from now until eternity.

Teach me to do your will, for you are my God! Let your good Spirit lead me on level ground! **(Psalm 143:10)**

Jesus said, "I am the good shepherd. The good shepherd lays down his life for the sheep." **(John 10:11)** Goodness breeds goodness. Just like all the fruit of the Spirit, goodness shows one more facet of God's nature and the nature He has put into each of us.

So, *Let us not grow weary of doing good, for in due season we will reap, if we do not give up.* **(Galatians 6:9)**

"But the greatest of these is love!"

DAY 123

But the fruit of the Spirit is love, joy, peace, patience, kindness, goodness, faithfulness, gentleness, self-control; against such things there is no law. (Galatians 5:22-23)

Great is his steadfast love toward us, and the faithfulness of the Lord endures forever. Praise the Lord! (Psalm 117:2)

Faithful: loyal, constant, devoted, unswerving, unwavering, staunch, steadfast, committed, trustworthy, dependable, reliable, unerring.

Know therefore that the Lord your God is God, the faithful God who keeps covenant and steadfast love with those who love him and keep his commandments, to a thousand generations. (Deuteronomy 7:9)

He is faithful to a thousand generations. That includes us. He has promised to never leave us nor forsake us. He is faithful and His word is true. We need to wrap this around our brain. He is faithful! Everything about God is, "yes and amen". We can count on Him regardless of what is going on around us.

He will guard the feet of his faithful ones, but the wicked shall be cut off in darkness, for not by might shall man prevail. (1 Samuel 2:9) *It* isn't what we do but what God does in us and through us that matters. We are His vessels, full of His glory!

Into your hand I commit my spirit; you have redeemed me, O Lord, faithful God. (Psalm 31:5) When was the last time you truly committed your life, or your families lives to Christ and left them there? Easier said than done. I cannot remember the number of times I have given my family to the Lord and then taken them back. But is there anything too hard for God? What can I do that He cannot do better?

The Lord preserves the faithful. (Psalm 31:23) That is a promise. He is faithful.

"But the greatest of these is love!"

DAY 124

But the fruit of the Spirit is love, joy, peace, patience, kindness, goodness, faithfulness, gentleness, self-control; against such things there is no law. (Galatians 5:22-23)

I will look with favor on the faithful in the land, that they may dwell with me. (Psalm 101:6)

Sometimes I feel like Ichabod is on our nation and our church. Where has the glory gone? Spirit of the Living God are you still in our midst? Have you given up on us? Where is your majesty and your glory? Then I remember that great is His faithfulness. He will never leave us nor forsake us. When I cannot feel His presence, I need to believe His word and keep on keeping on. He looks with favor on the faithful!

The works of his hands are faithful and just; all his precepts are trustworthy; they are established forever and ever, to be performed with faithfulness and uprightness. He sent redemption to his people; he has commanded his covenant forever. (Psalm 111:7-9)

When we begin to feel abandoned, we need to remember to *Trust in the Lord with all of your heart, and do not lean on your own understanding. In all your ways acknowledge him, and he will make straight your paths. Be not wise in your own eyes; fear the Lord and turn away from evil. It will be healing to your flesh and refreshment to your bones.* (Proverbs 3:7-8) Trust in His faithfulness!

Like all the fruit of the Spirit, faithfulness is a choice. The Spirit provides it, but we must act upon it. We must accept His faithfulness and step out in faith.

Now may the God of peace himself sanctify you completely and may your whole spirit and soul and body be kept blameless at the coming of our Lord Jesus Christ. He who calls you is faithful; he will surely do it. (1 Thessalonians 5:24-25)

"But the greatest of these is love!"

DAY 125

But the fruit of the Spirit is love, joy, peace, patience, kindness, goodness, faithfulness, gentleness, self-control; against such things there is no law. **(Galatians 5:22-23)**

Let us hold fast the confession of our hope without wavering, for he who promised is faithful. And let us consider how to stir up one another to love and good works. **(Hebrews 10:23-24)**

His faithfulness should prompt us to not only be faithful to Him but faithful to others, especially the body of Christ.

Our word is proof of who we are. If I can trust your word, then for sure I know I can trust His. Do trust and faithfulness go hand in hand?

Therefore, let those who suffer according to God's will entrust their souls to a faithful Creator while doing good. **(1 Peter 4:19)** Faithfulness shows itself through good works. Good works are the result of the fruit of the Spirit operating in us.

The Lord is faithful in all his words and kind in all his works. **(Psalm 145:13)**

No temptation has overtaken you that is not common to man. God is faithful, and he will not let you be tempted beyond your ability, but with the temptation he will also provide the way of escape that you may be able to endure it. **(1 Corinthians 10:13)**

This promise has sustained me many times. I have never gone through anything that others haven't also. I will never go through anything that others aren't going through. There are no pity parties in heaven. God is faithful and He will provide a way of escape either here or in heaven. God keeps His word. Therefore, we have nothing to fear but fear itself. So, we come full circle, ***Let us hold fast the confession of our hope without wavering, for he who promised is faithful.***

"But the greatest of these is love!"

DAY 126

But the fruit of the Spirit is love, joy, peace, patience, kindness, goodness, faithfulness, gentleness, self-control; against such things there is no law. (Galatians 5:22-23)

One who is faithful in a very little is also faithful in much, and one who is dishonest in a very little is also dishonest in much. (Luke 16:10)

Our faithfulness begins with little things. If we cannot be trusted in the little things, then dimes to donuts we cannot be trusted with bigger things. But we might say little things are not really important. That is where we are wrong. Just look at the word. Until we can handle the small things God tells us to do, we will not be given greater responsibility in the kingdom. Again, it comes down to faithfulness.

Now faith is the assurance of things hoped for, the conviction of things not seen. (Hebrews 11:1) I love the choice of words here. "Now faith" That means faith right now. It means faith "at the moment". How do we get this kind of faith? I believe it is line upon line and precept upon precept. I realized as I was praying about it that faith is the substance and faithfulness is the action. When we have faith in something or someone, we will be faithful.

By faith Sarah herself received power to conceive, even when she was past the age, since she considered him faithful who had promised. (Hebrews 11:11) I wonder how many miracles Sarah had seen God do before this time? Had He proven Himself to her? I think so.

And without faith it is impossible to please him, for whoever would draw near to God must believe that he exists and that he rewards those who seek him. (Hebrews 11:6)

"But the greatest of these is love!"

DAY 127

But the fruit of the Spirit is love, joy, peace, patience, kindness, goodness, faithfulness, gentleness, self-control; against such things there is no law. (Galatians 5:22-23)

Be faithful unto death, and I will give you the crown of life. He who has an ear, let him hear what the Spirit is saying to the churches. (Revelation 2:10-11)

I love this Christian walk, but when it comes to pain and suffering, I get a little nervous. Faithful might imply more than our American spirituality. I don't know anyone personally who has been threaten unto death. We have it really easy. I sometimes wonder if this is good. Has our faith really been tested?

The words of the Amen, the faithful and true witness, the beginning of God's creation. I know your works: you are neither cold nor hot. (Revelation 3:14-15)

Are we a lukewarm church? Are we lukewarm Christians? This question is one only you can answer. I think sometimes I am lukewarm and other times I am on fire for the Lord. But I have not been tested unto death.

They will make war on the Lamb, and the Lamb will conquer them, for he is Lord of lords, and King of kings, and those with him are called and chosen and faithful. (Revelation 17:14)

I pray that each one of us will be called, chosen and faithful. I am not sure what this requires on our part, but I want to be one of faithful ones and I am sure you do too.

Then I saw heaven opened, and behold, a white horse! The one sitting on it is called Faithful and True, and in righteousness he judges and makes war. (Revelation 19:11) Be faithful until the end!

"But the greatest of these is love!"

DAY 128

But the fruit of the Spirit is love, joy, peace, patience, kindness, goodness, faith-fulness, gentleness, self-control; against such things there is no law. (Galatians 5:22-23)

As I have said before, I am wondering if the fruits of the Spirit don't build upon each other. If we have love, we will have joy. If we have joy, we will have peace. If we have peace, we will have patience. If we have patience, we will have kindness. If we have kindness, we will have goodness. If we have goodness, we will have faith-fulness. If we have faithfulness, we will have gentleness and if we have gentleness, we will have self-control. But it all hinges on love. There are no accidents in the Word of God.

You have given me the shield of your salvation, and your right hand supported me, and your gentleness made me great. (Psalm 18:35)

What is gentleness? Kindness, tenderness, mercy, forgiveness, consideration, understanding, compassion, love, humility, tranquility, reverence, leniency, etc.

It is in interesting that the word gentleness is only mentioned twice in the Old Testament and the verses are almost identical. Do you suppose that true gentleness came with the Gentle Shepherd Jesus?

But in your hearts honor Christ the Lord as holy, always being prepared to make a defense to anyone who asks you for a reason for the hope that is in you; yet do it with gentleness and respect. (1 Peter 3:15)

In our zeal to share the Word, how often do we try to force our beliefs on others rather than gently leading them to the Lord through our actions and deeds? What really screams out to me in this verse is waiting to be asked, rather than plunging ahead like a bull in a China closet.

"But the greatest of these is love!"

DAY 129

But the fruit of the Spirit is love, joy, peace, patience, kindness, goodness, faithfulness, gentleness, self-control; against such things there is no law. (Galatians 5:22-23)

I therefore, a prisoner for the Lord, urge you to walk in a manner worthy of the calling to which you have been called, with all humility and gentleness, with patience, bearing with one another in love, eager to maintain the unity of the Spirit in the bond of peace. (Ephesians 4:1-3)

What more fitting verse could we have today? I urge you to walk in humility, gentleness, patience, and love. Walk in unity with one another. This does not mean we have to see eye to eye on everything. We must learn to agree to disagree in love. My friends, the Body of Christ is splintering, and we are part of the problem. We have chosen to disagree rather than to bond in friendship one to another. What has happened to the theme, "We will know them by their love"? Are all the things we are arguing about worth the friendships we are losing? Is my right to be right more important than my walk with the Lord? It is time to reevaluate.

What do you wish? Shall I come to you with a rod, or with love in a spirit of gentleness? (1 Corinthians 4: 21) A teaspoon of honey makes the medicine go down. I think we have forgotten this. It is time to sweeten our tongues and our hearts with gentleness. I am looking in the mirror and I do not like what I am seeing.

A gentle tongue is a tree of life, but perverseness in it breaks the spirit. (Proverbs 15:4) Lord forgive me. I have sinned against you, and you only have I sinned. But it is a new day and a new beginning. Let us choose to walk in gentleness.

"But the greatest of these is love!"

DAY 130

But the fruit of the Spirit is love, joy, peace, patience, kindness, goodness, faithfulness, gentleness, self-control; against such things there is no law. (Galatians 5:22-23)

Brothers, if anyone is caught in any transgression, you who are spiritual should restore him in a spirit of gentleness. Keep watch on yourself, lest you too be tempted. Bear one another's burdens, and so fulfill the law of Christ. (Galatians 6:1)

About the time I begin criticizing you, I find myself in need of forgiveness. It is amazing when we look into muddy water, we still see our reflection. I cannot think of the number of times I have been critical of another's actions and turned around and did something myself. Gentleness is not one of my strong suits, but I can definitely see the need for it in my life. Since self-control follows gentleness, I am beginning to realize that gentleness will produce self-control and self-control will produce gentleness. Count to ten!

But as for you, O man of God, flee these things. Pursue righteousness, godliness, faith, love, steadfastness, gentleness. Fight the good fight of faith. (1 Timothy 6:11)

There is a battle raging all around us and in most of us. Instead of pursuing the fruit of the Spirit, we seem to be pursuing me and mine. We are told to flee these things and put on the goodness of God. The battle is not against flesh and blood, and we need to remember this. So gently remind yourself!

But the wisdom from above is first pure, then peaceable, gentle, open to reason, full of mercy and good fruits, impartial and sincere. And a harvest of righteousness is sown in peace by those who make peace. (James 3:17) We have to sow it to reap it!

"But the greatest of these is love!"

DAY 131

But the fruit of the Spirit is love, joy, peace, patience, kindness, goodness, faithfulness, gentleness, self-control; against such things there is no law. (Galatians 5:22-23)

Have nothing to do with foolish, ignorant controversies; you know that they breed quarrels. And the Lord's servant must not be quarrelsome but be kind to everyone, able to teach, patiently enduring evil, correcting his opponents with gentleness. (2 Timothy 2:23-25)

Have you noticed that around some people your tongue begins to wag? Your total tone of conversation loses its holiness. You say things that you would not normally say. This is when we need to flee. Is my own ego part of the problem? Do I want to build myself up while tearing someone else down? I think we need to choose our friendships carefully lest we or they fall. It may not be the other persons fault but just our vibes together.

It is such a blessing to be around someone who edifies and builds up others and such a downer when we are with downers or are the downer. *Death and life are in the power of the tongue, and those who love it will eat its fruits.* (Proverbs 18:21)

For we never came with words of flattery, as you know, nor with a pretext for greed – God is our witness. Nor did we seek glory from people, whether from you or from others, though we could have made demands as apostles of Christ. But we were gentle among you, like a nursing mother taking care of her own children. (1 Thessalonians 2:5-7)

Let your adorning be the hidden person of the heart with the imperishable beauty of a gentle and quiet spirit, which in God's sight is very precious. (1 Peter 3:4)

"But the greatest of these is love!"

DAY 132

But the fruit of the Spirit is love, joy, peace, patience, kindness, goodness, faithfulness, gentleness, self-control; against such things there is no law. (Galatians 5:22-23)

We have reached the 9th fruit of the Spirit. Now if you have mastered all the above you can forget self-control because you have it. Have you noticed that the fruit of the Spirit is singular not plural? Do you suppose when we take a bite of the Tree of Life, we will get all of the fruit? Eve took one bite and look what happened. I hope the same can be said when we take a bite of the Tree of Life. We will be so full of all the fruit our lives will be instantly transformed. Just a crazy thought.

A man without self-control is like a city broken into and left without walls. (**Proverbs 25:28**) Self-control gives us control. Think about that for a minute.

Self-control: self-discipline, restraint, will power, composure, temperance, etc.

Every athlete exercises self-control in all things. They do it to receive a perishable wreath, but we are imperishable. So, I do not run aimlessly; I do not box as one beating the air. But I discipline my body and keep it under control. (1 Corinthians 9:25-26)

Honestly, self-control is probably the hardest fruit of the Spirit for each of us to master. When do we hold our tongue and when do we speak? Is it really important to always have my say or my way? Can I be right and remain silent? Do l take that second piece of cake? Do I really need to buy that outfit? Do I need a bigger house? Can I skip exercise for just one day? Can I skip Bible Study and prayer for just one day? Do I/can I_____ You fill in the blank.

"But the greatest of these is love!"

DAY 133

But the fruit of the Spirit is love, joy, peace, patience, kindness, goodness, faithfulness, gentleness, self-control; against such things there is no law. **(Galatians 5:22-23)**

Are you in control or have you relinquished your control to the One who can best keep you from stumbling?

For God gave us a spirit not of fear but of power and love and self-control. **(2 Timothy 1:7)**

If we believe that God is in control of our lives and our universe, then why are we so fearful? If He is in control, then we have nothing to fear. Self-control should give Him control.

For this reason, make every effort to supplement your faith with virtue, and virtue with knowledge, and knowledge with self-control, and self-control with steadfastness, and steadfastness with godliness, and godliness with brotherly affection, and brotherly affection with love. For if these qualities are yours and are increasing, they keep you from being ineffective or unfruitful in the knowledge of our Lord Jesus Christ. **(2 Peter 1:5-8)**

Self-control gives us steadfastness which produces godliness. When I pray self-control helps me to believe what I pray and wait patiently to see what God will do. I choose to rely on Him even when I do not instantly see results. That is self-control. I am back to, He said it! I believe it! That settles it!

For the grace of God has appeared, bringing salvation for all people, training us to renounce ungodliness and worldly passions, and to live self-controlled, upright, and godly lives in the present age. **(Titus 2:11-12)** Self-control is a choice.

"But the greatest of these is love!"

DAY 134

But the fruit of the Spirit is love, joy, peace, patience, kindness, goodness, faithfulness, gentleness, self-control, against such things there is no law. (Galatians 5:22-23)

I was thinking about this verse and realized I have left one section of it out entirely. *Against such things there is no law.* I get the fruit but what does this means? I began to think. You cannot legislate love or joy etc. It is something of the heart. It is a gift of the Holy Spirit which we can either accept or reject. Freebee!

No temptation has overtaken you that is not common to man. God is faithful, and he will not let you be tempted beyond your ability, but with the temptation he will also provide the way of escape, that you may be able to endure it. (1 Corinthians 10:13) This may seem like a strange verse to put with self-control. But think about it for a minute. Self-control helps us to endure all things. I can make it! I can do it! I can endure it! So just hang in there!

All things are lawful for me, but not all things are helpful. All things are lawful for me, but I will not be dominated by anything. (1 Corinthians 6:12) I will not be dominated by anything. The question is, "What are we dominated by or who?" Domination is not the same as desiring to please. The one is an act of force and the other an act of love. Self-control helps us to recognize the difference and act accordingly.

Know this, my beloved brothers: let every person be quick to hear, slow to speak, slow to anger, for the anger of man does not produce the righteousness of God. (James 1:19-20) Sometimes, I have to count to 10 before I speak. Many times, I speak before I count to 10. The gift of self-control helps me hold my tongue until my heart catches up with it.

"But the greatest of these is love!"

DAY 135

But the fruit of the Spirit is love, joy, peace, patience, kindness, goodness, faithfulness, gentleness, self-control: against such things there is no law. (Galatians 5:22-23)

I appeal to you therefore, brothers, by the mercies of God, to present your bodies as a living sacrifice, holy and acceptable to God, which is your spiritual worship. Do not be conformed to this world, but be transformed by the renewal of your mind, that by testing you may discern what is the will of God, what is good and acceptable and perfect. (Romans 12:1-2)

We will conclude our look at the Fruit of the Spirit by meditating on the above verses. Do not be conformed to this world but be transformed by the renewal of your mind. Self-control requires discipline and discipline requires desire and desire requires a heart change and the heart change comes from the Holy Spirit.

We need to discern what is the will of God, what is good and acceptable and perfect. How do we do that but by getting into His word and meditating on it day and night? How do we do that but by prayer? How do we do that but by fellowshipping with believers? We need each other. We are held accountable by each other. We are encouraged and uplifted by each other. We are able to share our joys and sorrows with each other. So, let's not be a Debbie Downer but ones who edifies and exhorts the Body of Christ.

Finally, be strong in the Lord and in the strength of his might. Put on the whole armor of God, that you may be able to stand against the schemes of the devil. (Ephesians 6:10-11)

For the fruit of the Spirit is love, joy, peace, patience, kindness, goodness, faithfulness, gentleness, self-control: against such there is no law.

"But the greatest of these is love!"

100 ATTRIBUTES OF GOD

DAY 136

"ATTRIBUTE OF GOD FROM A TO Z" (INTRODUCTION)

When we refer to God's attributes, we are referring to any and every part of God. Let's spend some time looking at some of His attributes from scripture.

1 Timothy 1:17 says, *Now to the King eternal, immortal, invisible, the only God, be honor and glory for ever and ever. Amen*

He is eternal. He is everlasting, never-ending, endless, without end, perpetual, undying, immortal, indestructible, permanent, timeless, enduring. He is eternal. **Deuteronomy 33:21** says, *The eternal God is your refuge, and underneath are the everlasting arms.*

He is immortal. He is exempt from oblivion, imperishable, not subject to death, not liable to perish or decay, everlasting. He is like the energizer bunny only He never runs out. He is immortal. 1 Timothy 6:16 says, *Who alone has immortality, who dwells in unapproachable light, whom no one has ever seen or can see. To him be honor and eternal dominion. Amen*

He is invisible. He is incapable by nature of being seen, not perceptible by vision, inaccessible to view, hidden. He is invisible. Hebrews 11:3 says, *By faith we understand that the universe was created by the word of God, so that what is seen was not made out of things that are visible.*

He is the only God. There is no other. John 17:3 says, *And this is eternal life, that they know you the only true God, and Jesus Christ whom you have sent.*

This is just a taste of what we will be studying for the next 100 days. Hopefully, you desire to know Him and will spend time meditating on His attributes.

For from him and through him and to him are all things. To him be glory forever. Amen. (Romans 11:36)

"Maranatha" Come Lord Jesus!

DAY 137

"ATTRIBUTES OF GOD FROM A TO Z" (A)

"Almighty"

Almighty: author, creator, deity, divinity, eternal, everlasting, Father, God, Godhead, Jehovah, King, Lord, Maker. We could go on and on. The Almighty is "all". All means all in all, every single bit, entire, whole, etc. That is who God is!

To Abram God said, *I am God Almighty; walk before me, and be blameless. (Genesis 17:1)*

To Jacob God said, *I am God Almighty: be fruitful and multiply. (Genesis 35:11)*

To Moses God said, *I appeared to Abraham, to Isaac and to Jacob, as God Almighty. (Exodus 6:3)*

Psalm 91:*1 says, He who dwells in the shelter of the Most High will abide in the shadow of the Almighty.*

God is known as El Shaddai, the all sufficient one. He said to Moses "I AM WHO I AM." (Exodus 3:14) God is everything. He is all encompassing. God tells us in the beginning of His Word who He is and then He proves to us through His word that He is who He says He is! Finally in Revelation He again reveals Himself as God Almighty.

"I am the Alpha and the Omega", says the Lord, "who is and who was and who is to come, the Almighty." (Revelation 1:8)

Holy, holy, holy, is the Lord God Almighty, who was and is and is to come! (Revelation 4:8)

And finally, *Hallelujah! For the Lord our God the Almighty reigns. Let us rejoice and exult and give him the glory. (Revelation 29:6)* Who is our God?

"El Shaddai!"

DAY 138

"Attributes of God from A to Z" (A)

"He is our Advocate."

The word advocate means counselor, comforter, champion, upholder, supporter, backer, protector, helper. Which part of the Trinity does this seem to describe? He is our parakletos or the Holy Spirit. God did not leave us defenseless but provided an advocate or a helper for us. I need all the above.

1 John 2:1 says, *If anyone does sin, we have an advocate with the Father, Jesus Christ the righteous. He is the propitiation for our sins, and not for ours only but also for the sins of the whole world.* Jesus has assured us that He will never leave us nor forsake us and the way He does this is through the Holy Spirit.

Jesus said, *I will ask the Father and he will give you another Helper, to be with you forever, even the Spirit of truth, whom the world cannot receive, because it neither sees him nor knows him. You know him, for he dwells with you and will be in you…He will teach you all things and bring to your remembrance all that I have said to you.* (John 14:16-17 & 26) In other words He is our counselor.

Have you ever noticed when you need a word from God it just seems to be there? When you are witnessing to someone you seem to have just the right words to say. Sometimes you say things that help another without realizing it. That comes from the Counselor who lives within you. He is your advocate.

But when the Helper comes, whom I will send to you from the Father, the Spirit of truth, who proceeds from the Father, he will bear witness about me. (John 15:26)

Not only will the Holy Spirit teach us, but He will reinforce what we know about Jesus. Sometimes we have a check in our spirit. That also comes from the Holy Spirit. He is protecting us against something or someone we need to back off from. I am so glad that I have an advocate; someone to support me and help me.

"He is my "Advocate".

DAY 139

"Attributes of God from A to Z" (A)

Jesus is the Author and finisher of our faith. (Hebrews 12:2)

What does the word "Author" mean? The beginning of the cause of, the one who forms, the creator, the originator, the composer, the one who goes before.

John 1:1 says, In the beginning was the Word and the Word was with God and the Word was God. God is the author and the finisher of the Word. Every word is inspired by God. It is so important that we believe this and walk in it. We cannot pick and choose.

For it became him, for whom are all things, and through whom are all things, in bringing many children to glory, to make the author of their salvation perfect through sufferings. (Hebrew 2:10) Jesus is the author of our salvation. He is the reason we are able to stand before the throne of God pure and holy. He is the spotless Lamb of God who takes away the sin of the world.

He is the author and finisher of our faith. *Looking to Jesus, the author and perfecter of faith, who for the joy that was set before him endured the cross, despising its shame, and has sat down at the right hand of the throne of God. (Hebrews 12:2)* and without faith it is impossible to please Him.

He is the author of our peace. *1 Corinthians 14:33 says, For God is not the author of confusion, but of peace. He says, Peace I leave with you, my peace I give to you. Not as the world gives do I give to you. (John 14:27)*

He is the author of life. *But you denied the Holy and Righteous One and asked for a murder to be granted to you, and you killed the Author of life, to which we are witnesses. (Acts 3:14-15) In the beginning, God created the heavens and the earth...Let us make man in our image, after our likeness. (Genesis 1:1 & 26)* He created us and wanted us to be like Him. He loves His creation!

He also wrote the end of the book. *The Spirit and the Bride say, "Come". And let the one who hears say, "Come. And let the one who is thirsty come; let the one who desires take the water of life without price. (Revelation 22:17)*

"He is the Author!"

DAY 140

"Attributes of God from A to Z" (A)

"The Anointed One"

The Spirit of the Lord is upon me, because the Lord has anointed me to bring good new to the poor, he has sent me to bind up the brokenhearted, to proclaim liberty to the captives, and the opening of the prison to those who are bound, to proclaim the year of the Lord's favor. **(Isaiah 61:1-2)** This is a prophecy concerning Jesus and it was fulfilled in the New Testament. (Luke 4:18)

What does anointing mean? Consecrate, sanctify, bless, ordain, hallow, chosen for a special job. Jesus was chosen by God, and He was God, to bring salvation to a dead and dying world.

Acts 10:38 says, *How God anointed Jesus of Nazareth with the Holy Spirit and with power. He went about doing good and healing all who were oppressed by the devil, for God was with him.*

Some attributes of Jesus because He was anointed were to preach, heal the broken hearted, set the captives free, heal the sick and proclaim liberty to each of us.

Acts 4:26 says, *The kings of the earth set themselves, and the rulers were gathered together, against the Lord and against his Anointed.*

We have found the Messiah. which literally means the Anointed One. **(John 1:41)** Jesus is not man but He is God. He is the anointed one of God. He is the Son of God. He is the Savior. He is filled with power. He is consecrated by God. He is blessed by God. He was ordained by God and chosen for a very special job by God. But He is God!

The woman at the well said, *I know that Messiah (the anointed one) is coming (he who is called Christ). When he comes, he will tell us all things. Jesus said to her, "I who speak to you am he."* **(John 4:25)**

"Jesus is the Anointed One!"

DAY 141

"Attributes of God from A to Z" (A)

"All-knowing" Omniscient

What does omniscient mean? Unlimited in creative power, aware of everything, timeless knowledge, knowing the past, present and the future, all-knowing.

Isaiah 37:28 says, *I know your sitting down and you're going out and coming in.*

There is nothing hidden from God. Sometimes I think we think we can do and say things that God does not hear and know, but God knows everything, and He still loves us.

He knows the way that I take; when he has tried me, I shall come out as gold. **(Job 23:10)**

He knows you're going through this great wilderness. **(Deuteronomy 2:7)**

Take comfort. He knows the wilderness we are in at the moment, and He has seen the end from the beginning. He knows and He cares!

Your Father knows what you need before you ask him. **(Matthew 6:8)**

A great example is Moses and the children of Israel in the wilderness. God provided everything that they needed. If He will do this for them, He will do it for us!

For he knows our frame; he remembers that we are dust. (Psalm 103:14) What a relief to know we do not have to be perfect. We can make mistakes.

He knows the secrets of the heart. **(Psalm 44:21)** Whether I say it or I just think it, He still knows.

The Lord knows those who are his. (2 Timothy 2:19) He knows us by name. He knew us before the foundation of the world. He knew us before we were formed in our mother's womb.

For whenever our heart condemns us, God is greater than our heart, and he knows everything. **(1 John 3:20)**

"He is Omniscient!"

DAY 142

"Attributes of God from A to Z" (A)

"All Powerful"

Yes, my God is "All powerful". He is strong, fierce, passionate, consuming, omnipotent, supreme, preeminent, unsurpassed, unequaled, matchless and on and on. He is God!

Psalm 29:4 says, The voice of the Lord is powerful; the voice of the Lord is full of majesty. If we listen, we can hear His still small voice. If we obey His voice will become more and more clear to us. That is how we know Him.

He who executes his word is powerful. (Joel 2:11)

For the Lord your God is a consuming fire, a jealous God. (Deuteronomy 4:24) He will have no other Gods before Him. He wants our entire allegiance.

Know therefore today that he who goes over before you as a consuming fire is the Lord you God. **(Deuteronomy 9:3)**

Earlier in the year we had just come home when our house was rocked like a bomb. As we looked out the window flames shot up, and the house across the street was totally demolished by a gas explosion. One moment it was a beautiful home and the next moment it was gone with one occupant inside. The power that emanated from this explosion is nothing like the consuming fire of God.

It is so comforting to know that this consuming fire goes before us. We have nothing to fear. All power is with us. All power is within us. We go forward in His strength.

So let us offer to God acceptable worship, with reverence and awe, for our God is a consuming fire. **(Hebrews 12:28-29)**

What more can we say?

He is "All Powerful!"

DAY 143

"ATTRIBUTES OF GOD FROM A TO Z" (A)

"Authority" And Jesus came and said to them, "All authority in heaven and on earth has been given to me." (Matthew 28:18)

Jesus has all authority in heaven and on earth. What does this mean? The dictionary says: inspiration, power to do, prerogative or right, ability. In the Old Testament authority was given to the prophets, priests, and kings. But in the New Testament authority begins with Jesus, then the Holy Spirit and finally we have been given authority through Him.

Romans 13:1 says, There is no authority except from God, and those that exist have been instituted by God. God is the final authority.

Colossians 2:9-10 says, For in him the whole fullness of deity dwells bodily, and you have been filled in him, who is the head of all rule and authority. About the time we think we are in charge we have a nudge from the Holy Spirit reminding us that, we are not our own but bought with a price and it is time to glorify God who is All in All.

Ephesians 1:20 says, That he worked in Christ when he raised him from the dead and seated him at his right hand in the heavenly places, far above all rule and authority and power and dominion, and above every name that is named...he put all things under his feet and gave him as head over all things to the church. Satan has no power over you and me. People have no power over you and me. Circumstances have no power over you and me. We are under the authority of the Lord Jesus Christ who has all power. So, relax we are well taken care of.

Now to him who is able to keep you from stumbling and to present you blameless before the presence of his glory with great joy, to the only God, our Savior, through Jesus Christ our Lord be glory, majesty, dominion, and authority, before all time and now and forever. Amen (Jude 1:24)

"He has all power and authority!"

DAY 144

"ATTRIBUTES OF GOD FROM A TO Z" (B)

"Blessed"

1 Timothy 6:15 says, *He who is the blessed and only Sovereign, the King of kings and the Lord of lords, who alone has immortality, who dwells in unapproachable light, whom no one has ever seen or can see. To him be honor and eternal domin-ion, Amen.*

Blessed: set apart, consecrated, esteemed, extolled, etc.

Blessed is the King who comes in the name of the Lord! Peace in heaven and glory in the highest!...I tell you, if these were silent, the very stones would cry out.. **(Luke 19:38-40)** So let us not be silent!

Bless the Lord, O my soul, and all that is within me bless his Holy Name! Bless the Lord, O my soul, and forget not all his benefits, who forgives all your iniquity, who heals all your diseases, who redeems your life from the pit, who crowns you with steadfast love and mercy. **(Psalm 103:1-4)**

He is the blessed, set apart, consecrated, esteemed, extolled because He is God!

Blessed be the God and Father of our Lord Jesus Christ, the Father of mercies and God of all comfort. **(2 Corinthians 1:3)**

Blessed be the God and Father of our Lord Jesus Christ, who has blessed us in Christ with every spiritual blessing in the heavenly places. **(Ephesians 1:3)**

As I am reading the blessed scriptures, I begin to see a pattern. Almost every time I see "He who is the blessed" I see immediately after some way that He is blessing us. His attribute of blessed spills over to us. He has redeemed us. He has healed us. He has forgiven us. He has crowned us with steadfast love and mercy. He comforts us. He has blessed us with every spiritual blessing in heavenly places. Therefore, should I not bless those around me because I have been so blessed by Him?

"He is our Blessing!"

DAY 145

"ATTRIBUTES OF GOD FROM A TO Z" (B)

"He is Beautiful!"

Have you ever considered that God is beautiful? Why shouldn't He be if He created so much beauty on the earth and in each of us. Beautiful means elegant, graceful, splendid, exquisite, magnificent, divine, radiant. Real beauty is manifest on the inside.

Psalm 27:4 says, One thing have I asked of the Lord, that will I seek after; that I may dwell in the house of the Lord all the days of my life, to gaze upon the beauty of the Lord and to inquire in his temple. Song of Solomon is an allegory of the Lord and His bride. He calls her beautiful and she calls Him beautiful. It is a mutual admiration. That bride is you and me.

Isaiah 33:17 says, Your eyes will behold the king in his beauty. I cannot begin to imagine the beauty of heaven and the beauty of our King! *For He has made everything beautiful in its time. (Ecclesiastics 3:11)*

Zechariah 9:17 says, For how great is his goodness, and how great his beauty. Do you think the King of Kings and the Lord of Lords would create anything that is not exquisite? He said, "It is good!" Every time we stand in awe and look at God's creation whether person, place, or thing we are seeing the fruit of God's beauty.

In that day, the Lord of hosts will be a crown of glory, and a diadem of beauty, to the remnant of his people. (Isaiah 28:5) Splendor and majesty are before him; strength and beauty are in his sanctuary. (Psalm 96:6)

Out of Zion, the perfection of beauty, God shines forth. (Psalm 50:2)

We haven't seen anything yet. We are still not at the end of the story. Revelation gives us a glimpse, but even that is inadequate to describe the Lord and what He has prepared for His bride. Appreciate the beauty around you but remember there is much more to come. I love the song, "Oh Lord you're beautiful, your face I long to seek and when your eyes are on this child your grace abounds in me."

"He is Beautiful!"

DAY 146

"Attributes of God from A to Z" (B)

He is the "Beginning".

God is the beginning of everything. He was, He is, and He is to come. He is the beginning and the end. He is the Creator. He is the One who said, "Let there be and there was". This is hard to wrap my mind around. In this tangible world we want things and thoughts that we can grasp. God does not fit into our neat little box.

In Revelation 22:13 He says, *I am the Alpha and the Omega, the first and the last, the beginning and the end.* In other words, He is all in all; all that was, all that is and all that is to come, and we are His creation. We are made in the very image of God.

Our story begins in **Genesis 1:1,** *In the beginning God and it does not end there. Then God said, "Let us make man in our image, after our likeness."* **(V26)** We have been in His mind since the very beginning, and He has not let go of us yet. He has not given up on us. Aren't you glad?

John 1:1 says, *In the beginning was the Word, and the Word was with God, and the Word was God. He was in the beginning with God.* When God said, *"Let us make man"* He was speaking of the Father, the Son, and the Holy Spirit. Not only did God create us but He gave us a Savior and a Comforter. We were not left to do life on our own.

Colossians 1:18-19 says, *He is the beginning, the firstborn from the dead, that in everything he might be preeminent. For in him all the fullness of God was pleased to dwell.*

Hebrews 1:10 says, *You Lord, laid the foundation of the earth in the beginning, and the heavens are the work of your hands. But you are the same, and your years will have no end.* He is the beginning, and He has a plan for the future. We will become His bride. We will live with Him forever. This beginning has no end. He is God and we are His. Alleluia!

"He is the Beginning!"

DAY 147

"Attributes of God from A to Z" (B)

"He is the Bread of Life"

Bread is the food that we require for physical sustenance. It is the spiritual food needed for a full life. When Jesus said, *"I am the Bread of Life"*, He was saying I am who you need to live life to the fullest. I am the One who will sustain you.

Nehemiah 9:15 says, You gave them bread from heaven for their hunger and brought water for them out of the rock for their thirst, and you told them to go in to possess the land that you had sworn to give them. In order to possess the land that God has given to you and me we must embrace the true Bread of Life.

For the bread of God is he who comes down from heaven and gives life to the world...Jesus said to them, "I am the bread of life; whoever comes to me shall not hunger, and whoever believes in me shall never thirst...I am the living bread that came down from heaven. If anyone eats of this bread, he will live forever." **(John 6:33-51)**

When many of his disciples heard it, they said, "This is a hard saying; who can listen to it?" (John 6:60) You will have to admit that many of the things that Jesus said were hard to understand but as we remain in His Word and listen to the voice of the Holy Spirit, we begin to understand at least in part.

Jesus on the night when he was betrayed took bread, and when he had given thanks, he broke it, and said, "This is my body, which is for you. Do this in remembrance of me." **(1 Corinthians 11:24-25)**

Jesus body was broken as bread, for you and me. At the time, the disciples did not understand what He meant. But after His death and resurrection it became clear to them. His sacrifice has given us life. His death as the sacrificial lamb was once and for all. Now we do not need to yearly sacrifice bulls and goats because "It is finished." His body as broken bread has given us life. He is our sustenance. As we eat the Bread, we remember His death until He comes.

"He is the Bread of Life!"

DAY 148

"ATTRIBUTES OF GOD FROM A TO Z" (B)

The Lord is my Banner! He is Jehovah Nissi.

And Moses built an altar and called the name of it, The Lord is My Banner. (Exodus 17:14)

What is the purpose of a banner? It is a symbol that advertises something or someone. It says follow me. The banner is a standard in battle. The warriors followed the banner. The serpent on the pole was a banner.

And the Lord said to Moses, "Make a fiery serpent and set it on a pole and everyone who is bitten, when he sees it, shall live." (Numbers 21:8)

As the Israelites looked to the banner they were healed. **1 Peter 2:24 says, *He himself bore our sins in his body on the tree, that we might die to sin and live to righteousness. By his wounds you have been healed.*** The Lord is My Banner.

And as Moses lifted up the serpent in the wilderness, so must the Son of Man be lifted up, that whoever believes in him may have eternal life. (John 3:14)

The cross is our banner and as we follow it, we are saved. **Psalm 60:4 says, *You have set up a banner for those who fear you.*** Jesus said, "Follow me!" and as we follow the banner, we have eternal life.

He brought me to his banqueting table, and his banner over me is love. (Song of Solomon 2:4) I love the song, "O what manner of love the Father has given unto us, that we might be called the Sons of God."

He is Jehovah Nissi. He is our banner. He is our leader. He is our commander. He is the King of Kings. He is the Lord of Lords.

For to this you have been called because Christ suffered for you, leaving you an example, so that you might follow in his steps. (1 Peter 2:20)

As he raises His banner, we are asked to follow Him and His banner over us is love.

"The Lord is my Banner!"

DAY 149

"Attributes of God from A to Z" (C)

"The Christ"

Christ means the anointed one, consecrated, sanctifies, blessed, ordained, hallowed. The prophet, priest or king is anointed, and Jesus is our prophet, priest, and king. In order to receive salvation, we must believe this.

For unto you is born this day in the City of David a Savior, who is Christ the Lord. (Luke 2:11) He has no beginning and no end, but He left His home in heaven and came to earth to live among us as a man. He came and experienced who we are, what we are and how we live so that He could become the *"Spotless Lamb of God that takes away the sin of the world."*

Simon Peter replied, *You are the Christ, the Son of the living God. (Matthew 16:16)* This is the most important confession that any one of us can make. "You are the Christ; the Son of the living God and I accept you as my Lord and Savior." Our true life begins with this confession.

For the law was given through Moses; grace and truth came through Jesus Christ. (John 1:17) We do not live under the law but under grace.

Now Jesus did many other signs in the presence of the disciple, which are not written in this book; but these are written so that that you may believe that Jesus is the Christ, the Son of God, and that by believing you may have life in his name. (John 20:31)

John 17 is the High Priestly Prayer. In it Jesus says, *And this is eternal life, that they know you the only true God and Jesus Christ whom you have sent. I glorified you on earth, having accomplished the work that you gave me to do. And now, Father, glorify me in your own presence with the glory that I had with you before the world existed.*

Jesus is the Christ, the anointed one, consecrated, sanctified, blessed, and hallowed by the Father and each of us who call him Lord.

"He is The Christ!"

DAY 150

"Attributes of God from A to Z" (C)

"The Comforter"

If you love me, you will keep my commands. And I will ask the Father, and he will give you another Helper, (Comforter, Advocate) to be with you forever, even the Spirit of truth. (John 14:15-17) We have not been left comfortless.

Comfort is defined as strengthen, console, encourage, stand along-side, helper, exhorter, advocate. We concede, we need all the above. If it were not for the Holy Spirit leading us and guiding us, we would be eternally lost.

John 16:7-8 says, Nevertheless, I tell you the truth: it is to your advantage that I go away, for if I do not go away, the Helper (Comforter) will not come to you. But if I go, I will send him to you. And when he comes, he will convict the world concerning sin and righteousness and judgment. Apart from the Comforter would we really know we need a Savior?

2 Corinthians 1:3-4 says, Blessed be the God and Father of our Lord Jesus Christ, the Father of all comfort, who comforts us in all our afflictions, so that we may be able to comfort those who are in any affliction, with the comfort with which we ourselves are comforted.

Have you noticed that everything God has done for us or given to us, He expects us to turn and give to someone else? We are to be a conduit which God pours His Spirit through, leaking out to those around us.

"Comfort ye, O comfort ye my people, says your God." (Isaiah 40:1) He is our strength. So, we are to strengthen others. He is our encouragement. So, we are to encourage others. He is our helper. So, we are to turn and help others. He stands along-side us. So, we are to stand along-side others.

Jesus said, All authority in heaven and on earth has been given to me. Go therefore… (Matthew 28:18) Not only are we to share the gospel, but we are to comfort the people of God. How do we do this? By following the leading of the Holy Spirit, the true Comforter.

"He is our Comforter!"

DAY 151

"Attributes of God from A to Z" (C)

"The Counselor"

For to us a child is born, to us a son is given; and the government shall be upon his shoulder, and his name shall be called Wonderful Counselor, Mighty God, Everlasting Father, Prince of Peace. (Isaiah 9:6)

A counselor is an advisor, teacher, instructor, advocate. We have a counselor in the Lord Jesus Christ and also in the Holy Spirit, who is here to lead us and guide us into all truth.

Job 12:13 says, With God are wisdom and might; he has counsel and understanding. About the time we begin to know it all, we realize that we don't, but He does. He knows the beginning from the end, and He counsels us if we will listen. He is our teacher and our advocate.

He says, *I will instruct you and teach you in the way you should go; I will counsel you with my eye upon you. (Psalm 32:8)*

The counsel of the Lord stands forever, the plans of his heart to all generations. **(Psalm 33:11)**

If we will just listen to His counsel and His plans, life will be so much easier. If we trust in Him, He will be our advocate. He cares for us with an undying love.

In him we have obtained an inheritance, having been predestined according to the purpose of him who works all things according to the counsel of his will. **(Ephesians 1:11)**

I can sure use some counsel and wisdom. There are so many things that I do not know or understand. Many times, I just need a word of wisdom. I need the Counselor and we have one!

The Spirit of the Lord shall rest upon him, the Spirit of wisdom and understanding, the Spirit of counsel and might, the Spirit of knowledge and the fear of the Lord. (Isaiah 11:2)

"He is our Counselor!"

DAY 152

"ATTRIBUTES OF GOD FROM A TO Z" (C)

"Jesus is the Cornerstone"

1 Peter 2:6 says, *Behold, I am laying in Zion a stone, a cornerstone chosen and precious and whoever believes in him will not be put to shame.*

A cornerstone is the first stone laid in a building and all the other stones are set in reference to this stone, determining the position of the entire structure. The cornerstone is the foundation, the basis, the mainstay, the core, the center, the backbone, the anchor. This is Jesus!

***Ephesians 2:20-22 says,** You are built on the foundation of the apostles and prophets, Christ Jesus himself being the cornerstone, in whom the whole structure, being joined together, grows into a holy temple in the Lord. In him you also are being built together into a dwelling place for God by the Spirit.* He is our firm foundation.

Psalm 118:22-23 says, *The stone that the builders rejected has become the cornerstone. This is the Lord's doing; it is marvelous in our eyes.*

This Jesus is the stone that was rejected by you, the builders, which has become the cornerstone. And there is salvation in no one else, for there is no other name under heaven given among men by which we must be saved. (Acts 4:11-12)

A cornerstone is not the whole building, but it is the true beginning. In order for a building to materialize there needs to be many stones or bricks. We are those stones.

You yourselves like living stones are being built up as a spiritual house, to be a holy priesthood, to offer spiritual sacrifices acceptable to God through Jesus Christ. (1 Peter 2:5)

So, the question is, "How are we building our spiritual house? Is it according to the specifications set by Christ?"

"He is our "Cornerstone!"

DAY 153

"ATTRIBUTES OF GOD FROM A TO Z" (C)

"The Carpenter"

For every house is built by someone, but the builder of all things is God. (Hebrews 3:4)

Is not this the carpenter, son of Mary? (Mark 6:3)

Jesus was a carpenter until He began to preach. He is still a carpenter as He builds up the Body of Christ.

Abraham was, *Looking forward to the city that has foundations, whose designer and builder is God. (Hebrews 11:10)*

Have you ever stopped to think that God from the very beginning has been creating a place for His people? He has designed it with great love. He has a master plan for us.

He says, *In my father's house are many rooms. If it were not so, would I have told you that I go to prepare a place for you? (John 14:2)* If He can create the Grand Canyon, the Seven Wonders of the World, etc. can we even begin to image what He has prepared for us.

For by him all things were created, in heaven and on earth, visible and invisible. (Colossians 1:15) All things were made through him, and without him was not anything made that was made. (John 1:3)

He says all things were created by Him. When He finished creating, He said, "It is good!" We are His creation. We are good! We need to wrap our heads around the fact that we are good. We were not haphazardly created. We were in His mind from the very beginning.

Do you not know that you are God's temple and that God's Spirit dwells in you? **(1 Corinthians 3:16)**

The Master Builder, the Carpenter makes no mistakes. His design is perfect, and His handiwork is perfect.

"He is The Carpenter!"

DAY 154

"ATTRIBUTES OF GOD FROM A TO Z" (D)

"God is Divine"

For what can be known about God is plain to them because God has shown it to them. For his invisible attributes, namely, his eternal power and divine nature, have been clearly perceived, ever since the creation of the world. (**Romans 1:19-20**)

What does the word divine mean? When I was young, women were always using the word divine to describe things. We don't hear that much anymore. In truth divine means Godly, heavenly, excellent in the highest degree, extraordinary, supreme, exalted. "He Is!" all the above.

Worthy is the Lamb who was slain, to receive power and wealth and wisdom and might and honor and glory and blessing! (Revelation 5:12) In other words He is divine!

For in him all the fullness of God was pleased to dwell, and through him to reconcile to himself all things, whether on earth or in heaven, making peace by the blood of his cross. (Colossians 1:19-20) He is divine!

His divine power has granted to us all things that pertain to life and godliness, through the knowledge of him who called us to his own glory and excellence. (2 Peter 1:3-4) He is divine!

It is hard for us to truly understand God. We can know Him by His word and by His interaction in our lives. But to truly know Him is going to take eternity. Several times in the last couple of days I have had this thought. Now I am not saying it is true but think about it. Heaven has no past and no future. It is only the present. If this is true, then everything that happened yesterday is forgotten and tomorrow has not come. Just a thought.

Therefore, God has highly exalted him and bestowed on him the name that is above every name, so that at the name of Jesus every knee should bow, in heaven and on earth and under the earth and every tongue confess that Jesus Christ is Lord, to the glory of God the Father. (**Philippians 2:9-11**)

"He is Divine!"

DAY 155

"ATTRIBUTES OF GOD FROM A TO Z" (D)

"He is our Deliverer"

The Lord is my rock and my fortress and my deliverer, my God, my rock, in whom I take refuge. (Psalm 18:2)

A deliverer is a rescuer, a savior, a helper, one who sets free or sets at liberty.

We have all found ourselves in places where we cried out to the Lord to help us or to set us free. I am reminded of a friend who does not believe in God. During the war he was in a fox hole and the bombs were exploding all around him. He cried out to God and then said, "Wait I don't even believe in God." He was delivered anyway. ***You are my help and my deliverer; do not delay, O my God! (Psalm 40:17)***

He is my steadfast love and my fortress, my stronghold and my deliverer, my shield and he in whom I take refuge. (Psalm 144:2) David knew the Lord as his deliverer. He was constantly running, and God was constantly saving him. I sometimes feel He is doing the same for me. Don't you too?

And lead us not into temptation but deliver us from evil. (Matthew 6:13) He also is constantly whispering in my ear. "Stop, don't do that, wait!"

He has delivered us from the domain of darkness and transferred us to the kingdom of his beloved Son, in whom we have redemption, the forgiveness of sins. (Colossians 1:13)

Despite all of the ways He physically saves us from danger, the most important thing that He does in each of our lives is to save us for eternity.

For God so loved the world, that he gave his only Son, that whoever believes in him should not perish but have eternal life. For God did not send his Son into the world to condemn the world, but in order that the world might be saved through him. (John 3:16-17)

"He is our Savior, our Rescuer, our Deliverer!"

DAY 156

"Attributes of God from A to Z" (D)

"The Defender"

He only is my rock and my salvation; he is my defense. I shall not be greatly moved. **(Psalm 62:2 KJV)**

When I think of the word defender, I associate it with one who stands by me to argue my case or one who stands by me to protect me from harm. I need someone constantly by my side protecting me from myself and from others. We have not been left defenseless because we have the Holy Spirit as our constant defender. (The word for defense in the ESV is fortress or shield.)

Do not be anxious about how you should defend yourself or what you should say, for the Holy Spirit will teach you in that very hour what you ought to say. **(Luke 12:11)**

But the Lord is my defense; and my God is the rock of my refuge. **(Psalm 94:22)**

When you were little did you ever build a snow fort or wall and throw snowballs as you defended your fort from other kids? As long as you were behind your fort, you could not be plummeted with snowballs. But if you stepped outside the fort, you were an open target to others. In the same way as we stand behind the Lord, we are safe from our enemies.

But I will sing of thy power; yea I will sing aloud of thy mercy in the morning: for thou has been my defense and refuge in the day of my trouble. **(Psalm 59:16 KJV)**
Whatever mess I get into; He is there as my defense. What a comfort as long as my mess is God ordained.

In you, O Lord, do I take refuge; let me never be put to shame; in your righteousness deliver me! Incline your ear to me; rescue me speedily! Be a rock of refuge for me, a strong fortress to save me! For you are my rock and my fortress. **(Psalm 31:1-3)**

"You are my Defender!"

DAY 157

"Attributes of God from A to Z" (E)

"The Everlasting Father!"

His name shall be called Wonderful Counselor, Mighty God, Everlasting Father, Prince of Peace. (Isaiah 9:6) Hallelujah!

Have you ever had an all-day sucker? I still remember the huge rainbow suckers we sometimes got at Christmas. Eventually we had to throw them away but never did we finish one. Our tongue was exhausted way before we saw the stick. This is what I visualize when I think of everlasting, but it is much more.

Everlasting means enduring forever, eternal, indefinite, no beginning, and no end, forever and forever.

Before the mountains were brought forth, or ever you had formed the earth and the world, from everlasting to everlasting you are God. **(Psalm 90:2)**

As a child I often ask where God came from? My parents had no explanation. "He always was", they said. This didn't satisfy me, but it was the best answer I got.

The steadfast love of the Lord is everlasting to everlasting on those who fear him and his righteousness to children's children. **(Psalm 103:7)**

Not only is He from everlasting to everlasting but His love is also. Can you image having a father that did not love us or care about us forever and ever?

For the Lord is good; his steadfast love endures forever, and his faithfulness to all generations. **(Psalm 100:5)**

Forever and forever God is good. Forever and forever, He is faithful. We can trust Him. We can stake our lives on His goodness and faithfulness.

But the Lord is the true God; he is the living God and the everlasting King. (Jeremiah 10:10) He will never leave us nor forsake us!

"He is Everlasting!"

DAY 158

"ATTRIBUTES OF GOD FROM A TO Z" (E)

"Emmanuel or Immanuel"

God is with us. God will protect us. He is always at our side. He is closer than a brother. He is in us. He surrounds us. He is all encompassing. He will never leave us nor forsake us. How much closer can you get than that?

Therefore, the Lord himself will give you a sign. Behold the virgin shall conceive and bear a son and shall call his name Emmanuel. (Isaiah 7:14) and (Matthew 1:23) God said it and then He did it! Have you noticed though that sometimes God tells us something and we must wait for it to happen as in the case of Emmanuel? That is where faith comes in.

And the Word became flesh and dwelt among us, and we have seen his glory, glory as of the only Son from the Father, full of grace and truth. (John 1:14) He not only is spiritually with us, but He physically sent His Son to walk among us and show us what the Father is like. "God with us!"

It is the Lord who goes before you. He will be with you; he will not leave you or forsake you. Do not fear or be dismayed. (Deuteronomy 31:6)

To me this is one of the most comforting scriptures in God's Word. He will not leave us or forsake us. He is with us in times of joy and times of sorrow. He knows our uprisings and our down sitting. He is with us, and He is for us!

For the Lord your God is a merciful God. He will not leave you or destroy you or forget the covenant with your fathers that he swore to them. (Deuteronomy 4:31) God says what He means, and He means what He says. There is no shadow of turning with the Him.

Peace I leave with you; my peace I give to you. Not as the world gives do I give to you. Let not your hearts be troubled, neither let them be afraid. (John 14:27)

We can walk in confidence because our Commander and Chief is none other than the Lord Himself and His name is

"Emmanuel God with us!"

DAY 159

"ATTRIBUTES OF GOD FROM A TO Z" (E)

"He is Exalted!"

The Lord lives, and blessed be my rock, and exalted be my God, the rock of my salvation. **(2 Samuel 22:47)**

Exalted means to raise in rank, power, or character, to elevate by praise, to esteem, to glorify, to lift up, to magnify. He is our rock. He is our salvation. We could keep right on going with words of praise for our Exalted Lord!

1 Chronicles 29:11 says, *Yours, O Lord is the greatness and the power and the glory and the victory and the majesty, for all that is in the heavens and in the earth is yours. Yours is the kingdom, O Lord, and you are exalted as head above all.*

We should pause and reflect on the above because that is who God is! He is all in all. He is over all and in all and above all. He is Lord of all!

Job 36:22 says, Behold, God is exalted in his power; who is a teacher like him? He is our teacher. He instructs us in the ways we should go. He guides us into all truth. He leads us in the path of righteousness.

Be still and know that I am God. I will be exalted among the nations; I will be exalted in the earth! (Psalm 46:10) Just about the time we begin to wonder who is in charge of our nation and our world, we are brought back to the fact that God is in charge of everything. He can handle it. We just need to yield to Him

God exalted him (Jesus) at his right hand as Leader and Savior, to give repentance to Israel and forgiveness of sins. **(Acts 4:31)**

Philippians 2:9-11 says, *Therefore God has highly exalted him (Jesus) and bestowed on him the name that is above every name, so that at the name of Jesus every knee should bow, in heaven and on earth and under the earth, and every tongue confess that Jesus Christ is Lord, to the glory of God the Father.*

"He is Exalted!"

DAY 160

"Attributes of God from A to Z" (E)

"God is Eternal"

He is without beginning or end of existence. He has always existed. He is everlasting and immortal. It is interesting that the word eternal is only used a couple of times in the Old Testament but is used in the New Testament almost exclusively to speak of eternal life or eternal punishment. Life will go on whether we believe it or not. We are eternal beings who serve an Eternal God.

Before the mountains were brought forth, or ever you had formed the earth and the world, from everlasting to everlasting you are God. (Psalm 90:2) He is eternal.

For thus says the One who is high and lifted up, who inhabits eternity whose name is Holy. (Isaiah 57:15) God lives in eternity. That is mind boggling. He lives in forever and He is forever.

He who is the blessed and only Sovereign, the King of kings and Lord of lords, who alone has immortality who dwells in unapproachable light, who no one has ever seen or can see. To him be honor and eternal dominion. Amen. (1 Timothy 6:15-16)

And we know that the Son of God has come and has given us understanding, so that we may know him who is true; and we are in him who is true, in his Son Jesus Christ. He is the true God and eternal life. (1 John 5:20)

He has told us that we may know Him, not only in eternity but right now. *My sheep hear my voice, and I know them, and they follow me. I give them eternal life, and they will never perish, and no one will snatch them out of my hand. (John 10:27-29)*

Eternal is a fact, and we are part of it. Whether we believe it or not, we are eternal beings who serve an Eternal God. Life will never end. It is for eternity. The question is, "Where will we be for eternity?"

"From everlasting to everlasting, you are God!"

DAY 161

"Attributes of God from A to Z" (F)

"God the Father"

My Father is invincible. He is too powerful to be defeated or overcome. He is indestructible, unconquerable, unbeatable, unshakeable. You do not want to mess with my Father! He hides me under the shadow of His wings and protects me from the evil one. And that is just the tip of the iceberg.

His name shall be called Wonderful counselor, Mighty God, Everlasting Father, Prince of Peace. (Isaiah 9:6) Let me tell you some more things about my Father.

1 Corinthians 1:3 says, Grace to you and peace from God our Father and the Lord Jesus Christ. He is the God of grace and peace. There is peace in my household.

Galatians 1:3 says, Grace to you and peace from God our Father and the Lord Jesus Christ, who gave himself for our sins to deliver us from the present evil age, according to the will of our God and Father, to whom be glory forever and ever. Amen. He takes what I deserve upon Himself. In other words, He takes my whipping.

Ephesians 1:3 says, Blessed be the God and Father of our Lord Jesus Christ, who has blessed us in Christ with every spiritual blessing in the heavenly places, even as he chose us in him before the foundation of the world. I am His and He has blessed me abundantly!

Ephesians 1:17 says, That the God of our Lord Jesus Christ, the Father of glory, may give you the Spirit of wisdom and of revelation in the knowledge of him, having the eyes of your hearts enlightened, that you may know what is the hope to which he has called you.

He has a plan for me. He has given me the equipment I need to fulfill that plan. What a mighty God we serve!

"God is My Father!"

DAY 162

"Attributes of God from A to Z" (F)

"God is Faithful"

Know therefore that the Lord your God is God, the faithful God who keeps covenant and steadfast love with those who love him and keep his commandments, to a thousand generations. (Deuteronomy 7:9) God was faithful. He is faithful and He will be faithful to a thousand generations.

Faithful - constant, loyal, steadfast, unwavering, staunch, unswerving, dependable, strong assurance, binding, dedicated, devoted, etc. These are just a few words that describe our Father.

Psalm 145:13 says, The Lord is faithful in all his words and kind in all his works. He is the same yesterday, today and forever! He is faithful.

Isaiah 49:7 says, Kings shall see and arise; princes, and they shall prostrate themselves; because of the Lord who is faithful, the Holy One of Israel, who has chosen you. He will never leave us nor forsake us. He is faithful.

1 Corinthians 1:9 says, God is faithful, by whom you were called into the fellowship of his Son, Jesus Christ our Lord. He has called us. He is faithful.

1 Corinthians 10:13 says, No temptation has overtaken you that is not common to man. God is faithful, he will not let you be tempted beyond your ability, but with the temptation he will also provide the way of escape, that you may be able to endure it. He is faithful.

1 Thessalonians 5:23-24 says, May your whole spirit and soul and body be kept blameless at the coming of our Lord Jesus Christ. He who calls you is faithful; he will surely do it. He is faithful.

2 Timothy 2:13 says, If we are faithless, he remains faithful - for he cannot deny himself. One of His attributes is faithfulness.

Then I saw heaven opened, and behold, a white horse! The one sitting on it is called Faithful and True. (Revelation 19:11) Now faith is the assurance of things hoped for, the conviction of things not seen. Not seeing we still believe!

"God is Faithful!"

DAY 163

ATTRIBUTES OF GOD FROM A TO Z (F)

"He is Forgiving!"

The Lord, the Lord, a God merciful and gracious, slow to anger, and abounding in steadfast love and faithfulness, keeping steadfast love for thousands, forgiving iniquity and transgression and sin. (Exodus 34:6-7)

God was about to reveal Himself to Moses again. In the burning bush He had declared to Moses, "I AM." Now God begins to expand what He means by "I AM". For us one of the most important revelations is that He is forgiving. Somedays I need His forgiveness over and over.

Forgiving means to pardon, exonerate, absolve, acquit, feel no resentment toward whether we actually deserve it or not. Whether we deserve it or not, God still forgives us. What a mighty God we serve!

In Numbers 14:18 He says, *The Lord is slow to anger and abounding in steadfast love, forgiving iniquity and transgression.*

Then in Psalm 86:5 He says, *For you, O Lord, are good and forgiving, abounding in steadfast love to all who call upon you.*

Have you noticed that He prefaces forgiveness with merciful, graciousness and love? Are these prerequisites for forgiving? I think so.

In Ephesians 4:32 He says, *Be kind to one another, tender-hearted, forgiving one another, as God in Christ forgave you.* The Golden Rule says to do unto others as you would have them do unto you. How many times have we been angry with God and then had to ask His forgiveness? He is forgiving!

Colossians 1:13-14 says, *He has delivered us from the domain of darkness and transferred us to the kingdom of his beloved Son, in whom we have redemption, the forgiveness of sins.*

If our Father were not a forgiving Father, we would all be headed toward hell. But He is forgiving and so should we be.

"He is Forgiving!"

DAY 164

ATTRIBUTES OF GOD FROM A TO Z (F)

"He is Forever!"

The Lord will reign forever and ever. (Exodus 15:18) This scripture is almost at the beginning of God's Word to us and as far as I know He is still reigning. Hallelujah!

The word forever means continually, perpetually, endlessly, always, never ending, eternally, everlasting…

Oh, give thanks to the Lord, for he is good; his steadfast love endures forever. (1 Chronicles 16:34) God is love, and whoever abides in love abides in God, and God abides in him. (1 John 416) He is love forever!

The counsel of the Lord stands forever, the plans of his heart to all generations. (Psalm 33:11) I know the plans I have for you. His plans stand forever!

For the Lord is good; his steadfast love endures forever, and his faithfulness to all generations. (Psalm 100:5) He is faithful forever!

The grass withers, the flower fades, but the word of our God will stand forever. (Isaiah 40:8) His word stands forever!

And he will reign over the house of Jacob forever, and of his kingdom there will be no end. (Luke 1:33) His kingdom is forever!

For from him and through him and to him are all things. To him be glory forever. (Romans 11:36) All things are His forever!

Your throne, O God, is forever and ever. (Hebrews 1:8) To him be dominion forever and ever. (1 Peter 5:11) His throne is forever, and He rules!

The kingdom of the world has become the kingdom of our Lord and of his Christ, and he shall reign forever and ever. (Revelation 11:15) The end of His word!

To the King of the ages, immortal, invisible, the only God be honor and glory forever and ever. Amen (1 Timothy 1:17) What more can we say but amen!

"He is Forever!"

DAY 165

ATTRIBUTES OF GOD FROM A TO Z (F)

"He is the Foundation!"

Behold, I am the one who has laid as a foundation in Zion, a stone, a tested stone, a precious cornerstone, of a sure foundation. (Isaiah 28:16)

A foundation distributes the load of a structure. It is the footing, the base, the substructure. It is the base on which the structure rests. The foundation is the most important part of the house. Apart from the foundation, a house cannot stand.

Of old you laid the foundation of the earth, and the heavens are the work of your hands. (Psalm 102:25)

In the beginning, Lord you laid the foundations of the earth, and the heavens are the work of your hands. Hebrews 1:10) He said, "Let there be and there was."

Righteousness and justice are the foundation of your throne; steadfast love and faithfulness go before you. (Psalm 89:14) His throne is built on righteousness and justice.

Jesus Christ is the cornerstone. **Behold, I am laying in Zion a stone, a cornerstone chosen and precious, and whoever believes in him will not be put to shame. (1 Peter 2:6) This Jesus is the stone that was rejected by you, the builders, which has become the cornerstone. (Acts 4:11)**

So, the honor is for you who believe, but for those who do not believe, "The stone that the builders rejected has become the cornerstone," and "a stone of stumbling, a rock of offense." (1 Peter 2:7-8)

There is only one foundation and one cornerstone. All others are wood, hay and stubble.

"He is our Foundation!"

DAY 166

"Attributes of God from A to Z" (G)

"He is God. He is Jehovah. He is Elohim."

In the beginning God created the heavens and the earth. (Genesis 1:1)

God is the creator, the ruler, the supreme being. He is perfect in power, wisdom and goodness. He is Omniscient or all knowing. He is Omnipotent or all powerful. He is Omnipresent or everywhere. He is God!

Psalm 45:6 says, Your throne, O God, is forever and ever. The scepter of your kingdom is a scepter of uprightness. God is, God was, and God always will be.

Be still and know that I am God. I will be exalted among the nations. I will be exalted in the earth! (Psalm 46:10)

Blessed is the nation whose God is the Lord, the people whom he has chosen as his heritage! (Psalm 33:12) Is "In God We Trust" still part of our nation and our hearts?

The Lord your God is in the midst, a mighty one who will save; he will rejoice over you with gladness; he will quiet you by his love; he will exult over you with loud singing. (Zephaniah 3:17) He is with us. He will never leave us nor forsake us. He enjoys his people!

Your throne, O God, is forever and ever, the scepter of uprightness is the scepter of your kingdom…You, Lord, laid the foundation of the earth in the beginning, and the heavens are the work of your hands…But you are the same, and your years will have no end. (Hebrews 1:8-12)

Now to him who is able to keep you from stumbling and to present you blameless before the presence of his glory with great joy, to the only God, our Savior through Jesus Christ our Lord, be glory, majesty, dominion, and authority, before all time and now and forever. Amen. (Jude 12:24-25) What more can we say?

"He is Jehovah!"

DAY 167

"Attributes of God from A to Z" (G)

"He is Goodness!"

I will make all my goodness pass before you and will proclaim before you my name "The Lord." **(Exodus 33:19)**

The Lord passed before him and proclaimed, "The Lord, the Lord, a God merciful and gracious, slow to anger, and abounding in steadfast love and faithfulness." (Exodus 34:6) The Lord, He is good!

Goodness means righteous, integrity, honest, truthful, worthy, blameless, impartial, kind, benevolent, compassionate, understanding, tolerant, etc. This is who God is!

Psalm 23:6 says, Surely goodness and mercy shall follow me all the days of my life. He has promised He is always with us!

Remember not the sins of my youth or my transgressions; according to your steadfast love remember me for the sake of your goodness, O Lord, (Psalm 25:7) I am sure you were perfect when you were young, but I am glad God does not remember my sins. They are as far away as the East is from the West.

Galatians 5:22 says, The fruit of the Spirit is love, joy, peace, patience, kindness, goodness, faithfulness, gentleness, self-control. This is who God is and what He wants us to become.

But when the goodness and loving kindness of God our Savior appeared, he saved us, not because of works done by us in righteousness, but according to his own mercy. (Titus 3:4) Not only has He forgiven us, but He has saved us and will one day welcome us home.

Romans 11:22 says, *Note then the kindness (goodness) and the severity of God: severity toward those who have fallen, but God's kindness (goodness) to you provided you continue in his kindness.*

"He is Goodness!"

DAY 168

ATTRIBUTES OF GOD FROM A TO Z (G)

"God is Gracious"

I will make all my goodness pass before you and will proclaim before you my name "The Lord" And I will be gracious to whom I will be gracious and will show mercy on whom I will show mercy. **(Exodus 33:19)**

Gracious means merciful, forgiving, compassionate, kind, lenient, tenderhearted, patient, generous etc.

I want God to be all of the above in my life because I need goodness. Pour it on Lord!

The Lord, the Lord, a God merciful and gracious, slow to anger, and abounding in steadfast love and faithfulness. (Exodus 34:5) These are the very words that the Lord spoke to Moses, and He is still speaking them to us today.

May the Lord make his face to shine upon you and be gracious to you; the Lord lift up his countenance upon you and give you peace. (Numbers 6:25) This is my prayer not only for myself but for my family and others. Lord let Your face shine upon us and be gracious to us. We desperately need you Lord!

The Lord is merciful and gracious, slow to anger and abounding in steadfast love. He will not always chide, nor will he keep his anger forever. (Psalm 103:8) Have you noticed that as you pray for someone many times the Lord will say, "Forgive them first." We are to follow in His Steps, and He does not keep His anger forever and neither should we.

Therefore, the Lord waits to be gracious to you and therefore he exalts himself to show mercy to you. (Isaiah 30:18) Each time He uses the word gracious, He also uses the word mercy. In the times we are in the moment, do we see much grace and mercy? Do we give grace and mercy?

"God is Gracious!"

DAY 169

"ATTRIBUTES OF GOD FROM A TO Z" (G)

"He is our Guide."

For you are my rock and my fortress; and for your name's sake you lead me and guide me. **(Psalm 31:3)**

I have absolutely no sense of direction. I can get lost in a store or a parking lot. I have no idea which is north, and which is south. I sing "When the golden sun sinks in the west" to determine which direction is east or west and then I think what difference does it make. I need a guide!

A guide is an escort, attendant, conductor, pilot, usher, chaperone, leader, shepherd. The Lord is my Shepherd.

That you may tell the next generation that this is God, our God forever and ever. He will guide us forever. (Psalm 48:14) Not only does He guide us, but He expects us to guide the next generation in the ways of the Lord. Recently I spent some time with my granddaughters. My youngest sat next to me and ask me all sorts of questions about God. It is thrilling to know that the next generation wants to know the truth that will set them free.

When the Spirit of truth comes, he will guide you into all the truth, for he will not speak on his own authority, but whatever he hears he will speak, and he will declare to you the things that are coming. (John 16:13) One of the things that my son asked was if I believed in the rapture. I said that I believed that Jesus was coming back to get his church. But whether I believe in pre-rapture, mid rapture, or post rapture, I had to say, I believe it will all pan out period. No one knows the day or the hour, but we must be ready.

For the Lamb in the midst of the throne will be their shepherd and he will guide them to springs of living water, and God will wipe away every tear from their eyes. **(Revelation 7:17)**

I believe heaven is a place of the "now". By that I mean there is no past, nor future but everything is right now. Am I right? Who knows but I want to find out?

"He is our Guide!"

DAY 170

"Attributes of God from A to Z" (G)

"The Glory of God"

O Lord, our Lord, how majestic is your name in all the earth! You have set your glory above the heavens. **(Psalm 8:1)**

Glory - renown, fame, honor, magnificence, splendor, grandeur, majesty, greatness, beauty, etc.

Matthew 25:31 says, **When the Son of Man comes in his glory, and all the angels with him, then he will sit on his glorious throne.** I cannot even begin to imagine what this will be like. Jesus will come with all his angels. Have you ever stopped to think how many angels that will be, and Jesus will be right in the midst of them? We saw a beautiful fireworks display recently, but that will not compare with Christ's coming. The question is, "Are you ready?"

Stephen was being stoned, **But he, full of the Holy Spirit, gazed into heaven and saw the glory of God and Jesus standing at the right hand of God. And he said, "Behold, I see the heavens opened, and the Son of Man standing at the right hand of God." (Acts 7:55)** He saw the majesty, the magnificence, the splendor, the beauty of God and he traveled right out of this world into the next. Hallelujah!

And the Word became flesh and dwelt among us, and we have seen his glory, glory as of the only Son from the Father, full of grace and truth. (John 1:14) Not only did Stephen see his glory but we too can witness it as we turn our eyes upon Jesus.

We were buried therefore with him by baptism into death, in order that, just as Christ was raised from the dead by the glory of the Father, we too might walk in newness of life. (Romans 6:4)

For I consider that the sufferings of this present time are not worth comparing with the glory that is to be revealed to us. (Romans 8:18)

For from him and through him and to him are all things. To him be glory forever. Amen. (Romans 11:36) We haven't seen anything yet! Just wait.

"Glory! Glory! Glory"

DAY 171

"Attributes of God from A to Z" (H)

"He is our Helper."

Hear, O Lord, and be merciful to me! O Lord be my helper. (Psalm 30:10)

A helper is an assistant, coworker, teammate, helpmate, aide, supporter, partner, Where would we be without the help of our Lord? How many times during the day do I say, "Help me Lord!"

The Lord is on my side as my helper; (Psalm 118:7) If God is for us, who can be against us? (Romans 8:31) God is on our side even if at times it seems like He has turned His back on us. He hasn't. He has our best interest at heart. He is our helper.

God is our refuge and strength, a very present help in trouble. (Psalm 46:1) David knew what he was talking about because God was always rescuing him from one trouble or another. He was David's helper. He is our helper!

Hebrews 13:6 says, The Lord is my helper; I will not fear; what can man do to me? The Lord is my helper!

Psalm 54:4 says, Behold, God is my helper; the Lord is the upholder of my life. I am His and He is mine and His banner over me is love.

Jesus said, **I will ask the Father, and he will give you another Helper, to be with you forever, even the Spirit of truth. (John 14:16)** He has not left us defenseless.

But the Helper, the Holy Spirit, whom the Father will send in my name, he will teach you all things and bring to your remembrance all that I have said to you. (John 14:26) The moment I was filled with the Holy Spirit, I began to understand the Word of God in a new way. I was able to remember scriptures that before I had struggled with. He is my helper.

But when the Helper comes, whom I will send to you from the Father, the Spirit of truth, who proceeds from the Father, he will bear witness about me. (John 15:26)

"He is our Helper!

DAY 172

"ATTRIBUTES OF GOD FROM A TO Z" (H)

"The Lord our Healer."

I am the Lord, your healer. (Exodus 15:26) And the Lord will take away from you all sickness, and none of the evil diseases of Egypt, which you knew, will he inflict on you. (Deuteronomy 7:15) And for 40 years they had no diseases and even their clothes did not wear out. I am the Lord, your healer.

To heal means, restore to health, cure, get better, become sound or healthy again, recover, mend, free from ailments, etc. There are all sorts of things in each of us that need healed; not only physical but mental, emotional, etc. The Lord is my Healer.

O Lord, my God, I cried to you for help, and you have healed me. (Psalm 30:2) The Lord hears us as we cry out to Him in faith, and He is there to meet all our needs according to His riches in Christ Jesus. Do we really believe He is our Healer?

Psalm 103:2 says, Bless the Lord, O my soul, and forgets not all his benefits, who forgives all your iniquity, who heals all your diseases.

Psalm 107:20 says, He sent out his word and healed them, and delivered them from their destruction. He is the same yesterday, today and forever!

He himself bore our sins in his body on the tree, that we might die to sin and live to righteousness. By his wounds you have been healed. (1 Peter 2:24) I have heard that there are 40 different kinds of diseases and each stripe on Jesus' back was for one of those diseases. I don't know if this is true, but it is worth thinking about.

James 5:16 says, Therefore, confess your sins to one another and pray for one another, that you may be healed. The prayer of a righteous person has great power as it is working. When I need prayer, which we all do, I want someone to pray for me who can really believe God will answer without a lot of but's.

"He is the Healer!"

DAY 173

"Attributes of God from A to Z" (H)

"He is my Hope!"

And now, O Lord, for what do I wait? My hope is in you. (Psalm 39:7) Hope: aspiration, desire, wish, expectation, ambition, aim, dream, longing, yearning, craving, a feeling of trust.

Psalm 62:5 says, For God alone, O my soul, wait in silence, for my hope is from him. He only is my rock and my salvation, my fortress; I shall not be shaken.

He is my hope. If I put my trust in anyone or anything other than Him, I am on shaky ground.

May the God of hope fill you with all joy and peace in believing, so that by the power of the Holy Spirit you may abound in hope. (Romans 15:13)

Hope is the ability to put one foot in front of the other and go on in life. Without hope we would be destitute. Suicide happens because people have lost hope. Hope is the anchor on which our faith is built. Hope brings us to a place of knowing.

2 Thessalonians 2:16 says, Now may our Lord Jesus Christ himself, and God our Father, who loved us and gave us eternal comfort and good hope through grace, comfort your hearts and establish them in every good work and word. Our hope is in Christ Jesus. He alone is our salvation.

For to this end, we toil and strive, because we have our hope set on the living God, who is the Savior of all people, especially of those who believe. (1 Timothy 4:10)

Let us hold fast the confession of our hope without wavering, for he who promised is faithful. (Hebrews 10:23)

The Lord takes pleasure in those who fear him, in those who hope in his steadfast love. (Psalm 147:11)

"He is our Hope!"

DAY 174

"ATTRIBUTES OF GOD FROM A TO Z" (H)

"He is Holy!"

Cast me not away from your presence and take not your Holy Spirit from me. Restore to me the joy of your salvation and uphold me with a willing spirit. (Psalm 51:11)

Holy: sacred, consecrated, hallowed, sanctified, venerated, revered, divine, blessed, exalted, worthy of complete devotion.

Your way, O God, is holy. What god is great like our God? (Psalm 77:13)

Rejoice in the Lord, O you righteous, and give thanks to his holy name. (Psalm 97:12)

God is holy. He is divine. He is worthy of complete devotion. His name should be used only in reverence because He is exalted.

Exalt the Lord our God, worship at his footstool! Holy is he! (Psalm 9:5)

Proverbs 9:10 says, *The fear of the Lord is the beginning of wisdom, and the knowledge of the Holy One is insight."*

Today we do not understand the word holy. We do not understand what true worship really is. We are so centered on self, me and my, that we have lost true reverence. When was the last time you bowed down to the Lord or truly held Him in awe?

For he who is mighty has done great things for me, and holy is his name. (Luke 1:49)

But in your hearts honor Christ the Lord as holy, always being prepared to make a defense to anyone who asks you for a reason for the hope that is in you. (1 Peter 3:15)

When we consider His holiness and live as holy vessels unto Him, we honor Him. He has told us to be holy because He is holy.

"He is Holy!"

DAY 175

"ATTRIBUTES OF GOD FROM A TO Z" (I)

"I AM" He is the great I AM!

God said to Moses, "I AM who I AM." (Exodus 3:14)

This is my name forever, and thus I Am to be remembered throughout all genera-tions. (Exodus 3:15) He is everything to everyone. He is all in all. He is the begin-ning and the end. He is from everlasting to everlasting. I am the Lord!

Be still and know that I am God. I will be exalted among the nations. I will be exalted in the earth. (Psalm 46:10)

When we begin to think we are in control of our lives, we have a huge revelation. We are Not! He is! I am so thankful I am not in control. I don't know the beginning from the end. I do not know what is best for me and my family. I do not know, but I know the One who does.

When I am afraid, I put my trust in you. In God, whose word I praise, in God I trust; I shall not be afraid. (Psalm 56:3) What a comfort it is to know the Great I Am is in charge and every good and perfect gift comes from Him.

I am the Lord your God, who brought you up out of the land of Egypt. Open your mouth wide, and I will fill it. (Psalm 81:10) We were in the Land of Egypt, but the Lord has delivered us. He has saved us. He has sanctified us. He has set us apart to himself. I am his and He is mine. I need not worry what to say or when because He has promised to fill my mouth with His words.

I am with you to deliver you, declares the Lord! I am watching over my word to perform it. (Jeremiah 1:8 & 1:12) Is there anything too hard for God?

I am the Lord your God and there is none else. And my people shall never again be put to shame. (Joel 2:27) And he asked them, "But who do you say I am?" Peter answered him "You are the Christ." (Mark 8:29) This is the most important confession we will ever make. "You are the Christ!"

"I AM who I AM!"

DAY 176

"ATTRIBUTES OF GOD FROM A TO Z" (I)

"He is Immortal"

To the King of the ages, immortal, invisible, the only God, be honor and glory forever and ever. Amen **(1 Timothy 1:17)**

Immortal: undying, eternal, everlasting, constant, abiding, indestructible, enduring

The word immortal is only used two times in the Bible so we will use other words that mean the same thing such as eternal.

The eternal God is your dwelling place, and underneath are the everlasting arms. (Deuteronomy 33:27) When I think of everlasting arms, I picture God holding me up, comforting me, rescuing me from myself. He says He will be there to do that forever because He is immortal.

For his invisible attributes, namely his eternal power and divine nature, have been clearly perceived, ever since the creation of the world, in the things that have been made. (Romans 1:20) Everywhere we look we can see God. We see Him in the heavens and on the earth. We see Him in those He has created, and we see Him in his Son, Jesus Christ. We just need to take the time to look.

Psalm 93:2 says, Your throne is established from of old; you are from everlasting. He has always been and will always be. He is immortal.

Psalm 145:13 says, Your kingdom is an everlasting kingdom, and your dominion endures throughout all generations. He will rule forever.

You have been born again, not of perishable seed but of imperishable through the living and abiding word of God. (1 Peter 1:23) Not only is He immortal but His word is immortal. It never changes.

Oh, give thanks to the Lord, for he is good; for his steadfast love endures forever! (I Chronicles 16:34) His love is forever! *Whoever does the will of God abides forever. (1 John 2:17)* We too are immortal. We will live forever and forever, hopefully with him.

"He is Immortal!"

DAY 177

"Attributes of God from A to Z" (I)

"He is Indescribable!"

Though you have not seen him you love him. Though you do not now see him, you believe in him and rejoice with joy that is inexpressible and filled with glory, obtaining the outcome of your faith, the salvation of your souls. **(1 Peter 1:8)**

Indescribable means indefinable, beyond description, incredible, impossible, overwhelming, inexpressible, unspeakable. The word indescribable is not found in the Bible but its meaning is everywhere.

Great is our Lord, and abundant in power; his understanding is beyond measure. **(Psalm 147:5)** He is indescribable!

The Word became flesh and made his dwelling among us. We have seen his glory, the glory of the one and only Son who came from the Father, full of grace and truth. **(John 1:14)** He is indescribable!

How great is God - beyond our understanding! The number of his years is past finding out. **(Job 36:26)**

Job said, *Surely, I spoke of things I did not understand, things too wonderful for me to know.* **(Job 42:3)** He is indescribable!

That you may know the hope to which he has called you, the riches of his glorious inheritance in his holy people and his incomparably great power for us who believe. **(Ephesians 1:18)**

My mouth will tell of your righteous deeds, of your saving acts all day long though I know not how to relate to them all. I will come and proclaim your mighty acts, Sovereign Lord; I will proclaim your righteous deeds, yours alone. **(Psalm 71:15)**

Our Father is indescribable. He is inexpressible. He is indefinable. He is beyond description. He is beyond our understanding. When we begin to think we know Him, He shows us another of His attributes and we begin to realize we have not seen anything yet.

"He is Indescribable!"

183

DAY 178

"Attributes of God from A to Z" (I)

"He is Infinite!"

Infinite means boundless, unlimited, never-ending, immeasurable, fathomless, immense, without limits. He is everywhere! He is omnipotent.

But will God really dwell on earth? The heavens, even the highest heaven, cannot contain you. (1 Kings 8:27) He is everywhere. We cannot hide from Him. He knows us completely and He still loves us with a boundless love.

This grace was given me: to preach to the Gentiles the boundless riches of Christ, and to make plain to everyone the administration of this mystery, which for ages past was hidden in God who created all things. (Ephesians 3:8)

Heaven and earth cannot contain God. He is so much more than we can fathom. HIs boundless riches surpass our wildest imagination.

Job 11:7 says, *Can you fathom the mysteries of God? Can you probe the limits of the Almighty? They are higher than the heavens above.*

Great is the Lord and most worthy of praise; his greatness no one can fathom. (Psalm 145:3)

He has made everything beautiful in its time. He has also set eternity in the human heart; yet no one can fathom what God has done from beginning to end. (Ecclesiastes 3:11)

Who can fathom the Spirit of the Lord, or instruct the Lord as his counselor? (Isaiah 40:13)

Job 42:1-3 & 5 says, *Who is this that obscures my plans without knowledge? Surely, I spoke of things I did not understand, things too wonderful for me to know...My ears had heard of you, but now my eyes have seen you.*

God is boundless, unlimited, never-ending, immeasurable, unfathomable, without limits. He is God!

"He is Infinite!"

DAY 179

"ATTRIBUTES OF GOD FROM A TO Z" (I)

"God is Immutable!"

God is not man, that he should lie, or a son of man that he should change his mind. **(Numbers 23:19)**

Immutable means unchanging, consistent, fixed, unbending, permanent, established, unshakeable, constant, abiding, enduring, set, unyielding, etc.

For I the Lord do not change. **(Malachi 3:6)** He said it. I believe it. That settles it!

The Lord has sworn and will not change his mind, "You are a priest forever." **(Hebrews 7:21)** He was speaking of Jesus, but it is important for us to know that God means what He says and says what He means.

If what you heard from the beginning abide in you, then you too will abide in the Son and in the Father. And this is the promise that he made to us - eternal life. **(1John 2:24)** He has promised to abide in us forever. His promise is immutable.

And I will establish my covenant between me and you and your offspring after you throughout their generations for an everlasting covenant, to be God to you and to your offspring after you. **(Genesis 17:7)** He will be God to us forever!

Thus says the Lord who made the earth, the Lord who formed it to establish it - the Lord is his name: Call to me and I will answer you and will tell you great and hidden things that you have not known. **(Jeremiah 33:2)** He will always communicate with us if we will take the time to listen.

But the Lord is faithful. He will establish you and guard you against the evil one. **(2 Thessalonians 3:3)** He is immutable!

For I said, "Steadfast love will be built up forever; in the heavens you will establish your faithfulness." **(Psalm 89:2)**

The Lord does not change. His son Jesus is our lifeline. If we abide in Him, we have eternal life. He will be our God forever. He hears us and answers. He will guard us against the evil one. His steadfast love is forever.

"He is Immutable!"

DAY 180

Attributes of God from A to Z (J)

"He is Jesus!" (Some of the Old Testament proof. There is much more.)

In the beginning was the Word, and the Word was with God, and the Word was God. He was in the beginning with God. (John 1:1-2)

He shall bruise your head, and you shall bruise his heel. (Genesis 3:15) God had said *"Let us make man in our own image."* Speaking of the Trinity. Here He is speaking specifically of Jesus. He has taken care of the serpent on the Cross!

He was born in Bethlehem. ***From you shall come forth for me one who is to be ruler in Israel whose coming forth is from old, from ancient days. (Micah 5:2)***

He was born of a virgin. ***Therefore, the Lord himself will give you a sign. Behold the virgin shall conceive and bear a son and shall call his name Immanuel. (Isaiah 7:14)***

His family escaped to Egypt when all the children 2 and under were killed. ***When Israel was a child, I loved him, and out of Egypt I called my son. (Hosea 11:1)***

He was announced by John the Baptist. ***A voice cries: In the wilderness prepare the way of the Lord; make straight in the desert a highway for our God. (Isaiah 40:3)***

He was rejected by His own people. ***He was despised and rejected by men, a man of sorrows, and acquainted with grief; and as one from whom men hide their faces he was despised, and we esteemed him not. (Isaiah 53:3)***

His ministry included the following: ***The Spirit of the Lord God is upon me, because the Lord has anointed me to bring good news to the poor; he has sent me to bind up the broken hearted, to proclaim liberty to the captives, and the opening of the prison to those who are bound; to proclaim the year of the Lord's favor, and the day of vengeance of our God; to comfort all who mourn. (Isaiah 61:1-2)***

He was betrayed by Judas for 30 pieces of silver. ***So, I took the thirty pieces of silver and threw them into the house of the Lord, to the potter. (Zechariah 11:13)***

He was crucified. ***He poured out his soul to death and was numbered with the transgressors; yet he bore the sin of many. (Isaiah 53:12)***

He was nailed to the cross and a sword pierced his side. ***When they look on me, on him whom they have pierced. (Zechariah 12:10)***

"He is Jesus!"

DAY 181

ATTRIBUTES OF GOD FROM A TO Z (J)

"He is the Judge!"

The Lord judges the people; judge me, O Lord, according to my righteousness and according to the integrity that is in me. **(Psalm 7:8)**

Judge: magistrate, hear cases in court, pronounce judgment, sentence, with power to punish, enforce order, decision maker, advocate,

Not only is God a loving Father, but He also is a judge. He investigates our hearts to determine our motives. Are we truly sold out to Him? Are we lukewarm?

Then shall the trees of the forest sing for joy before the Lord, for he comes to judge the earth. **(1 Chronicles 16:33)**

He calls to the heavens above and to the earth, that he may judge his people. **(Psalm 50:4)** He is the judge!

I said in my heart, God will judge the righteous and the wicked, for there is a time for every matter and for every work. **(Ecclesiastes 3:1)** God will judge both the good and the bad.

Yet I do not seek my own glory; there is One who seeks it, and he is the judge. **(John 8:50)**

And he commanded us to preach to the people and to testify that he is the one appointed by God to be judge of the living and the dead. **(Acts 10:42)**

For we know him who said, "Vengeance is mine; I will repay." And again, "The Lord will judge his people." It is a fearful thing to fall into the hands of the living God. **(Hebrews 10:30-31)** Sometimes, I feel we are playing games with God. We want His blessings, but we do not want His discipline.

There is only one lawgiver and judge, he who is able to save and destroy. **(James 4:11)** He tells us to let Him be the judge.

But they will give account to him who is ready to judge the living and the dead. **(1Peter 4:5)** Thank goodness we are judged through the blood of Jesus Christ!

"He is the Judge!"

DAY 182

"ATTRIBUTES OF GOD FROM A TO Z" (J)

"The Lord is full of Joy!"

The joy of the Lord is your strength. (Nehemiah 8:10)

Joy: delight, pleasure, jubilation, triumph, rejoicing, happiness, exhilaration, exuberance, rapture, radiance, gratification

Did you know that joy is mentioned 180 times in the Bible? God cannot give joy unless He has it to give. He is full of joy. He wants His people to be joyful. He has told us that joy is our strength. Have you ever laughed so hard that your sides ached but afterwards you felt so good, so free, so refreshed?

Then shall the trees of the forest sing for joy before the Lord, for he comes to judge the earth. (1 Chronicles 16:33) Even nature rejoices. The trees of the field clap their hands. God has created joy in everything and everyone. We just need to find it.

You make known to me the path of life; in your presence there is fullness of joy; at your right hand are pleasures forever-more. (Psalm 16:11) I want to be around people who are full of joy, and I want to experience the joy of the Lord.

Your words were found, and I ate them, and your words became to me a joy and the delight of my heart for I am called by your name, Lord, God of host. (Jeremiah 15:16) Even His words bring joy to my heart. When my phone rings and one of my children says, "Hi mom!" I feel joy. The Lord feels the same way when we talk to Him.

Looking to Jesus, the founder and perfecter of our faith, who for the joy that was set before him endured the cross, despising the shame, and is seated at the right hand of the throne of God. (Hebrews 12:2) Even in suffering Jesus found joy. This should be an example to us, but it is hard to find joy in pain.

Now to him who is able to keep you from stumbling and to present you blameless before the presence of his glory with great joy, to the only God, our Savior. (Jude 1:24)

"The Lord is full of Joy!"

DAY 183

"Attributes of God from A to Z" (J)

"God is a Jealous God!"

For I the Lord your God am a jealous God, visiting the iniquity of the fathers on the children to the third and fourth generation of those who hate me, but showing steadfast love to thousands of those who love me and keep my commandments. (**Exodus 20:5-6**)

Jealous: envious, covetous, resentful, protective, defensive, vigilant, watchful

I may discipline my children, but don't let anyone else even speak a negative word about them, because I am like a mother bear. I am protective and defensive. In other words, I am jealous over them. So is our God!

For you shall worship no other god, for the Lord, whose name is Jealous, is a jealous God. (**Exodus 34:14**) He wants our undivided devotion. I am His and He is mine and His banner over me is love.

The Lord is a jealous and avenging God; the Lord is avenging and wrathful; the Lord takes vengeance on his adversaries and keeps wrath for his enemies. (**Nahum 1:2**)

This sounds like a really frightening verse, but God isn't talking about you and me. He is speaking of those who are not His. Even though He is a loving God, He still has an angry side. We do not want to be part of His wrath.

For the Lord your God is a consuming fire, a jealous God. (**Deuteronomy 4:24**)

We had an explosion across the street that totally leveled the house and destroyed one person inside. The flames were so high from the fire that the whole sky was lit up. It not only consumed the house but everything around it. Our God is a consuming fire. I am so thankful I will not experience His wrath.

You shall not go after other gods, the gods of the peoples who are around you - for the Lord your God in your midst is a jealous God. (**Deuteronomy 6:14**)

"God is a Jealous God!"

DAY 184

"ATTRIBUTES OF GOD FROM A TO Z" (J)

"He is the Judge!"

For the Lord is our judge; the Lord is our lawgiver; the Lord is our king; he will save us. (Isaiah 33:22)

This is probably the most difficult but also the most important message I will send. We need to realize regardless of how loving and kind and good God is; He is also the judge. Maybe it is my age. Maybe it is all that is going on in the world. Maybe it is just my imagination, but I feel an urgency to talk a little about what is to come. I am not an expert on these things, but I am grieving right now for those who have not made Jesus Lord of their lives. I believe in the Rapture, and I believe it is close upon us even though no one knows the day nor the hour.

If I were to die tonight, I believe I would have at least a moment to cry out to the Lord. But if we are taken up in the rapture there will not be a moment of decision. We will either be gone, or we will be left behind. It will be in a twinkling of an eye. There will be no time to repent and be saved.

Behold! I tell you a mystery. We shall not all sleep, but we shall all be changed, in a moment, in the twinkling of an eye, at the last trumpet. For the trumpet will sound, and the dead will be raised imperishable, and we shall be changed. (1 Corinthians 15:51-52) I believe this is what we have labeled the rapture. I believe this is the church being taken out of this world before the great tribulation.

The times of ignorance God overlooked, but now he commands all people everywhere to repent, because he has fixed a day on which he will judge the world. (Acts 17:30)

The Lord will judge his people. It is a fearful thing to fall into the hands of the living God. (Hebrews 10:30-31)

But they will give account to him who is ready to judge the living and the dead. (1 Peter 4:5)

Behold, now is the favorable time; behold now is the day of salvation. (2 Cor. 6:2)

"He is the Judge!"

DAY 185

"ATTRIBUTES OF GOD FROM A TO Z" (J)

"He is Just!"

The Rock, his work is perfect, for all his ways are justice. A God of faithfulness and without iniquity, just and upright is he. (**Deuteronomy 32:4**)

Just: fair, equitable, impartial, unbiased, objective, open-minded, honorable, upright, righteous, virtuous, trustworthy, incorruptible. This is our God!

Now I Nebuchadnezzar, praise and extol and honor the King of heaven, for all his works are right and his ways are just; and those who walk in pride he is able to humble. (**Daniel 4:37**)

Remember King Nebuchadnezzar had said, *Is not the great Babylon, which I have built by my mighty power as a royal residence and for the glory of my majesty?* (**Daniel 4:30**) For 7 years he reaped the benefit of these words. Then he realized who is really in charge. So often I think we put too much responsibility on ourselves instead of allowing God to be God. What a relief when we realize we are not in charge. In the process He is forgiving and just.

If we confess our sins, he is faithful and just to forgive us our sins and to cleanse us from all unrighteousness. (**1 John 1:9**) He is fair!

The Almighty - we cannot find him; he is great in power; justice and abundant righteousness he will not violate. Therefore, men fear him; he does not regard any who are wise in their own conceit. (**Job 37:23-24**) Total proof of His justice. He is God and there will be no other.

He loves righteousness and justice; the earth is full of the steadfast love of the Lord. (**Psalm 33:5**) He says, "I am the Lord. I change not!"

For the Lord is a God of justice; blessed are all those who wait for him. (**Isaiah 30:18**)

The Lord within her is righteous; he does no injustice; every morning he shows forth his justice; each dawn he does not fail. (**Zephaniah 3:5**) He is fair. He is impartial. He is trustworthy and He is incorruptible.

"He is Just!"

DAY 186

"Attributes of God from A to Z" (K)

"He is the King of Kings!"

He who is the blessed and only Sovereign, the King of kings and the Lord of lords, who alone has immortality who dwells in unapproachable light, whom no one has ever seen or can see. To him be honor and eternal dominion. Amen. **(1 Timothy 6:14)**

King: ruler, sovereign, monarch, majesty, emperor, potentate, lord

It is interesting to note that only two times in the Bible is our Father called the King of kings even though we often call him that. When I began to think of King of Kings, I realized that there could be no one higher than a King of Kings. There could be no one higher than the monarch or the emperor or the Lord. He is above all, and in all, and over all. He is the King of Kings!

The Lord is slow to anger and great in power. **(Nahum 1:3)** He is great in power. He is the source of all power. He is our powerhouse.

The Lord is good, a stronghold in the day of trouble; he knows those who take refuge in him. **(Nahum 1:7)** He is a stronghold. He is our protector.

And the Lord will be king over all the earth. On that day the Lord will be one and his name one. **(Zechariah 14:9)** It hasn't happened yet, but it will. The Lord will be King over all the earth. At this moment Satan has rule but it is just for a moment. His rule will end.

For I am a great King, say the Lord of hosts, and my name will be feared among the nations. **(Malachi 1:14)**

If you will fear the Lord and serve him and obey his voice and not rebel against the commandment of the Lord, and if both you and the king who reigns over you will follow the Lord your God, it will be well. **(1 Samuel 12:14)**

He has promised to never leave us nor forsake us. He has promised to be our God and we, his people. *On his robe and on his thigh he has a name written, King of kings and Lord of lords.* **(Revelation 19:16)**

"He is the King of kings!"

DAY 187

"Attributes of God from A to Z" (K)

"God is All Knowing!"

God is greater than our heart, and he knows everything. **(1 John 3:20)**

There is nothing hidden from God. He knows our down sitting and our uprising. He knows the beginning from the end. He knows everything about us. Nothing is hidden from God.

To know: be aware of, realize, be informed, perceive, see, sense, understand

The Lord knows the days of the blameless, and their heritage will remain forever. **(Psalm 37:18)** He knows our life span. Our days will not be stolen by the evil one.

He knows the way that I take; when he has tried me, I shall come out as gold. **(Job 23:10)** He knows what I will do even before I do it.

He knows the secrets of the heart. **(Psalm 44:21)** He even knows my heart!

The Lord knows the thoughts of man, that they are but a breath. **(Psalm 94:11)**

He knows what is in the darkness, and the light dwells with him. **(Daniel 2:22)** We cannot hide from Him. All things done in darkness will be brought to the light!

Your Father knows what you need before you ask him. **(Matthew 6:8)** He knows our need, but we do need to ask Him. He wants to talk with us.

But concerning that day and hour no one knows, not even the angels of heaven, nor the Son, but the Father only. **(Matthew 24:36)** Only the Father knows when He will say enough is enough.

You are those who justify yourselves before men, but God knows your hearts. **(Luke 16:15)** Sometimes we don't even know our own hearts, but God does.

The Lord knows those who are his. **(2 Timothy 2:19)**

"God is All Knowing!"

DAY 188

"Attributes of God from A to Z" (K)

"The Lord is full of Loving Kindness!"

Thy loving kindness is better than life, my lips will praise you thus will I bless you. I will lift up my hands in your name. **(Psalm 63:3)** (My song version)

Kindness: affection, gentleness, tenderness, concern, care, consideration, thoughtfulness, compassion, sympathy, understanding, generosity, patience

Praise be to the Lord, the God of my master Abraham who has not abandoned his kindness and faithfulness to my master. **(Genesis 24:27)** He has not abandoned His kindness to us either.

But show me unfailing kindness like the Lord's kindness as long as I live. **(1 Samuel 20:14)** Kindness is one of the Fruits of the Spirit.

I have loved you with an everlasting love; I have drawn you with unfailing kindness. **(Jeremiah 31:3)** What an amazing promise!

God's kindness is intended to lead you to repentance. **(Romans 2:4)** So often we try to beat salvation into others rather than loving them and showing them God's kindness. A little bit of honey makes the medicine go down.

And God raised us up with Christ and seated us with him in the heavenly realms in Christ Jesus, in order that in the coming ages he might show the incomparable riches of his grace, expressed in his kindness to us in **Christ Jesus. (Ephesians 2:6-7)**

But when the kindness and love of God our Savior appeared, he saved us, not because of righteous things we had done, but because of his mercy. **(Titus 3:4)**

Jesus did not come to earth with a rod in His hand but in love and mercy. His kindness is what drew people to Him. We should follow in His steps!

With everlasting kindness, I will have compassion on you, says the Lord your Redeemer. **(Isaiah 54:8)**

"The Lord is full of Loving Kindness!"

DAY 189

"Attributes of God from A to Z" (K)

"The Lord is our Keeper!"

You will keep in perfect peace those whose minds are steadfast because they trust in you. Trust in the Lord forever, for the Lord, the Lord himself, is the Rock eternal. **(Isaiah 26:3-4)**

Keeper: guardian, protector, defender, guard, chaperone

The Lord will keep you from all harm - he will watch over your life. The Lord will watch over your coming and going both now and forevermore. **(Psalm 121:7-8)** He is our guardian and protector. Nothing shall harm us. He stands at the door of our hearts.

Keep me as the apple of your eye; hide me in the shadow of your wings. **(Psalm 17:8)** He is my chaperone. I like that.

For the Lord will be at your side and will keep your foot from being snared. **(Proverbs 3:26)** He is always there to keep us from falling. The Holy Spirit is there as a check and balance to our lives, if we will listen to His still small voice.

The eyes of the Lord keep watch over knowledge, but he frustrates the words of the unfaithful. **(Proverbs 22:12)** This verse speaks to me right now. We are hearing so many things, especially on the news. What is true? What is not? Are we walking in fear or in faith? He will show us what is really true!

You, Lord, keep my lamp burning; my God turns my darkness into light. **(Psalm 18:28)** This speaks to me about depression which I think most of us are feeling right now. Is there a light at the end of the tunnel? Yes, He is there!

He will also keep you firm to the end, so that you will be blameless on the day of our Lord Jesus Christ. God is faithful, who has called you into fellowship with his Son, Jesus Christ our Lord. **(1 Corinthians 1:8-9)** He has promised to never leave us nor forsake us. He is at our right hand. We cannot be shaken!

"The Lord is our Keeper!"

DAY 190

"Attributes of God from A to Z" (K)

"He holds the Keys!"

And I will place on his shoulder the key of the house of David. He shall open, and none shall shut; and he shall shut, and none shall open. (Isaiah 22:22)

Keys: a means of gaining or preventing entrance: A key will lock or unlock something.

Often when I am praying, I ask the Lord to open or shut the door to the thing I am praying about. I want His perfect will in the situation. He holds the key.

The words of the holy one, the true one, who has the key of David, who opens, and no one will shut, who shuts, and no one opens. (Revelation 3:7)

This is my prayer. *Set a guard, O Lord, over my mouth; keep watch over the door of my lips.* (Psalm 141:3) In other words show me when to speak and when to be silent. Have you ever noticed that sometimes when someone wants us to be still, he will put his hand over his mouth and turn it to lock our lips?

At the same time, pray also for us, that God may open to us a door for the word, to declare the mystery of Christ. (Colossians 4:3) He holds the key to witnessing.

And I tell you, ask, and it will be given to you; seek, and you will find; knock, and it will be opened to you. (Matthew 7:7) He holds the key to prayer.

I will give you the keys of the kingdom of heaven, and whatever you bind on earth shall be bound in heaven, and whatever you lose on earth shall be loosed in heaven. (Matthew 16:19) This is an awesome responsibility. My first thought is forgiveness. When we forgive we are forgiven. What we give we receive in return. What we curse is cursed and what we bless is blessed. We also hold the keys.

Fear not, I am the first and the last, and the living one. I died, and behold I am alive forevermore, and I have the keys of Death and Hades. (Revelation 1:18)

"He holds the Keys to our lives, and He is good Gatekeeper."

DAY 191

"Attributes of God from A to Z" (L)

"Jesus Christ is Lord!"

The word "Lord" is used 6,675 times in the Bible. The word Lord must be very important to be in the Word that many times. It suggests a person in authority who has subjects under him. It is defined as master, overlord, governor, owner, ruler, leader, superior, monarch, sovereign, king, commander. Jesus is our Lord. I don't think most of us in the United States understand lordship.

Our theme is "I will do it my way." Therefore, it is hard for us to submit to leadership but if we would, our lives would be so much better. Below are a few things that would be ours if we would yield our lives to His.

Therefore, since we have been justified by faith, we have peace with God through our Lord Jesus Christ. (Romans 5:1) We have peace!

Blessed be the God and Father of our Lord Jesus Christ, the Father of mercies and God of all comfort. (2 Corinthians 1:3) We have mercy and comfort!

Grace to you and peace from God our Father and the Lord Jesus Christ, who gave himself for our sins to deliver us from the present evil age. (Galatians 1:3) He is our delivered not only from our sins but from this present evil age!

Blessed be the God and Father of our Lord Jesus Christ, who has blessed us in Christ with every spiritual blessing in the heavenly places. (Ephesians 1:3)

Grace, mercy, and peace from God the Father and Christ Jesus our Lord. (1 Timothy 1:2) He is merciful to us! I need His mercy daily. All these gifts are from the Father and the Son.

Blessed be the God and Father of our Lord Jesus Christ! According to his great mercy, he has caused us to be born again to a living hope through the resurrection of Jesus Christ from the dead, to an inheritance that is imperishable, undefiled, and unfading, kept in heaven for you. (1 Peter 1:3) We are saved!

"Jesus Christ is Lord!"

DAY 192

"ATTRIBUTES OF GOD FROM A TO Z" (L)

"God is Love!"

***God is love, and whoever abides in love abides in God, and God abides in him.
(1 John 1:16)***

Love: intimacy, devotion, compassion, care, friendship, kindness, relationship

***But I have trusted in your steadfast love; my heart shall rejoice in your salva-
tion. (Psalm 13:5)*** When we truly learn to trust God and His great love for us it
becomes easier to follow in His steps. We need to decide once and for all that God
loves us and has only our best interest in mind and He does!

***The steadfast love of the Lord never ceases; his mercies never come to an end;
they are new every morning; great is your faithfulness. (Lamentations 3:22-23)***

***I will betroth you to me in righteousness and in justice, in steadfast love and in
mercy. I will betroth you to me in faithfulness. And you shall know the Lord.
(Hosea 2:19)*** He loves us with an everlasting love. He wants us to know Him. He
says, ***"I am the Lord I change not!"***

***But God shows his love for us in that while we were still sinners, Christ died for
us. (Romans 5:8)*** He even loved us while we were still sinners. He does not love
our sin, but He loves us. What a mighty God we serve!

***Who shall separate us from the love of Christ? Shall tribulation, or distress, or
persecution, or famine, or nakedness, or danger, or sword? No, in all these things
we are more than conquerors through him who loved us. (Romans 8:35,37)***
Nothing shall separate us from the love of Christ. Nothing!

***See what kind of love the Father has given to us, that we should be called children
of God; and so, we are. (1 John 3:1)***

If you do not see anything today in what you have read but this, I want you to
know without a shadow of doubt that God loves you and truly has your best interest at heart. He will not give up on you. He wants a personal relationship with you.

"God is Love!"

DAY 193

"ATTRIBUTES OF GOD FROM A TO Z" (L)

"The Lamb of God!"

And Isaac said to his father Abraham, "My Father!" And he said, "Here I am, my son." He said, "Behold, the fire and the wood but where is the lamb for a burnt offering?" Abraham said, "God will provide for himself the lamb for a burnt offering my son." (**Genesis 22:7**)

He was oppressed, and he was afflicted, yet he opened not his mouth; like a lamb that is led to the slaughter, and like a sheep that before its shearers is silent, so he opened not his mouth etc. (**Isaiah 53:7**) This is one of the many prophecies about Jesus.

Behold, the Lamb of God, who takes away the sin of the world! (**John 1:29**)

For Christ, our Passover lamb has been sacrificed. Let us therefore celebrate the festival. (**1 Corinthians 6:7**)

He himself bore our sins in his body on the tree, that we might die to sin and live to righteousness. By his wounds you have been healed. (**1 Peter 2:24**)

For our sake he made him to be sin who knew no sin, so that in him we might become the righteousness of God. (**2 Corinthians 5:21**) He became the Passover Lamb. He took our place. He became our sin. He took the punishment that we deserve. It is the blood of the Lamb that kept the death angel away from the children of Israel as they were leaving Egypt. It is also the Lamb that keeps the death angel away from us as we leave our Egypt (sin).

For the Lamb in the midst of the throne will be their shepherd, and he will guide them to springs of living water, and God will wipe away every tear from their eyes. (**Revelation 7:17**)

Worthy is the Lamb who was slain, to receive power and wealth and wisdom and might and honor and glory and blessing! (**Revelation 5:11**)

To him who sits on the throne and to the Lamb be blessing and honor and glory and might forever and ever! (**Revelation 5:13**)

"The Lamb of God!"

DAY 194

"Attributes of God from A to Z" (L)

"Jesus is the Light of the World!"

The Lord is my light and my salvation; whom shall I fear? The Lord is the stronghold of my life; of whom shall I be afraid? **(Psalm 27:1)**

Light: illumination, brightness, brilliance, radiance, to light is to set on fire, through Him we come to the light.

Lift up the light of your face upon us, O Lord! **(Psalm 4:6)** In the midst of the darkest times we can still see Him. His light shines upon us. We are never really in the dark as long as our eyes are on Him.

The true light, which gives light to everyone, was coming into the world. **(John 1:9)**

I am the light of the world. Whoever follows me will not walk in darkness but will have the light of life. **(John 8:12)** Jesus is the light of the world. In Him there is no darkness. Did you know there is no shadow to a flame? There is no shadow of turning with Him. Jesus said, *As long as I am in the world, I am the light of the world.* **(John 9:5)**

The god of this world has blinded the minds of the unbelievers, to keep them from seeing the light of the gospel of the glory of Christ, who is the image of God. **(2 Corinthians 4:4)** Either we walk in the light or in darkness. There is no middle ground.

But you are a chosen race, a royal priesthood, a holy nation, a people for his own possession, that you may proclaim the excellencies of him who called you out of darkness into his marvelous light. **(1 Peter 2:9)**

By a pillar of cloud, you led them in the day, and by a pillar of fire in the night to light for them the way in which they should go. **(Nehemiah 9:11)** He is still leading us in the way we should go.

And the city has no need of sun or moon to shine on it, for the glory of God gives it light, and its lamp is the Lamb. **(Revelation 21:23)**

"Jesus is Our Light!"

DAY 195

"Attributes of God from A to Z" (L)

"He is our Life!"

The Lord is my light and my salvation; whom shall I fear? The Lord is the stronghold of my life; of whom shall I be afraid? (Psalm 27:1)

Life: Life is what you do, what you love, what you hate, what you dislike. It is our soul, our spirit, our very being. It is every breath we take.

For whoever finds me finds life and obtains favor from the Lord, but he who fails to find me injures himself; all who hate me love death. (Proverbs 8:35) Where would we go or what would we do apart from the Lord. I cannot even begin to imagine the void in my life if I did not have the Lord. He is my life!

In him was life, and the life was the light of men. The light shines in the darkness and the darkness has not overcome it. (John 1:4)

You make known to me the path of life; in your presence there is fullness of joy; at your right hand are pleasures forevermore. (Psalm 16:11) The joy of the Lord is our strength. We know a merry heart doth good like medicine. A life full of joy is a full life.

Jesus said to them, I am the bread of life; whoever comes to me shall not hunger, and whoever believes in me shall never thirst. (John 6:35) We know that without food and water we will die, but many of us do not understand that food and water are not enough. We need to be full of the Spirit of God to truly have life.

That which was from the beginning which we have heard, which we have seen with our eyes, which we looked upon and have touched with our hands, concerning the word of life - the life was made manifest, and we have seen it, and testify to it and proclaim to you the eternal life, which was with the Father and was made manifest to us. (1 John 1:1-2)

Jesus is the way, and the truth, and the Life! Our life begins and ends with Him. There is no life apart from Him. So, take a deep breath and breathe in His life.

"He is the Breath of Life!"

DAY 196

"Attributes of God from A to Z" (M)

"God is Mighty!"

O Lord God, you have only begun to show your servant your greatness and your mighty hand. For what god is there in heaven or on earth who can do such works and mighty acts as yours? **(Deuteronomy 3:24)**

Mighty: fearsome, ferocious, big, tough, dominant, influential, strong, powerful, important, enormous, immense, tremendous etc.

We used to sing a song, "What a mighty God we serve. Angels bow before him. Heaven and earth adore him. What a mighty God we serve!"

For the Lord, your God is God of gods and Lord of lords, the great, the mighty, and the awesome God. **(Deuteronomy 10:17)** Sometimes we need to pause and think of all the mighty things God has done in our lives.

I had a text from my youngest son last night. My granddaughter had 5 girls over to spend the night. Before the evening was over, she had witnessed to them, and they had decided to start a Bible Study. She is 13 and has just moved to K.C. That isn't stopping her from sharing Jesus.

Who is this King of glory? The Lord, strong and mighty, the Lord, mighty in battle! **(Psalm 24:8)** He has not left us defenseless!

O Lord God of hosts, who is mighty as you are, O Lord, with your faithfulness all around you? **(Psalm 89:8)** Look around and see the mighty hand of God at work in your life and in the lives of those around you.

For he who is mighty has done great things for me, and holy is his name. **(Luke 1:49)**

Humble yourselves, therefore, under the mighty hand of God so that at the proper time he may exalt you, casting all your anxieties on him, because he cares for you. **(1 Peter 5:6)**

"God is Mighty!"

DAY 197

"Attributes of God from A to Z" (M)

"The Lord is Merciful!"

The Lord passed before him (Moses) and proclaimed, "The Lord, the Lord, a God merciful and gracious, slow to anger, and abounding in steadfast love and faithfulness." (Exodus 34:6)

Merciful: forgiving, compassionate, gracious, lenient, tenderhearted, kind, patient, generous, benevolent, gracious, courteous, polite, accommodating, charitable. I think in every scripture I read merciful and gracious were side by side. They are very similar words.

The Lord is gracious and merciful, slow to anger and abounding in steadfast love. The Lord is good to all, and his mercy is over all that he has made. (Psalm 145:8-9) We serve a merciful God.

Return to the Lord your God, for he is gracious and merciful, slow to anger, and abounding in steadfast love; and he relents over disaster. (Joel 2:13) I am banking on the fact that He relents over disaster because that is all that we seem to see around us at the moment. Come Lord Jesus, Come!

He has told us to *Be merciful, even as your Father is merciful. (Luke 6:36)*

For I will be merciful toward their iniquities, and I will remember their sins no more. (Hebrews 8:12) Apart from His mercy we would be lost. Apart from His mercy we would be wallowing in our sins. Apart from His mercy we would have no Savior, nor eternal life.

For the Lord, your God is a merciful God. He will not leave you or destroy you or forget the covenant with your fathers that he swore to them. (Deuteronomy 4:30) His rainbow in the sky is a constant reminder that He keeps His promises.

The Lord is merciful and gracious, slow to anger and abounding in steadfast love. He will not always chide, nor will he keep his anger forever. He does not deal with us according to our sins, nor repay us according to our iniquities. (Psalm 103:8-9)

"The Lord is Merciful!"

DAY 198

"Attributes of God from A to Z" (M)

"He is Majestic!"

***Who is like you, O Lord, among the gods? Who is like you, majestic in holiness, awesome in glorious deeds, doing wonders?* (Exodus 15:11)**

Majestic: exalted, great, awesome, elevated, magnificent, splendid, glorious, awe-inspiring, marvelous, sovereign

***O Lord, our Lord, how majestic is your name in all the earth!* (Psalm 8:1)**

I have noticed as we look at some of the attributes of God that every attribute is in the Psalms. David knew God and he knew how to praise and worship Him. When I look in the New Testament it seems to me, we know how to work for God, but it is very hard to find His attributes. Have we lost worship for works? I don't know.

***Glorious are you, more majestic than the mountains full of prey.* (Psalm 76:4)** When I look up at the mountains am I seeing the majesty of the mountains or am I seeing the majesty of the One who made them?

***For when he received honor and glory from God the Father, and the voice was borne to him by the Majestic Glory, "This is my beloved Son, with whom I am well pleased," we ourselves heard this very voice borne from heaven, for we were with him on the holy mountain.* (2 Peter 1:17-18)** (We were with Him!)

***Great is the Lord and greatly to be praised in the city of our God! His holy mountain, beautiful in elevation, is the joy of all the earth.* (Psalm 48:1)** When I first became a Christian, we used the King James Bible and sang many of the Psalms. This was one of my favorites and singing God's word is a way to memorize scripture and to worship.

***After it, his voice roars; he thunders with his majestic voice, and he does not restrain the lightning when his voice is heard.* (Job 37:4)**

Listen today and maybe you will hear His voice in the thunder and see His majesty in the bolts of lightning that stream across the sky.

"He is Majestic!"

DAY 199

"Attributes of God from A to Z" (M)

"He is our Master!"

Behold, as the eyes of servants look to the hand of their master, as the eyes of a maidservant to the hand of her mistress, so our eyes look to the Lord our God, till he has mercy upon us. (Psalm 123:2)

Master: lord, ruler, sovereign, monarch, overseer, leader, commander, director, controller, head, magistrate. He is in charge.

It is interesting that in the Old Testament the word master is never used to describe God except in Psalm 123 and even there it is implied, but it is used often by the disciples in the New Testament.

And Simon answered, Master, we toiled all night and took nothing! But at your word I will let down the nets. (Luke 5:5) He is Master of the Word.

And they went and woke him, saying, "Master, Master, we are perishing!" And he awoke and rebuked the wind and the raging waves, and they ceased, and there was calm. (Luke 8:24) He is Master of the wind and waves.

He was met by ten lepers, who stood at a distance and lifted up their voices, saying, "Jesus, Master, have mercy on us." (Luke 17:13) He is the Master of miracles.

He who is both their Master and yours is in heaven, and that there is no partiality with him. (Ephesians 6:9) With Him there is no partiality. He has no favorites. He loves us all equally. He is the Master of justice.

Masters, treat your bondservants justly and fairly, knowing that you also have a Master in heaven. (Colossians 4:1) He is a just and fair Master.

For certain people have crept in unnoticed who long ago were designated for this condemnation, ungodly people, who pervert the grace of our God into sensuality and deny our only Master and Lord, Jesus Christ. (Jude 1:4) He is our Master. He is sovereign. He is the ruler. He is the magistrate. He is the leader. He is our commander. He is Lord! Praise God!

"He is our Master!"

DAY 200

"ATTRIBUTES OF GOD FROM A TO Z" (M)

"He is the Mediator!"

For there is one God, and there is one mediator between God and men, the man Christ Jesus. (1 Timothy 2:5)

Mediator: arbitrator, negotiator, go-between, middleman, moderator, intercessor, peacemaker, umpire, judge, conciliator

There are two very good examples of mediation in the Old Testament. The first is when Abraham interceded for Sodom. He asked God if He would sweep away the righteous with the wicked. Finally, they arrived at the number ten righteous but there were not even ten righteous men in Sodom. It was destroyed. **(Genesis 18)**

In Numbers 14 Moses interceded for the people after they refused to believe Joshua and Caleb's report. *And the Lord said to Moses, "How long will this people despise me? How long will they not believe in me, in spite of all the signs that I have done among them?"* God wanted to destroy them. *"I will make of you a nation greater and mightier than they."* **(V12)** But Moses became the mediator between God and man. They were spared.

Therefore he (Christ) is the mediator of a new covenant, so that those who are called may receive the promised eternal inheritance, since a death has occurred that redeems them from the transgressions committed under the first covenant. **(Hebrews 9:15)** Christ is our mediator. He stands between us and God and says, "They are mine. I have bought them with my life."

Jesus is the mediator of a new covenant which he purchased by giving his life for each of us. **(Hebrews 12:24)**

The Spirit himself intercedes for us with groaning too deep for words. And he who searches hearts knows what is the mind of the Spirit, because the Spirit intercedes for the saints according to the will of God. **(Roman 8:26-27)**

"He is our Mediator!"

DAY 201

"ATTRIBUTES OF GOD FROM A TO Z" (N)

"He is the Name Above All Names!"

O Lord, our Lord, how majestic is your name in all the earth! You have set your glory above the heavens. (Psalm 8:1)

Name: A name is a term used for identification. The word or words that a person, thing, or place are known by. A name can bring honor or dishonor.

Stand up and bless the Lord your God from everlasting to everlasting. Blessed be your glorious name, which is exalted above all blessing and praise. (Nehemiah 9:5)

When I hear someone use the name of the Lord in any way other than in praise, I hurt inside. His name is to be honored. It is the name above all names and any use other than praise is an affront to Him. We are not to take the name of the Lord in vain.

I bow down toward your holy temple and give thanks to your name for your steadfast love and your faithfulness, for you have exalted above all things your name and your word. (Psalm 138:2) The children of Israel considered His name so holy that they did not even utter it. Today we use it as a by-word rather than the name above all names. O Lord forgive us!

What is the immeasurable greatness of his power toward us who believe, according to the working of his great might that he worked in Christ when he raised him from the dead and seated him at his right hand in heavenly places, far above all rule and authority and power and dominion, and above every name that is named not only in this age but also in the one to come. (Ephesians 1:20)

Therefore, God has highly exalted him and bestowed on him the name that is above every name, so that at the name of Jesus every knee should bow, in heaven and on earth and under the earth, and every tongue confess that Jesus Christ is Lord, to the glory of God the Father. (Philippians 2:9-10)

"He is the Name Above All Names!"

DAY 202

"ATTRIBUTES OF GOD FROM A TO Z" (N)

"Jesus the Nazarene!"

There shall come forth a shoot from the stump of Jesse, and a branch from his roots shall bear fruit. And the Spirit of the Lord shall rest upon him, the Spirit of wisdom and understanding, the Spirit of counsel and might, the Spirit of knowledge and the fear of the Lord. And his delight shall be in the fear of the Lord. (Isaiah 11:1-3)

Nazareth means branch or watch tower. If you study the meaning of words in the Bible you will be amazed that they all mean something and fit together. Jesus is the branch and a watch tower. He is the Nazarene.

Behold, the days are coming, declares the Lord, when I will raise up from David a righteous Branch, and he shall reign as king. (Jeremiah 23:5)

The name of the Lord is a strong tower; the righteous man runs into it and is safe. (Proverbs 18:10)

And he came to Nazareth, where he had been brought up. He went to the synagogue, and this is what he said. *"The Spirit of the Lord is upon me, because he has anointed me to proclaim good news to the poor. He has sent me to proclaim liberty to the captives and recovering of sight to the blind, to set at liberty those who are oppressed, to proclaim the year of the Lord's favor.* (Luke 4:18 -19)

Nathanael said to him, 'Can anything good come out of Nazareth?" (John 1:46)

The unclean spirit cried out, "What have you to do with us, Jesus of Nazareth? Have you come to destroy us? I know who you are - the Holy One of God." (Mark 1:23) He is the branch, the strong tower.

And I fell to the ground and heard a voice saying to me, "Saul, Saul, why are you persecuting me?" And I answered, "Who are you, Lord'" And he said to me, "I am Jesus of Nazareth, whom you are persecuting." (Acts 22:7-8) Of all the ways Jesus could have identified himself, why did he say Jesus of Nazareth?

Pilate wrote, Jesus of Nazareth, the King of the Jews. (John 19:19)

"Jesus the Nazarene!"

DAY 203

"Attributes of God from A to Z" (N)

"God is Near!"

The Lord is near to all who call on him, to all who call on him in truth. He fulfills the desire of those who fear him; he also hears their cry and saves them. (**Psalm 145:18-19**)

Near: close by, at hand, within reach, alongside, nigh, imminent

Seek the Lord while he may be found; call upon him while he is near. (**Isaiah 55:6**) I picture a young child playing outside with new friends. Every now and then he looks up to be sure his mother is nearby. This is our Father.

You came near when I called on you; you said, "Do not fear!" (**Lamentations 3:57**)

The Lord is near to the brokenhearted and saves the crushed in spirit. (**Psalm 34:18**) What a fantastic promise!

In the midst of a crisis we often say, "Where are you Lord?" But He has promised to never leave us nor forsake us. He is near!

Surely his salvation is near to those who fear him, that glory may dwell in our land. (**Psalm 85:9**) Our land desperately needs the Lord to be near right now, and He is if we will call upon Him. The problem is we think we can live without Him until we are desperate. He is not a magic wand but a Father wanting a relationship with His children.

But you are near, O Lord, and all your commandments are true. (**Psalm 119:151**)

But what does it say? The word is near you, in your mouth and in your heart" *(that is, the word of faith that we proclaim); because, if you confess with your mouth that Jesus is Lord and believe in your heart that God raised him from the dead, you will be saved.* (**Romans 10:8-9**) The most important words we will ever utter are, "Jesus is Lord. I believe." He will hear and answer because He is as near as a heartbeat, ready to forgive and offer us eternal life.

Draw near to God, and he will draw near to you. (**James 4:8**)

"God is Near!"

DAY 204

"ATTRIBUTES OF GOD FROM A TO Z" (O)

"God is Omnipotent!"

The word omnipotent is not found in the word of God but the meaning is everywhere. Omnipotent means all powerful, almighty, most high, preeminent, invincible. This is our God!

With man this is impossible, but with God all things are possible. (**Matthew 19:26**) Never underestimate the power of God or His love.

Be exalted, O Lord, in your strength! We will sing and praise your power. (**Psalm 21:13**) He is the God of strength and of power.

He who dwells in the shelter of the Most High will abide in the shadow of the Almighty. (**Psalm 91:1**) He is the Almighty!

I will give to the Lord the thanks due to his righteousness, and I will sing praise to the name of the Lord, the Most High. (Psalm 7:17)

They remembered that God was their rock, the Most High God their redeemer. (**Psalm 78:35**)

Yet the Most High does not dwell in houses made by hands, as the prophet says, "Heaven is my throne, and the earth is my footstool." (Acts 7:48-49)

And he is the head of the body, the church. He is the beginning, the firstborn from the dead, that in everything he might be preeminent. For in him all the fullness of God was pleased to dwell. (**Colossians 1:18**)

I sometimes wonder if we understand the omnipotence of God. Do we understand that He is all powerful, almighty, the most high, preeminent, and invincible? He is not a puppet on a string but a powerhouse of goodness!

Now to him who is able to do far more abundantly than all that we ask or think, according to the power at work within us, to him be glory in the church and in Christ Jesus throughout all generations. (**Ephesians 3:20**)

"He is Omnipotent!"

DAY 205

"Attributes of God from A to Z" (O)

"God is Omnipresent!"

"Can a man hide himself in secret places so that I cannot see him?" declares the Lord. "Do I not fill heaven and earth? declares the Lord." (Jeremiah 23:24)

Omnipresent means everywhere, infinite, boundless, far reaching, widespread, extensive, present everywhere at the same time.

Where shall I go from your Spirit? Or where shall I flee from your presence? If I ascend to heaven, you are there! If I make my bed in Sheol, you are there! If I take the wings of the morning and dwell in the uttermost parts of the sea, even there your hand shall lead me, and your right hand shall hold me. (Psalm 139:7-10)

Remember as a little child how you would put your hands over your eyes and say, "You can't see me." Many times, I think we are still saying this to God. "You can't see me!" But He is omnipresent! He sees everything and everyone. He is aware of our uprising and our down sitting. He knows, He sees, and He cares!

The Lord looks down from heaven; he sees all the children of man; from where he sits enthroned, he looks out on all the inhabitants of the earth. (Psalm 33:13)

For he looks to the ends of the earth and sees everything under the heavens. (Job 28:24) There is nothing hidden from Him. He knows our joys and our sorrows. He knows our pain and our pleasure. He knows everything about us. He sees us and He loves us.

But when you pray, go into your room, and shut the door and pray to your Father who is in secret. And your Father who sees in secret will reward you. (Matthew 6:6) Have you ever wondered how God can see and hear us all at the same time?

He is Omnipresent. I do not understand this, but I know He hears and answers my prayers. I am so thankful for His salvation and His boundless love toward me. I am so thankful for His presence in my life.

"He is Omnipresent!"

DAY 206

"ATTRIBUTES OF GOD FROM A TO Z" (O)

"God is Omniscient!"

But he knows the way that I take; when he has tried me, I shall come out as gold. (Job 23:10)

Omniscient: All-knowing, all-wise, all-seeing. This is God alone. There is no man or woman that can say he or she knows everything even Solomon in all his glory did not know everything. God is the wisest. He is all wisdom.

The Lord knows the days of the blameless and their heritage will remain forever; they are not put to shame in evil times; in the days of famine, they have abundance. (Psalm 37:18) God knows those who are His and He cares.

He knows the secrets of the heart. (Psalm 44:21)

The Lord knows the thoughts of man, that they are but a breath. (Psalm 94:11)

There is a difference between the secrets of the heart and our thoughts, I think. When I think thoughts, I am mulling over things in my life but when I think of secrets of the heart, I am thinking about what I wish I were or what I wish I could be or what I wish to become. God knows what I am thinking and what I am wishing.

He reveals deep and hidden things; he knows what is in the darkness, and the light dwells with him. (Daniel 2:22) There is nothing hidden from him!

Your Father knows what you need before you ask him. (Matthew 6:8) He is aware of every need we have, but he wants us to ask so that we have a relationship with him. He wants to talk with us.

But concerning that day or that hour, no one knows, not even the angels in heaven, nor the Son, but only the Father. (Mark 13:32) He knows when it began and when it will end.

God is greater than our heart, and he knows everything. (1 John 3:20)

"He is Omniscient!"

DAY 207

"Attributes of God from A to Z" (P)

"He keeps His Promises!"

Not one word of all the good promises that the Lord had made to the house of Israel had failed; all came to pass. **(Joshua 21:44)** *"I am the Lord. I change not."*

Promises: word of honor, assurance, pledge, vow, guarantee, oath, agreement, commitment, contract, covenant

Blessed be the Lord who has given rest to his people Israel, according to all that he promised. Not one word has failed of all his good promises. **(1 Kings 8:56)**

Let your steadfast love come to me, O Lord, your salvation according to your promise. **(Psalm 119:41)**

Behold, I am sending the promise of my Father upon you. But stay in the city until you are clothed with power from on high. **(Luke 24:49)**

For all the promises of God, find their "Yes" in him. **(2 Corinthians 1:20)** The question is, "Can we trust God?" This may be one of the most important questions we have to ask ourselves. "Do we trust Him? Do we trust His word?"

By which he has granted to us his precious and very great promises, so that through them you may become partakers of the divine nature. **(2 Peter 1:4)**

The Lord is not slow to fulfill his promise as some count slowness, but is patient toward you, not wishing that any should perish, but that all should reach repentance. **(2 Peter 3:9)**

I will be a father to you, and you shall be sons and daughter to me, says the Lord Almighty. Since we have these promises, beloved, let us cleanse ourselves from every defilement of body and spirit, bringing holiness to completion in the fear of God. **(2 Corinthians 6:18 - 7:1)**

He has promised to never leave us nor forsake us. He has promised to meet our needs. He has promised to lead us and guide us into all truth.

"He has Promised!"

DAY 208

"ATTRIBUTES OF GOD FROM A TO Z" (P)

"He is the God of Peace!"

For to us a child is born, to us a son is given; and the government shall be upon his shoulder, and his name shall be called Wonderful Counselor, Mighty God, Everlasting Father, Prince of Peace. **(Isaiah 9:6)**

Peace: tranquility, calm, quiet, silence, stillness, solitude

Peace I leave with you; my peace I give to you. Not as the world gives do I give to you. Let not your hearts be troubled, neither let them be afraid. **(John 14:27)**

For the kingdom of God is not a matter of eating and drinking but of righteousness and peace and joy in the Holy Spirit. **(Romans 14:17)**

May the God of peace be with you all. **(Romans 15:32)** If you could have only one attribute of God what would it be? I think that mine would be peace. It would be a quiet spirit. It would be a quiet assurance that God is in control of my life and of the world around me.

For God is not a God of confusion but of peace. **(1 Corinthians 14:33)** Where there is confusion there is no peace. Right now, it feels like we are in a state of confusion. What to do? What not to do? Where to go? Where not to go? What to think? What not to think? This is not God!

And let the peace of Christ rule in your hearts, to which indeed you were called in one body. And be thankful. **(Colossians 3:15)** The command is to let the peace of God rule. This says to me I have a part in this. I am to choose peace over confusion, doubt, anxiety, etc.

And he shall stand and shepherd his flock in the strength of the Lord, in the majesty of the name of the Lord his God. And they shall dwell secure, for now he shall be great to the ends of the earth. And he shall be their peace. **(Micah 5:4-5)**

May mercy, peace, and love be multiplied to you. **(Jude 1:2)** This is my prayer.

"He is the God of Peace!"

DAY 209

"Attributes of God from A to Z" (P)

"He is our Provider!"

My God will provide all your needs according to the riches of his glory in Christ Jesus. (Philippians 4:19)

Provide: supply, give, furnish, dispense, bestow, impart, produce, yield, deliver, contribute, distribute,

He struck the rock so that water gushed out and streams overflowed. Can he also give bread or provide meat for his people? (Psalm 78:20) Is anything too hard for God?

No temptation has overtaken you that is not common to man. God is faithful, and he will not let you be tempted beyond your ability, but with the temptation he will also provide the way of escape that you may be able to endure it. (1 Corinthians 10:13)

Not only does He provide for our physical needs, but He also provides for every other part of our lives. He has promised to provide for all our needs! He is aware of where we are and what we have need of at the moment. He will never leave us nor forsake us.

So, Abraham called the name of that place, "The Lord will provide" as it is said to this day. "On the mount of the Lord it shall be provided." (Genesis 22:14)

His greatest provision for each of us is the spotless Lamb of God who takes away the sin of the world, Jesus.

He who supplies seed to the sower and bread for food will supply and multiply your seed for sowing and increase the harvest of your righteousness. (2 Corinthians 9:10)

"He is our Provider!"

DAY 210

"Attributes of God from A to Z" (P)

"He is Perfect in all of His ways!"

The Rock, his work is perfect, for all his ways are justice. A God of faithfulness and without iniquity, just and upright is he. (Deuteronomy 32:4)

Perfect: ideal, faultless, flawless, exemplary, ultimate, superb, excellent, wonderful, marvelous, beautiful, magnificent, unrivaled, unequaled, matchless, unparalleled, beyond compare... What more can we say? He is perfect.

This God - his way is perfect; the word of the Lord proves true; he is a shield for all those who take refuge in him. (2 Samuel 22:31)

Down to the smallest detail He is perfect. Just look at a butterfly or a bird or an insect. Study the patterns and designs. Look at the cloud formations or the formations of rocks. Look at your fingerprint. Everywhere we look we see His perfection.

The law of the Lord is perfect, reviving the soul; the testimony of the Lord is sure, making wise the simple, the precepts of the Lord are right, rejoicing the heart; the commandment of the Lord is pure, enlightening the eyes; (Psalm 19:7-8) and we could go on and on about the perfection of God!

You therefore must be perfect, as your heavenly Father is perfect. (Matthew 5:48) But we ask, "How can we be perfect? There is only One who is perfect." But through the blood of Jesus Christ, we are made perfect. For when God looks at us, He does not see us, but He sees Jesus the author and finisher of our faith.

And being made perfect, he became the source of eternal salvation to all who obey him, being designated by God a high priest after the order of Melchizedek. (Hebrews 5:8) Not only is the Father perfect but so is His son Jesus Christ.

There is no fear in love, but perfect love casts out fear. For fear has to do with punishment, and whoever fears has not been perfected in love. (1 John 4:18)

"He is Perfect!"

DAY 211

"ATTRIBUTES OF GOD FROM A TO Z" (P)

"He is our Protector!"

May the Lord answer you in the day of trouble! May the name of the God of Jacob protect you! (Psalm 20:1)

Protector: defender, bodyguard, guardian, keeper, shield, buffer

Deliver me from my enemies, O my God; protect me from those who rise up against me; deliver me from those who work evil. (Psalm 59:1)

Because he holds fast to me in love, I will deliver him; I will protect him, because he knows my name. (Psalm 91:14)

We know that everyone who has been born of God does not keep on sinning, but he who was born of God protects him, and the evil one does not touch him. (1 John 5:18)

God is our protector, and the enemy cannot touch His children. He is like a mother bear protecting her cubs. He went so far as to give His life to protect those who call upon His name.

Like birds hovering, so the Lord of host will protect Jerusalem; he will protect and deliver it; he will spare and rescue it. (Isaiah 31:5) God has no favorites so I believe the promise applies to you and me too. He is hovering over us. I like this picture of God.

The glory of the Lord shall be your rear guard. (Isaiah 58:8) In Ephesians when we are told to put on the whole armor of God, have you noticed there is not protection behind. That is because God is our rear guard.

For you shall not go out in haste, and you shall not go in flight, for the Lord will go before you, and the God of Israel will be your rear guard. (Isaiah 52:12) In other words we are not to run. God is always with us, and He protects our backside.

"He is our Protector!"

DAY 212

"Attributes of God from A to Z" (P)

"He is our High Priest!"

Therefore, he had to be made like his brothers in every respect, so that he might become a merciful and faithful high priest in the service of God, to make propitiation for the sins of the people. (Hebrews 2:17) As high priest He is the satisfactory payment for sin. He became our substitute for sin. He has taken our punishment upon Himself.

Priest: pastor, father, reverend, minister, and high priest is the highest!

It is interesting to note that Jesus as our High Priest is only found in Hebrews, and we are not sure who wrote Hebrews, but it is a wonderful book.

Since then, we have a great high priest who has passed through the heavens, Jesus, the Son of God, let us hold fast our confession. For we do not have a high priest who is unable to sympathize with our weaknesses, but one who in every respect has been tempted as we are, yet without sin. (Hebrews 4:14-15)

He was able to walk our walk and live our lives without stumbling and falling.

So also, Christ did not exalt himself to be made a high priest, but was appointed by him who said to him, "You are my Son, today I have begotten you." (Hebrews 5:5)

Notice He did not elevate Himself but allowed God to place Him where He wanted Him. This should be a lesson to us. Let God be God in our lives. Let Him decide the direction of our lives. Then we will live to the fullest.

We have such a high priest, one who is seated at the right hand of the throne of the Majesty in heaven, a minister in the holy places, in the true tent that the Lord set up not man. (Hebrews 8:1-2) The Lord set up not man!

But when Christ appeared as a high priest of the good things that have come, then through the greater and more perfect tent (not made with hands, that is not of this creation) he entered once for all into the holy places…securing an eternal redemption. (Hebrews 9:11-12)

"He is our High Priest!"

DAY 213

"Attributes of God from A to Z" (Q)

"Sometimes God is Quiet!"

Have you noticed that sometimes God is quiet? We pray and we pray but we hear no answer. Then we begin to doubt God. But He is there. Maybe He is waiting for us to finally give up and let Him be God. Maybe He is trying to teach us to wait upon Him. Maybe He has something better for us then what we are asking for. Maybe He is just being God. I love this story about Elijah and God.

Go out and stand on the mount before the Lord. And behold the Lord passed by, and a great and strong wind tore the mountains and broke in pieces the rocks before the Lord, but the Lord was not in the wind. And after the wind an earthquake, but the Lord was not in the earthquake. And after the earthquake a fire, but the Lord was not in the fire. And after the fire the sound of a low whisper. (1 Kings 19:11-12)

What do you think would have happened if Elijah had given up after the strong wind, or the earthquake or the fire? But Elijah waited on the Lord. He waited knowing, that eventually God would speak to him. Do we have the same confidence when we pray?

But they who wait for the Lord shall renew their strength; they shall mount up with wings like eagles; they shall run and not be weary; they shall walk and not faint. (Isaiah 40:31)

Blessed is the one who listens to me, watching daily at my gates, waiting beside my doors. For whoever finds me finds life and obtains favor from the Lord. (Proverbs 8:34)

What does waiting have to do with quiet? I believe everything. Unless we learn to wait, we will not hear the still small voice of God. If we do not hear His still small voice, we will miss out on so many gems the Lord has to tell us.

We know that God does not listen to sinners, but if anyone is a worshiper of God and does his will, God listens to him. (John 9:31)

"Sometimes God is Quiet!"

DAY 214

"Attributes of God from A to Z" (R)

"He is our Redeemer!"

For I know that my Redeemer lives, and at the last he will stand upon the earth. **(Job 19:25)** Job had come face to face with God and now he knew without a doubt that God was his redeemer. Before his encounter he knew about God but now he knew God. It was no longer a theory but a fact in his life. God was real!

Redeemer: guardian, savior, champion, avenger, deliverer, messiah

Let the words of my mouth and the meditation of my heart be acceptable in your sight, O Lord, my rock, and my redeemer. **(Psalm 19:14)** This is my prayer and I hope it is yours. Let my thoughts line up with yours Lord. Let my words be a sweet incense to your ears. Keep me steadfast and strong in you.

They remembered that God was their rock, the Most High God their redeemer. **(Psalm 78:35) O** Lord put me in remembrance of you daily.

Thus says the Lord, the King of Israel and his Redeemer, the Lord of hosts; I am the first and I am the last; besides me there is no god. **(Isaiah 44:6)** Just think for a moment about all the little gods we put before God. Is it time, talent, money, friends, stuff? Let's place God where He belongs in our lives and live for Him.

"For a brief moment. I deserted you, but with great compassion I will gather you. In overflowing anger for a moment, I hid my face from you, but with everlasting love I will have compassion on you," says the Lord your Redeemer. **(Psalm 54:7)** He hasn't forgotten us even though, at the moment, it may seem like it. He is still in the redeeming business.

Thus says the Lord, your Redeemer, the Holy One of Israel: I am the Lord your God who teaches you to profit, who leads you in the way you should go. Oh, that you had paid attention to my commandments! Then your peace would have been like a river, and your righteousness like the waves of the sea. **(Isaiah 48:17)**

It is time to turn our eyes upon Jesus. It is time to pay attention to Him.

"He is our Redeemer!"

DAY 215

"ATTRIBUTES OF GOD FROM A TO Z" (R)

"God is our Refuge!"

You have been a refuge for the poor, a refuge for the needy in their distress, a shelter from the storm and a shade from the heat. (**Isaiah 25:4**)

Refuge: shelter, protection, safety, security, hiding place, strong hold, shield

God is our refuge and strength, an ever-present help in trouble. Therefore, we will not fear, though the earth gives way, and the mountains fall into the heart of the sea. (**Psalm 46:1-2**) God is our refuge. So often we look to man for our help, when our help comes from the Lord who made heaven and earth. Our eyes are focused on man rather than our Maker. When a child is lost, he cries for his mother not for a stranger in the street. Why is it so difficult for us to cry out to God?

You are my hiding place; you will protect me from trouble and surround me with songs of deliverance. I will instruct you and teach you in the way you should go; I will counsel you with my loving eye on you. (**Psalm 32:7-8**) What a promise!

My God is my rock, in whom I take refuge, my shield and the horn of my salvation. He is my stronghold, my refuge and my savior. (**2 Samuel 22:3**)

The Lord is good, a refuge in times of trouble. He cares for those who trust in him. (**Nahum 1:7**) What am I putting my trust in? This may be the key to where I am spiritually.

The Lord is a refuge for the oppressed, a stronghold in times of trouble. Those who know your name trust in you, for you, Lord, have never forsaken those who seek you. (**Psalm 9:9-10**)

Why do I use scripture more than just telling you what I think? Because, *The word of God is alive and active, sharper than any double-edged sword, it penetrates even to dividing soul and spirit, joints, and marrow; it judges the thoughts and attitudes of the heart.* (**Hebrews 4:12**) The word speaks where I can't!

The Lord is my rock, my fortress, and my deliverer. (**Psalm 18:2**)

"God is My Refuge!"

DAY 216

"TTRIBUTES OF GOD FROM A TO Z" (R)

"He is Righteous!"

We have an advocate with the Father - Jesus Christ, the Righteous One. He is the atoning sacrifice for our sins, and not only for ours but also for the sins of the whole world. (1 John 2:1)

Righteous: just, faultless, blameless, irreproachable, sinless, upright, honest, innocent, guiltless, uncorrupted, pure

But the Lord Almighty will be exalted by his justice, and the holy God will be proved holy by his righteous acts. (Isaiah 5:16)

For in the gospel the righteousness of God is revealed. (Romans 1:17)

My mouth will tell of your righteous deeds, of your saving acts all day long. (Psalm 71:15)

This is the name by which he will be called: The Lord Our Righteous Savior. (Jeremiah 23:6)

For the Lord is righteous, he loves justice; the upright will see his face. (Psalm 11:7)

The Lord is gracious and righteous; our God is full of compassion. (Psalm 116:5)

So many times, I say Lord I do not understand. But then I must yield to Him because His ways are not my ways, and His thoughts are not my thoughts. He is always right. He knows what is best. He is pure and holy, and we need to trust Him regardless of whether we understand or not.

You are righteous, Lord, and your laws are right. The statutes you have laid down are righteous; they are fully trustworthy. (Psalm 119:37) The question is do we trust Him and His ways?

The Lord is righteous in all his ways and faithful in all he does. The Lord is near to all who call on him, to all who call on him in truth. (Psalm 145:17)

"He is Righteous!"

DAY 217

"Attributes of God from A to Z" (R)

"He is the Rock!"

He is the Rock, his works are perfect, and all his ways are just. A faithful God who does no wrong, upright, and just is he. (**Deuteronomy 32:4**)

Rock symbolizes strength and stability.

There is no one holy like the Lord; there is no one besides you; there is no Rock like our God. (**1 Samuel 2:2**)

The Lord is my rock, my fortress, and my deliverer; my God is my rock in whom I take refuge, my shield, and the horn of my salvation. He is my stronghold, my refuge, and my savior. (**2 Samuel 22:2-3**) In other words He is everything! He is able to do abundantly above all that I ask or think! He is the solid rock on which I stand.

See, I lay in Zion a stone that causes people to stumble and a rock that makes them fall, and the one who believes in him will never be put to shame. (**Romans 9:33**) Don't fall on the rock but cling to Him. He is our life preserver.

The Lord is my rock, my fortress and my deliverer, my God is my rock, in whom I take refuge, my shield and the horn of my salvation, my stronghold. (**Psalm 18:2**)

There is nothing too hard for Him. He is steadfast. He is immovable. He is dependable. He is always there.

Trust in the Lord forever, for the Lord, the Lord himself is the Rock eternal. (**Isaiah 26:4**) He does not change.

"Who do you say I am'" Simon Peter answered, "You are the Messiah, the Son of the living God." Jesus replied, "Blessed are you, Simon son of Jonah for this was not revealed to you by flesh and blood, but by my Father in heaven. And I tell you that you are Peter, and on this rock, I will build my church, and the gates of Hades will not overcome it." (**Matthew 16:15-18**)

Upon this rock I will build my church. Believing that Jesus is the Christ the Son of the Living God offers us entrance into His kingdom. The door is always open to those who will receive and believe in Him. He is our rock and our salvation.

"He is our Rock!"

DAY 218

"Attributes of God from A to Z" (R)

"He is the Resurrection!"

I am the resurrection and the life. The one who believes in me will live, even though he dies. Do you believe this? **(John 11:25)**

Resurrection: raising from the dead, restoring to life, return from the dead, rebirth

I want to know Christ - yes, to know the power of his resurrection and participation in his sufferings, becoming like him in his death, and so, somehow, attaining to the resurrection from the dead. **(Philippians 3:10)**

Praise be to the God and Father of our Lord Jesus Christ! In his great mercy he has given us new birth into a living hope through the resurrection of Jesus Christ from the dead, and into an inheritance that can never perish, spoil, or fade. This inheritance is kept in heaven for you. **(1 Peter 1:3-4)**

Seeing what was to come, he spoke of the resurrection of the Messiah, that he was not abandoned to the realm of the dead, nor did his body see decay. God has raised this Jesus to life, and we are all witnesses of it. **(Acts 2:31-32)**

What does all of this mean to you and me? Everything! As Christ died and rose from the dead, so we to will die but not forever. We will be raised from the dead and spend eternity with Christ in heaven, if we confess with our mouth and believe in our heart that God raised Christ from the dead. Where we spend eternity is totally decided by one question. Do we believe that Jesus is the Christ? Our future depends upon our answer.

Through him you believe in God, who raised him from the dead and glorified him, and so your faith and hope are in God. **(1 Peter 1:21)**

Whoever wants to be my disciple must deny themselves and take up their cross daily and follow me. For whoever wants to save their life will lose it, but whoever loses their life for me will save it. **(Luke 9:23)**

"I am the resurrection and the life. Do you believe this?" See you in eternity!

"He is the Resurrection!"

DAY 219

"Attributes of God from A to Z" (S)

"Christ is our Sacrifice!"

Therefore, as dearly loved children walk in the way of love, just as Christ loved us and gave himself up for us as a fragrant offering and sacrifice to God. (Ephesians 5:2)

Sacrifice: act of giving up something for someone else, something that costs me

For the life of a creature is in the blood, and I have given it to you to make atonement for yourselves on the altar; it is the blood that makes atonement for one's life. (Leviticus 17:11) I will never forget a woman saying to me, "Stop talking about the blood. I hate that." We were standing in front of the church. I have never forgotten this conversation because, *Without the shedding of blood there is no forgiveness.* (Hebrews 9:22)

God presented Christ as a sacrifice of atonement, through the shedding of his blood - to be received by faith. (Romans 3:25) Do I understand this? Absolutely not but God said it. I believe it. That settles it.

For by one sacrifice, he has made perfect forever those who are being made holy. (Hebrews 10:14) Once and for all. Christ only had to die once, and we are the recipients of His death.

He is the atoning sacrifice for our sins, and not only for ours but also for the sins of the whole world. (1 John 2:2) Does this mean that the whole world is saved? No, it means the whole world has the choice to be saved but the choice is ours.

Just as Moses lifted up the snake in the wilderness, so the Son of Man must be lifted up, that everyone who believes may have eternal life in him. (John 3:14)

This is love: not that we loved God, but that he loved us and sent his Son as an atoning sacrifice for our sins. (1 John 4:10)

For God so loved the world that he gave his one and only Son, that whoever believes in him shall not perish but have eternal life. For God did not send his Son into the world to condemn the world, but to save the world through him." (John 3:16-17)

"Christ is our Sacrifice!"

DAY 220

"ATTRIBUTES OF GOD FOR A TO Z" (S)

"Jesus Christ is our Savior!"

The Lord lives! Praise be to my Rock! Exalted be my God, the Rock, my Savior! (2 Samuel 22:47)

Savior: Redeemer, Messiah, Lord, Lamb of God, Son of God, Prince of Peace, King of Kings, Emmanuel. He has rescued us from the pit of hell and brought us into His kingdom as sons and daughters of the Most High.

Guide me in your truth and teach me, for you are God my Savior, and my hope is in you all day long. (Psalm 25:5)

Today in the town of David a Savior has been born to you; he is the Messiah, the Lord. (Luke 2:11)

This grace was given us in Christ Jesus before the beginning of time, but it has now been revealed through the appearing of our Savior, Christ Jesus, who has destroyed death and has brought life and immortality to light through the gospel. (2 Timothy 1:10)

Christ Jesus has saved us from death to life. He has rescued us from the powers of hell and seated us in heavenly places with Him. We have been redeemed by the blood of the Lamb!

But when the kindness and love of God our Savior appeared, he saved us, not because of righteous things we had done, but because of his mercy. He saved us through the washing of rebirth and renewal by the Holy Spirit, whom he poured out on us generously through Jesus Christ our Savior, so that, having been justified by his grace, we might become heirs having the hope of eternal life. (Titus 3:4-6) What a promise!

To him who is able to keep you from stumbling and to present you before his glorious presence without fault and with great joy - to the only God our Savior be glory, majesty, power and authority, through Jesus Christ our Lord, before all ages, now and forevermore! Amen. (Jude 1:24-25)

"He is our Savior!"

DAY 221

"He is the Good Shepherd!"

The Lord is my shepherd, I lack nothing. He makes me lie down in green pastures, he leads me beside quiet waters, he refreshes my soul. He guides me along the right paths for his name's sake. Even though I walk through the darkest valley, I will fear no evil, for you are with me; your rod and your staff, they comfort me. You prepare a table before me in the presence of my enemies. You anoint my head with oil, my cup overflows. Surely your goodness and love will follow me all the days of my life, and I will dwell in the house of the Lord forever. (Psalm 23)

Take a minute to really reflect on this. The Lord is our shepherd. He leads and guides us. He comforts us. He never leaves us nor forsakes us. He provides for us. He loves us!

Shepherd: keeper, caretaker, guard, herder, leader, pastor, teacher, watchman, etc.

He tends his flock like a shepherd; He gathers the lambs in his arms and carries them close to his heart. (Isaiah 40:11)

As a shepherd looks after his scattered flock when he is with them, so will I look after my sheep. (Ezekiel 34:12)

But you, Bethlehem, in the land of Judah, are by no means least among the rulers of Judah; for out of you will come a ruler who will shepherd my people Israel. (Matthew 2:6)

For you were like sheep going astray, but now you have returned to the Shepherd and Overseer of your souls. (1 Peter 2:25)

I am the good shepherd. The good shepherd lays down his life for the sheep...I am the good shepherd; and I know my sheep and my sheep know me. (John 10:11 & 14)

"He is the Good Shepherd!"

DAY 222

"Attributes of God from A to Z" (S)

"God is Sovereign!"

As I was studying God's sovereignty, I began to notice that the Old Testament saints spoke often of it, but sovereignty was only mentioned 6 times in the New Testament. I have also noticed other attributes of God that are spoken of countless times in the Old Testament but not in the New and I wondered why? Do we not have the awesome reverence that people of old experienced? Have we forgotten who God really is? I don't know.

Sovereign: ruler, king, lord, supreme, absolute, unlimited, infinite, unconditional

But Abram said, *"Sovereign Lord, how will I know?"* **(Genesis 15:8)**

Moses said, *Sovereign Lord, you have begun to show your servant your greatness and your strong hand.* **(Deuteronomy 3:24)**

Joshua said, *"Alas, Sovereign Lord, why did you ever bring this people across the Jordan to deliver us into the hands of the Amorites to destroy us?"* **(Joshua 7:7)**

Gideon said, *"Alas, Sovereign Lord! I have seen the angel of the Lord face to face!"* **(Judges 6:22)**

Then Samson prayed to the Lord, *"Sovereign Lord, remember me. Please, God, strengthen me just once more."* **(Judges 16:28)**

David said, *"How great you are, Sovereign Lord! There is no one like you, and there is no God but you."* **(2 Samuel 7:22)**

Isaiah said, *"See, the Sovereign Lord comes with power, and he rules with a mighty arm."* **(Isaiah 40:10)**

Jeremiah said, *"Ah, Sovereign Lord, you have made the heavens and the earth by your great power and outstretched arm. Nothing is too hard for you."* **(Jeremiah 32:17)**

Simeon said, *"Sovereign Lord, as you have promised, you may now dismiss your servant in peace."* **(Luke 2:29)**

"God is Sovereign!"

DAY 223

"Attributes of God from A to Z" (S)

"He is the Son of God!"

For to us a child is born, to us a son is given, and the government will be on his shoulders. And he will be called Wonderful Counselor, Mighty God, Everlasting Father, Prince of Peace. Of the greatness of his government and peace there will be no end. (Isaiah 9:6-7)

The most important thing that any of us will ever do is to believe that Jesus is the Christ, the Son of the Living God and ask Him to make His permanent dwelling in us. Believing in Jesus is a matter of life and death. Today we are seeing people wearing masks, social distancing, washing their hands frequently, waiting for a vaccine but in the same frantic manner are we seeking the One who can truly save us? We should be desperate for Him!

He will be great and will be called the Son of the Most High. The Lord God will give him the throne of his father David and he will reign over Jacob's descendants forever; his kingdom will never end. (Luke 1:32-33)

I have been crucified with Christ and I no longer live, but Christ lives in me. The life I now live in the body, I live by faith in the Son of God, who loved me and gave himself for me. (Galatians 2:20)

Therefore, since we have a great high priest who has ascended into heaven, Jesus the Son of God, let us hold firmly to the faith we profess. (Hebrews 4:14)

In the same way, Christ did not take on himself the glory of becoming a high priest. But God said to him, "You are my Son; today I have become your Father." (Hebrews 5:5)

If anyone acknowledges that Jesus is the Son of God, God lives in them and they in God. (1 John 4:15)

"He is the Son of God!"

DAY 224

"Attributes of God from A to Z" (T)

"He is the Teacher!"

God is exalted in his power. Who is a teacher like him? Who has prescribed his ways for him, or said to him, "You have done wrong?" (Job 36:22)

Teacher: educator, tutor, instructor, school master, coach, trainer, guide, mentor, counselor,

When the Pharisees saw this, they asked his disciples, "Why does your teacher eat with tax collectors and sinners?" (Matthew 9:11) The Pharisees called Him Teacher.

Just then a man came up to Jesus and asked, "Teacher, what good thing must I do to get eternal life?" (Matthew 19:16) The common man called Him Teacher.

The disciples woke him and said to him, "Teacher, don't you care if we drown?" (Mark 4:38) The disciples called Him Teacher.

On one occasion an expert in the law stood up to test Jesus. "Teacher," he asked, "what must I do to inherit eternal life?" (Luke 10:25) A lawyer called Him Teacher.

So, the spies questioned him: "Teacher, we know that you speak and teach what is right and that you do not show partiality but teach the way of God in accordance with the truth." (Luke 20:21) Even the spies called Him Teacher.

Jesus replies, ***"Go into the city to a certain man and tell him, The Teacher says: My appointed time is near. I am going to celebrate the Passover with my disciples at your house." (Matthew 26:18)***

Jesus called Himself the Teacher. He is our instructor, our guide, our mentor, our counselor. Even as students are expected to pay attention to their teachers, we are expected to pay attention to Jesus and His words because they bring life both now and eternally to us. So don't be a dunce but a doer of His Word.

"He is our Teacher!"

DAY 225

"ATTRIBUTES OF GOD – FROM A TO Z" (T)

"He is the Truth!"

Guide me in your truth and teach me, for you are God my Savior, and my hope is in you all day long. (Psalm 25:5)

Truth: sincerity, honesty, genuineness, accuracy, correctness, rightness, authenticity, certainty

Jesus answered, "I am the way and the truth and the life. No one comes to the Father except through me." (John 14:6)

The Word became flesh and made his dwelling among us. We have seen his glory, the glory of the one and only Son who came from the Father, full of grace and truth. (John 1:14)

For the law was given through Moses; grace and truth came through Jesus Christ. (John 14:17)

Sanctify them by the truth; your word is truth. (John 17:17)

Jesus and His Word are one and the same. **In the beginning was the Word, and the Word was with God, and the Word was God. He was with God in the beginning. (John 1:1)**

This is how we know that we belong to the truth and how we set our hearts at rest in his presence: If our hearts condemn us, we know that God is greater than our hearts, and he knows everything. (1 John 3:19-20)

The Spirit is also called the Spirit of Truth. It is the Spirit living in each of us that speaks God's secrets into our hearts. He is the third part of the Trinity and is living in us until the return of Christ. Jesus said, **Do not leave Jerusalem, but wait for the gift my Father promised, which you have heard me speak about. For John baptized with water, but in a few days, you will be baptized with the Holy Spirit. (Acts 1:4-5)**

"He is the Spirit of Truth!"

DAY 226

"Attributes of God from A to Z" (T)

"The Godhead is called the Trinity!"

In the beginning God (the Father) created the heavens and the earth. Now the earth was formless and empty, darkness was over the surface of the deep, and the Spirit of God was hovering over the waters. And God said. (Jesus the World) (Genesis 1:1)

I will proclaim the Lord's decree: He said to me, "You are my son; today I have become your father." (Psalm 2:7)

Because you are his sons, God sent the Spirit of his Son into our hearts, the Spirit who calls out, "Abba, Father." (Galatians 4:6)

Trinity means three. When I was baptized the pastor said, "I baptize you in the name of the Father, the Son and the Holy Spirit." All through the Word of God we see the workings of the Trinity.

Now what I am going to say is just me so please don't take it for honest truth. I see the Father as the inspiration for all things. I see Jesus as the Word that brought forth all that God thought, and I see the Holy Spirit as the one who helps us live out God's Word.

I have always thought of the Trinity as an egg. There is the shell, the white and the yoke. They are all one, but they are all different with a different purpose. Now that is just my childlike mind trying to figure out God, which no one can.

The Holy Spirit will come on you, and the power of the Most High will over-shadow you. So, the holy one to be born will be called the Son of God. (Luke 1:35) This is a good example of the Trinity in action. Do I understand this? "No" but do I believe it? The answer is "Yes".

We proclaim to you what we have seen and heard, so that you also may have fellowship with us. And our fellowship is with the Father and with his Son, Jesus Christ. (1 John 1:3)

"God, Three in One, the Trinity!"

DAY 227

"Attributes of God from A to Z" (T)

"He is Trustworthy!"

The law of the Lord is perfect, reviving the soul; the testimony of the Lord is sure, making wise the simple; the precepts of the Lord are right, rejoicing the heart; the commandment of the Lord is pure, enlightening the eyes; the fear of the Lord is clean, enduring forever; the rules of the Lord are true, and righteous altogether. **(Psalm 19:7-9)** In other words He is trustworthy!

Trustworthy: reliable, dependable, honest, upright, truthful, incorruptible, faithful, guaranteed, unfailing

The works of his hands are faithful and just; all his precepts are trustworthy. **(Psalm 111:7)**

Righteous are you, O Lord, and right are your rules. You have appointed your testimonies in righteousness and in all faithfulness. **(Psalm 119:137-138)** He is trustworthy!

Your kingdom is an everlasting kingdom, and your dominion endures throughout all generations. The Lord is faithful in all his words and kind in all his works. **(Psalm 145:13)** He is trustworthy!

And now, O Lord God, you are God, and your words are true. **(2 Samuel 7:28)**

The only way we will ever know how trustworthy God is, is to be tested. It is easy to spout off scriptures, but until they become a tested reality in our lives, we do not truly know how trustworthy our God is. The question is, "Can we trust Him with our families, with our lives? The answer is "yes" but the answer does not come without trials and tribulation.

And he said to me, "These words are trustworthy and true. And the Lord, the God of the spirits of the prophets, has sent his angel to show his servants what must soon take place. And behold, I am coming soon. Blessed is the one who keeps the words of the prophecy of this book. **(Revelation 22:6-7)**

"He is Trustworthy!"

DAY 228

"Attributes of God from A to Z" (U)

"He is Unchangeable!"

So, when God desired to show more convincingly to the heirs of the promise the unchangeable character of his purpose, he guaranteed it with an oath, so that by two unchangeable things, in which it is impossible for God to lie, we who have fled for refuge might have strong encouragement to hold fast to the hope set before us. **(Hebrews 6:17-18)**

Unchanging: consistent, constant, predictable, steady, lasting, ceaseless, never-ending, eternal

God is not man, that he should lie, or a son of man, that he should change his mind. Has he said, and will he not do it? Or has he spoken, and will he not fulfill it? **(Numbers 23:19)** He is unchangeable!

And also, the Glory of Israel will not lie or have regret, for he is not a man, that he should regret. **(1 Samuel 15:29)**

The Lord has sworn and will not change his mind. You are a priest forever after the order of Melchizedek. **(Psalm 110:4)**

The Lord knew us even before we were born in our mother's womb. He knew our names. He knew our purpose in life. He knew the talents and abilities He had given us. He knew our personalities. He said, "It is good!" and He will not change His mind. He has complete confidence in what He has created.

For I the Lord do not change; therefore you, O children of Jacob, are not consumed. **(Malachi 3:6)** This is proof of the above statement.

In our ever-changing world it is hard to believe the steadfast love of the Lord never changes. His mercies are new every day. Great is His faithfulness!

But I have trusted in your steadfast love; my heart shall rejoice in your salvation. I will sing to the Lord, because he has dealt bountifully with me. **(Psalm 13:5-6)**

"He is Unchangeable!"

DAY 229

"Attributes of God from A to Z" (U)

"He is Unsearchable in all His ways!"

Oh, the depth of riches and wisdom and knowledge of God! How unsearchable are his judgments and how inscrutable his ways! **(Romans 11:33)**

Unsearchable: hidden, unfathomable, mysterious, inscrutable, beyond the power of man to explore

Call to me and I will answer you and will tell you great and hidden things that you have not known. **(Jeremiah 33:3)** He will show us mysteries.

Now to him who is able to strengthen you according to my gospel and the preaching of Jesus Christ, according to the revelation of the mystery that was kept secret for long ages but has now been disclosed. **(Romans 16:25)**

But we impart a secret and hidden wisdom of God, which God decreed before the ages for our glory...What no eye has seen, nor ear heard, nor the heart of man imagined, what God has prepared for those who love him. **(1 Corinthians 2:7-9)** *He* is unsearchable in all of his ways!

In him we have redemption through his blood, the forgiveness of our trespasses, according to the riches of his grace, which he lavished upon us, in all wisdom and insight making known to us the mystery of his will, according to his purpose, which he set forth in Christ as a plan for the fullness of time, to unite all things in him, things in heaven and things on earth. **(Ephesians 1:8-10)**

The mystery hidden for ages and generations but now revealed to his saints. To them God chose to make known how great among the Gentiles are the riches of the glory of this mystery, which is Christ in you, the hope of glory. **(Colossians 1:26-27)** This is a very important verse to me because I am not of Jewish descent. I would be hopelessly lost apart from the grace and mercy of God.

He was manifested in the flesh, vindicated by the Spirit, seen by angels, proclaimed among the nations, believed on in the world, taken up in glory. **(I Timothy 3:16)**

"He is Unsearchable in all of His Ways!"

DAY 230

"Attributes of God from A to Z" (V)

"He is Our Victory!"

For the Lord, your God is he who goes with you to fight for you against your enemies to give you the victory. **(Deuteronomy 20:4)**

Victory: success, triumph, conquest, win, conquering, overpowering, supremacy, trouncing, saving

Now I know that the Lord saves his anointed: he will answer him from his holy heaven with the saving might of his right hand. Some trust in chariots and some in horses, but we trust in the name of the Lord our God. **(Psalm 20:6-7)** He is our victory!

But you have saved us from our foes and have put to shame those who hate us. **(Psalm 44:7)**

With God we shall do valiantly, it is he who will tread down our foes. **(Psalm 108:13)** He is our victory!

The horse is made ready for the day of battle, but the victory belongs to the Lord. **(Proverbs 21:31)**

So often we think we are fighting battles by ourselves. We think "If it is to be, it is up to me." We can walk this way, but we will walk in frustration and defeat. The victory belongs to the Lord. When we let Him take over, everything in life becomes a breath of fresh air. He is able and He wants to be a part of each of our lives. He is our Father.

A bruised reed he will not break, and a smoldering wick he will not quench, until he brings justice to victory; and in his name the Gentiles will hope. **(Matthew 12:20)** That's you and me!

When the perishable puts on the imperishable, and the mortal puts on immortality, then shall come to pass the saying that is written: Death is swallowed up in victory. O death, where is your victory? O death, where is your sting? **(1 Corinthians 15:54-55)**

"The final Victory is life eternal!"

DAY 231

"Attributes of God from A to Z" (V)

"He is the Vine!"

Turn again, O God of hosts! Look down from heaven and see; have regard for this vine, the stock that your right hand planted, and for the son whom you made strong for yourself. **(Psalm 80:14)**

Vine: A plant whose stem requires support.

I am the true vine, and my Father is the vinedresser. Every branch in me that does not bear fruit he takes away, and every branch that does bear fruit he prunes, that it may bear more fruit. **(John 15:1-2)**

Have you ever felt pruned? Sometimes we grumble and blame God for things that are happening in our lives. But have we ever considered the fact that He may be pruning us so that we will bear more fruit? It hurts to be pruned, but the end result is worth the pain. We just need to remember this in the middle of the pain.

Abide in me, and I in you. As the branch cannot bear fruit by itself, unless it abides in the vine, neither can you, unless you abide in me. **(John 15:4)**

Abide: obey, observe, follow, stick to, stand by, accept, go along with, acknowledge, respect

Today we so often want instant pudding rather than the real thing. But with God abiding is the real thing. The closer we walk with Him and the more time we spend with Him, the more we know about Him, the more we abide in Him.

I am the vine; you are the branches. Whoever abides in me and I in him, he it is that bears much fruit, for apart from me you can do nothing. **(John 5:5)**

Some of the most important instructions in the Word are, "Apart from me you can do nothing." In our society that believes, "I will do it my way!" we do not understand this statement. No wonder things are in such a mess. Let's begin to abide in the vine and see what a difference it will make in our lives.

"He is the Vine!"

DAY 232

"Attributes of God from A to Z" (W)

"He is the Word!"

In the beginning was the Word, and the Word was with God, and the Word was God…In him was life, and the life was the light of men. **(John 1:1 & 4)**

The Word has been manifest to us through the Father, Son and Holy Spirit. Prophets of old proclaimed the Word. The Word has come in dreams and visions. Many times, the word will come to us in a still small voice or a thought. God is still speaking to His people. He tells us to be still and know that He is God.

It is written, "Man shall not live by bread alone, but by every word that comes from the mouth of God." **(Matthew 4:4)** Jesus demonstrated for us the way to fight the devil. Speak the Word of God to him and he will flee.

That evening they brought to him many who were oppressed by demons, and he cast out the spirits with a word and healed all who were sick. **(Matthew 8:16)**

Truly, truly, I say to you, if anyone keeps my Word, he will never see death. **(John 8:51)** We need to hide the word in our hearts. The more of the word that is hidden in our hearts the easier it is to know and believe the truth which will set us free.

Sanctify them in the truth; your word is truth. **(John 17:17)**

So, then faith comes from hearing, and hearing through the word of Christ. **(Romans 10:17)** When was the last time you needed a little extra faith? Just pick up the Word and speak it. Watch and see what God will do.

And take the helmet of salvation, and the sword of the Spirit, which is the word of God, praying at all times in the Spirit. **(Ephesians 6:17-18)** Part of putting on the whole armor of God is picking up the sword of the Spirit and using it.

For the word of God is living and active, sharper than any two-edged sword, piercing to the division of soul and of spirit, of joints and of marrow, and discerning the thoughts and intentions of the heart. **(Hebrews 4:12)**

So, the next time the enemy assaults you,

"Speak the Word!"

DAY 233

"Attributes of God from A to Z" (X)

"He is X-cellent!" (Now be lenient with my spelling!)

Praise him for his mighty deeds; praise him according to his excellent greatness! **(Psalm 150:2)**

Excellent: superb, outstanding, magnificent, marvelous, wonderful, matchless, splendid, awesome, perfect, supreme, superior

This also comes from the Lord of hosts; he is wonderful in counsel and excellent in wisdom. **(Isaiah 28:29)** How can we describe the Lord? He is beyond words.

Having become as much superior to angels as the name he has inherited is more excellent than theirs. For to which of the angels did God ever say, "You are my Son, today I have begotten you?"' **(Hebrews 1:4-5)**

Declare his glory among the nations, his marvelous works among all the peoples! For great is the Lord, and greatly to be praised, and he is to be feared above all gods. **(I Chronicles 16:24-25)** He is excellent!

As for me, I would seek God, and to God would I commit my cause, who does great things and unsearchable, marvelous things without number. **(Job 5:8-9)**

All we have to do is look around and we will see who God is and what He has done for each of us. He created us in His image. He gave us His Holy Spirit to lead and guide us into all truth. He will never leave us comfortless. He is always with us. He has a plan for each of us that will lead us into eternity. There is not one thing that God has left undone. He is excellent in all of His ways!

But you are a chosen race, a royal priesthood, a holy nation, a people for his own possession, that you may proclaim the excellencies of him who called you out of darkness into his marvelous light. **(1 Peter 2:9)**

Today let us spend a few minutes thinking about how excellent our God is and how much He loves us and wants us to draw close to Him.

"He is X-cellent in all of His Ways!"

DAY 234

"ATTRIBUTES OF GOD FROM A TO Z" (Y)

"He is Yahweh!"

God said to Moses, "I Am Who I Am." (Exodus 3:14)

Who is Yahweh?

He has no beginning.

He has no end.

He is absolute reality.

He is utterly independent. What He says He will do.

Everything that is not God depends totally on God. Think about that statement. We can do nothing apart from God. Every breath we take is a gift from Him. Everything in the universe is controlled by Him.

Nothing compares to God. He is altogether lovely.

He is constant. He is the same yesterday, today and forever. We can trust Him and His word.

He has the highest standard of truth, goodness, and beauty. Our standards are nothing compared to His. The outward expression of this is the sacrifice of His only Son on the cross. The ultimate gift to us.

God does what He pleases. He is not influenced by any other. He is totally in charge. He knows the beginning from the end of everything.

He holds the universe in His hands. That is a literal statement. Think what would happen if He let loose of it and everything in it.

He is Yahweh the Lord God Almighty! The King of Kings! The Lord of Lords! The Only True God!

Prayerfully, He is your Lord!

"He is Yahweh!"

DAY 235

"ATTRIBUTES OF GOD FROM A TO Z" (Z)

"He is Zealous!"

Of the increase of his government and of peace there will be no end, on the throne of David and over his kingdom, to establish it and to uphold it with justice and with righteousness from this time forth and forevermore. The zeal of the Lord of hosts will do this. (Isaiah 9:7)

Zeal: passion, love, fervor, fire, devotion, eagerness, enthusiasm

O Lord, your hand is lifted up, but they do not see it. Let them see your zeal for your people and be ashamed. (Isaiah 26:11) I am guilty of saying, "Where are you Lord?" when I do not see an immediate answer to a prayer or see someone hurting or a tragedy. Give me eyes to see You in every part of my life. Let Your zeal consume me!

My zeal consumes me because my foes forget your words. (Psalm 119:139) Does it ever bother you when someone rejects what you believe? It hurts me to the core, especially when I am trying to share the Holy Spirit and what a marvelous gift, He is to each of us.

He put on righteousness as a breastplate, and a helmet of salvation on his head; he put on garments of vengeance for clothing and wrapped himself in zeal as a cloak. (Isaiah 59:17) I think of Paul and the other apostles and the zeal that they had. They were not afraid to say it as it is. They were not afraid of being rejected and they were.

For zeal for your house has consumed me, and the reproaches of those who reproach you have fallen on me. (Psalm 69:9) It is not hurting me when I am reproached for the gospel, but it hurts the Lord. If I can only keep this in mind and not take every reproach as an affront to me, I will be free to share the Good News!

100 attributes and that is only the beginning. I hope you have enjoyed spending this time reflecting on the goodness of God.

"Let His Zeal Consume You!"

THE MIRACLES OF JESUS

DAY 236

There are 35 miracles recorded in the New Testament. I am wondering if these are a shadow and a type or an admonition for us? We know that the first one is for sure. So, let's go exploring and see what your think. John recorded 8 miracles and only 1 was written in the other gospels. I wonder why?

Matthew 8:16 says, *That evening they brought to him many who were oppressed by demons, and he cast out the spirits with a word and healed all who were sick. This was to fulfill what was spoken by the prophet Isaiah: "He took our illnesses and bore our disease."*

I have heard it said that there are only 40 different types of illness and that by His stripes we are healed. If so, He has taken care of all our diseases on the cross.

The first miracle recorded in the New Testament is the Wedding at Cana. Only John records this miracle. Remember John saw the beginning from the end in Rev.

On the 3rd day there was a wedding at Cana...Everyone serves the good wine first...but you have kept the good wine until now. **(John 2:1 & 10)**

Hallelujah! For the Lord, our God the Almighty reigns. Let us rejoice and exult and give him the glory, for the marriage of the Lamb has come, and his Bride has made herself ready. **(Revelation 19: 6-7)**

We begin with a wedding, and we go into eternity with another wedding. The first wedding is an appetizer and the second is the real thing. I love what Mary said to the servants, *Whatever he tells you to do, do it.* **(John 2:5)**

Her words ring through my mind many times. Whatever He tells you to do, do it!

And the angel said to me, "Write this: Blessed are those who are invited to the marriage supper of the Lamb." **(Revelation 19:9)**

If we have invited Jesus into our hearts and confess him as our Lord and Savior, we will be part of this marriage supper.

DAY 237

The 2nd miracle recorded that Jesus preformed was healing the official's son. This also was only spoken of in John's gospel. Here is what I find interesting. Jesus' ministry had just begun and here was an official already convinced that Jesus had healing power.

When this man heard that Jesus had come from Judea to Galilee, he went to him and asked him to come down and heal his son, for he was at the point of death. **(John 4:47)**

We are not told what was wrong with the son, only he was at the point of death and the official was desperate. In the 2nd miracle the illness was not specified. But Jesus is the healer. Have you ever been there? I am sure some of us have.

So, Jesus said to him, "Unless you see signs and wonders you will not believe." **(V 48)**

This is still the question that Jesus is asking us today. *Have you believed because you have seen me? Blessed are those who have not seen and yet have believed.* **(John 20:29)** Sometimes I cry out for the Lord to just give me a sign. "Become real to me today, Lord." If we are honest, we have all done this.

The key here is the persistence of the official. Jesus has said, *Ask and keep on asking and it will be given to you; seek and keep on seeking and you will find; knock and keep on knocking, and it will be opened to you.* **(Matthew 7:7)** (my version) Sometimes, we have to keep on keeping on.

The official said to him, "Sir, come down before my child dies." Jesus said to him, "Go, your son will live." **(V 49-50)**

Now here is the 2nd key to this miracle. *The man believed the word that Jesus spoke to him and went on his way.* **(V 50)**

The result was that - *He himself believed, and all his household.* **(V 53)** Jesus had more in mind than just healing the son. Salvation came to that whole family.

DAY 238

It is interesting in the New Testament Jesus drives out evil spirits five times and He heals the blind five times. These two events are recorded more than any other healings. I am wondering why? Does our blindness cause us to allow things into our lives that we wouldn't allow if we could see the outcome?

And in the synagogue, there was a man who had the spirit of an unclean demon, and he cried out with a loud voice, "Ha! What have you to do with us, Jesus of Nazareth? Have you come to destroy us? I know who you are – the Holy One of God." But Jesus rebuked him, saying, "Be silent and come out of him!" And when the demon had thrown him down in their midst, he came out of him, having done him no harm. And they were all amazed and said to one another, "What is this word? For with authority and power he commands the unclean spirits, and they come out!" **(Luke 4:33-36 or Mark 1:23-27)**

The demons know who Jesus is. He is the Holy One of God. They know He has more power than they do. He says, *The thief comes only to steal and kill and destroy. I came that they may have life and have it abundantly.* **(John 10:10)**

(Having done him no harm.) **So, if the Son sets you free, you will be free indeed. (John 8:36)** This man had been bound by the devil. He no longer was able to react on his own. He was possessed. He had allowed evil to enter in and it had consumed him. But Jesus! Never believe that anything is impossible with Jesus. He is able to do exceedingly, abundantly more than we ask or think.

Every miracle that He performed had a purpose. Yes, it was to heal but it had a far-reaching purpose. Each miracle was to set someone free so that they and others might believe that Jesus is the Christ, the Son of the Living God, and that He wants to draw all men unto Himself. We think in the here and now. We think in creature comforts, but Jesus thinks in the beyond. He would have none perish but all come to eternal life. He speaks with authority and power. His love is able to heal the very worst of sinners. He reaches out to whosoever will. He is God!

DAY 239

The 4th miracle Jesus performed was healing Peter's Mother-in-Law who was sick with a fever. 1st Jesus showed us the beginning from the end with the wedding at Cana. Then he healed the official's son. We have no idea what was wrong with the son which makes me wonder if the reason it doesn't say is because Jesus wants us to know He is the healer regardless of the need. Then He drove out evil spirits from a man in Capernaum. Before Adam and Eve sinned, there were no evil spirits able to touch them. The spirits know Jesus and that their time on earth is short. There will be no sin or sickness in heaven. Now we come to Peter's mother-in-law.

And when Jesus entered Peter's house, he saw his mother-in-law lying sick with a fever. He touched her hand, and the fever left her, and she rose and began to serve him. (Matthew 8:14-15, Mark 1:30-31, Luke 4:38-39)

Luke says he rebuked the fever in the same way he rebuked the evil spirit. God never intended for sin and sickness to be part of our lives. He wanted us to love Him, serve Him and obey Him. Sin and sickness are not His fault.

His kingdom shall be an everlasting kingdom, and all dominions shall serve and obey him. (Daniel 7:27)

As in each miracle the healing was marvelous, but the purpose behind the healing was what was most important. Peter's mother-in-law immediately got up and began to serve Jesus.

These are the ones coming out of the great tribulation. They have washed their robes and made them white in the blood of the Lamb. Therefore, they are before the throne of God and serve him day and night in his temple. (Revelation 7:14-15)

Has healing brought service in our lives? When Jesus has answered our prayers do we immediately get up and begin to serve Him or do we give Him a small thanks and instantly forget what He has done? Lord forgive us!

DAY 240

For God so loved the world, that he gave his only Son, that whoever believes in him shall not perish but have eternal life. For God did not send his Son into the world to condemn the world, but in order that the world might be saved. **(John 3:16 & 17)**

We can all repeat this scripture, but do we realize that Jesus whole purpose coming to earth was to save you and me. The 5th miracle performed by Jesus really emphasizes this point. Let's look at it now.

And when he had finished speaking, he said to Simon, "Put out into the deep and let down your nets for a catch." And Simon answered, "Master, we toiled all night and took nothing! But at your word I will let down the nets." And when they had done this, they enclosed a large number of fish, and their nets were breaking. They signaled to their partners in the other boat to come and help them. And they came and filled both boats, so that they began to sink. But when Simon Peter saw it, he fell down at Jesus' knees, saying "Depart from me, for I am a sinful man, O Lord." (Luke 5:4-8)

This scripture is full of meaning. 1st Peter was obedient even though he was a seasoned fisherman. 2nd At Jesus word he let down the nets. 3rd His obedience brought a huge catch. 4th He shared what he had caught. 5th Finally he realized his own sinful nature and confessed Jesus as Lord.

Follow me, and I will make you fishers of men. Immediately they left their nets and followed him. **(Matthew 4:19)**

The fish were not Jesus' primary goal. Just as Peter's mother-in-law rose and began to serve, the disciples were to switch professions and become fishers of men. As they obeyed and shared the word, they received a huge catch.

So those who received his word were baptized, and there were added that day about three thousand souls. **(Acts 2:41)** What are we fishing for?

DAY 241

And behold, a leper came to him and knelt before him, saying, "Lord, if you will, you can make me clean." And Jesus stretched out his hand and touched him, saying, "I will, be clean." And immediately his leprosy was cleansed. And Jesus said to him, "See that you say nothing to anyone, but go, show yourself to the priest and offer the gift that Moses commanded, for a proof to them." (Matthew 8:2-4; Mark 1:40-45 and Luke 5:12-14)

It is interesting in Mark it says, *"Jesus was moved with pity."* Does compassion have anything to do with healing? Jesus warned him to say nothing to anyone but go show the priest. In Mark it says, *But he went out and began to talk freely about it, and to spread the news, so that Jesus could no longer openly enter a town, but was out in desolate places, and people were coming to him from every quarter.*

What can we learn from this miracle? 1st the man said, "If you will" and Jesus said, "I will." Jesus wants everyone whole physically, mentally, emotionally, and spiritually. That is His desire, and it will be completely accomplished in heaven. There is hope for everyone who believes in Him.

2nd He told the man to go to the priest and say nothing on the way. Now Jesus knew he was not going to obey. He was so excited to be healed that he had to tell everyone he saw. When Jesus does something in our lives do, we immediately go and tell others? We should. We should constantly be bragging about our Savior and Lord.

3rd because he did not obey, *Jesus could no longer enter a town but was out in desolate places, and people were coming to Him from every quarter.* I like the fact that people had to come to Him. It meant that they really wanted to be with Him. It took effort on their part. So, from this miracle we see that Jesus cares about us and our response should be excitement. It costs us something to follow Him. We need to seek Him with all of our hearts, and we will be found by Him.

DAY 242

When he had entered Capernaum, a centurion came forward to him, appealing to him, "Lord, my servant is lying paralyzed at home, suffering terribly." And he said to him, "I will come and heal him." But the centurion replied, "Lord, I am not worthy to have you come under my roof, but only say the word, and my servant will be healed. For I too am a man under authority, with soldiers under me. And I say to one, Go, and he goes, and to another, Come, and he comes and to my servant, Do this, and he does it." (Mathew 8:5-9 & Luke 7:6-8)

Jesus said, I tell you, not even in Israel have I found such faith. (Luke 7:9)

What can we learn from this miracle? We know the servant was healed the moment Jesus spoke the word. We also know that it wasn't necessary for Jesus to lay hands on the servant for him to be healed.

I believe what Jesus was trying to show the people was the importance of faith. The centurion had no trouble believing that Jesus could and would heal his servant. He did not need a great display of power. He did not beg and plead. He said, *Say the word and let my servant be healed.* At that very moment, the servant was healed.

Jesus said, *Whatever you ask in prayer, you will receive if you have faith.* (Mathew 21:22)

And Jesus answered them, "Truly, I say to you, whoever says to this mountain, be taken up and thrown into the sea, and does not doubt in his heart, but believes that what he says will come to pass, it will be done for him." (Mark 11:22-23)

Were these promised only for the early disciples, or can we still take them to the bank today? Our answer may determine our power in prayer. It is not easy to believe what we cannot see. This is the reason many do not believe Christianity. We must put our faith in the unseen in order to see. The centurion understood this, and the results were amazing.

DAY 243

And the power of the Lord was with him to heal. And behold, (love that) some men were bringing on a bed a man who was paralyzed, and they were seeking to bring him in and lay him before Jesus, but finding no way to bring him in, because of the crowd, they went up on the roof and let him down with his bed through the tiles into the midst before Jesus. And when he saw their faith, he said, "Man, your sins are forgiven you." ... which is easier to say, "Your sins are forgiven you, or to say, rise and walk? But that you may know that the Son of Man has authority on earth to forgive sins he said to the man who was paralyzed, I say to you, rise, pick up your bed and go home" ...And amazement seized them all, and they glorified God and were filled with awe, saying, "We have seen extraordinary things today." (Luke 5:17-20, 23-26; Matthew 9:1-8 and Mark 3:1-6)

First, I want friends like this man's. They were determined to see their friend healed at any expense. They totally believed that Jesus was the healer and that He was going to heal their friend. No doubts! This is a key to healing.

Second, when Jesus saw their faith…I don't know whether this included the man's faith or not. But for sure Jesus saw the carrier's faith. This tells me that sometimes it is the faith of those who are standing by that brings a miracle. Sometimes the person needing a miracle is just too overwhelmed. Jesus understands!

Then it seems like in this particular case the man had sins that needed attention before the healing could take place. Does this mean all sickness is because of sin? Definitely not. But his sins had paralyzed him. Unconfessed sin can do this.

Then Jesus told him to pick up his bed and go home. The man had a part in this healing. He was to stand up, pick up and go home. If he said, "I can't!" I wonder what would have happened.

The result was that that all the people glorified God and were filled with awe. Even though we know Jesus is God, they did not understand this yet. What is important is that they did not glorify the man Jesus, but God!

DAY 244

Again, he entered the synagogue, and a man was there with a withered hand. And they watched Jesus, to see whether he would heal him on the Sabbath, so that they might accuse him. And he said to the man with the withered hand, "Come here." And he said to them, "Is it lawful on the Sabbath to do good or to do harm, to save life or to kill?" But they were silent. And he looked around at them with anger, grieved at their hardness of heart, and said to the man, "Stretch out your hand." He stretched it out, and his hand was restored. (Mark 3:1-5; Matthew 12:9-14 and Luke 6:6-11)

It is interesting that the man did not ask for healing. Also, it is interesting that it was in the synagogue, the very place that we should expect miracles. It makes me wonder if our hearts haven't become hardened in the church. Do we expect God to move or are we looking around for someone or something to criticize? Did the music not suit our taste? Was the sermon boring? Did someone not speak to me? Was I the only one with or without a mask on? You fill in the blank checking your own heart. I am guilty. Forgive me Lord!

It wasn't so much the healing of the man's hand, but the healing of man's heart. Did you know that the word heart is found 714 times in the Bible? It must be a very important part of our body.

Let not steadfast love and faithfulness forsake you; bind them around your neck; write them on the tablet of your heart. (Proverbs 3:3)

Sadly, this miracle did not change the Pharisees for they went out and immediately held counsel with the Herodians against Him, how to destroy Him. Church is over. Does praise or criticism fill your vehicle? Oops! I am meddling.

Let us draw near with a true heart in full assurance of faith, with our hearts sprinkled clean from an evil conscience and our bodies washed with pure water. Let us hold fast the confession of our hope without wavering, for he who promised is faithful. (Hebrews 10:22-23) I have some repenting to do.

DAY 245

As he drew near to the gate of the town, (Nain) behold, a man who had died was being carried out, the only son of his mother, and she was a widow, and a considerable crowd from the town was with her. And when the Lord saw her, he had compassion on her and said to her, "Do not weep." Then he came up and touched the bier, and the bearers stood still. And he said, "Young man, I say to you. Arise." And the dead man sat up and began to speak, and Jesus gave him to his mother. (*Luke* 7:11-15)

It is interesting that this is only mentioned in Luke and yet it was a huge miracle. We know that the disciples were with Him. We also know a person was unclean if he touched a dead body. And we know that he was a young man. In those days there was not social security, so the mother was left destitute plus alone.

Jesus had compassion on her. Many of Jesus's miracles were done out of compassion.

For the Lord has comforted his people and will have compassion on his afflicted. (Isaiah 49:13)

But Luke goes on to say, *Fear seized them all, and they glorified God, saying, "A great prophet has arisen among us! And God has visited his people."* (V 16)

The result of the miracle was that fear seized them and they glorified God. Many of the miracles that Jesus performed brought the people to a sense of fear and awe. I wish we could say that today. But because we have all sorts of ways to be healed, I am afraid most of the time we give glory to the wrong source. Ultimately God is always the healer regardless of the method used.

Finally, *And this report about him spread through the whole of Judea and all the surrounding country.* (V 17)

Go tell it on the mountain, over the hills and everywhere. That Jesus Christ is Lord!

DAY 246

On that day, when evening had come, he said to them, "Let us go across to the other side." And leaving the crowd, they took him with them in the boat, just as he was. And other boats were with him. And a great windstorm arose, and the waves were breaking into the boat, so that the boat was already filling. But he was in the stern, asleep on the cushion. And they woke him and said to him, "Teacher, do you not care that we are perishing?" And he awoke and rebuked the wind and said to the sea, "Peace! Be still!" And the wind ceased, and there was a great calm. He said to them. "Why are you so afraid? Have you still no faith?" And they were filled with great fear and said to one another, "Who then is this, that even the wind and the sea obey him?" (**Mark 4:35-41, Matthew 8:23-27 and Luke 8:22-25**)

1st Jesus said, *Let us go across to the other side.* When I pray and I hear God speak I need to instantly obey. What He says He will do. The disciples were assured that they would reach the other side because Jesus said so.

2nd I wonder what was meant by *Just as he was.* He was worn out. He had just taught them the parable of the Sower, a lamp under a basket, the seed growing and the mustard seed. He knew that they still did not understand. Exhausting!

3rd There were other boats with them. They also were fighting the storm. They must have realized that Jesus spoke the word and the storm ceased. What happened in their hearts?

4th *Teacher do you not care that we are perishing?* This really spoke to me. Most of my prayers are about me and mine. They are about what I need, what I want and what is bothering me. They do not center on who He is but who I am.

5th *He said to them, "Why are you so afraid? Have you still no faith?"* Can't you hear your mother saying, "How many times do I have to tell you?" I am sure Jesus was more tired of their unbelief than He was in His physical body.

Today is the 1st day of the rest of your life. Put your trust in Him. Believe Him! He is able to do exceeding, abundantly more than you ask or think.

DAY 247

And when Jesus had stepped out of the boat, immediately there met him out of the tombs a man with an unclean spirit. He lived among the tombs. And no one could bind him anymore, not even with chains, for he had often been bound with shackles and chains, but he wrenched the chains apart, and he broke the shackles in pieces. No one had the strength to subdue him. Night and day among the tombs and on the mountains he was always crying out and cutting himself with stones. And when he saw Jesus from afar, he ran and fell down before him. And crying out with a loud voice, he said, "What have you to do with me, Jesus, Son of the Most High God? I adjure you by God, do not torment me." For he was saying to him, "Come out of the man, you unclean spirit!" And Jesus asked him, "What is your name?" He replied, "My name is Legion, for we are many." And he begged him earnestly not to send them out of the country…and the unclean spirits came out and entered the pigs; and the herd, numbering about two thousand, rushed down the steep bank into the sea and drowned in the sea. (Mark 5: 1-13, Matthew 8:28-32 and Luke 8:26-33)

1st Sometimes we are asked to do things that require more faith than we think we have. Like Jesus we must get out of the boat. No miracle happens apart from faith and faith is an action.

2nd Evil spirits are strong. They are not something to play around with. Remember when Jesus said, *"This kind comes out with prayer and fasting."* This is serious business.

3rd The man would cry out and cut himself. I do not believe he wanted to be demon possessed but something had happened, and he had allowed these evil spirits in. Then the spirits began to speak to Jesus. They knew who He was, Son of the Most High God. *Even the demons believe – and shudder!* (James 2:19)

4th Spirits have names. My question is, "Can a spirit be destroyed or is it only transferred to another place?" If you have ever messed with an "Ouija Board" or been to a fortune teller, you need to confess this and ask God's forgiveness.

DAY 248

While he was saying this, a synagogue leader came and knelt before him and said, "My daughter has just died. But come and put your hand on her, and she will live." Jesus got up and went with him, and so did his disciples. Just then a woman who had been subject to bleeding for twelve years came up behind him and touched the edge of his cloak. She said to herself, "If I only touch his cloak, I will be healed." Jesus turned and saw her. "Take heart daughter," he said, "your faith has healed you." And the woman was healed at that moment. (Matthew 9:19-22)

Interestingly in both instances it was the faith of the person that produced healing. They believed Jesus could and would heal. The woman said to herself, *If only I touch his cloak.* The synagogue leader said, *But come and put your hand on her, and she will live.* When we pray in faith God is honored. When we pray in fear and unbelief we are spitting in the wind. Now that sounds rather cruel, but I honestly believe God honors faith. The word says *Without faith it is impossible to please him.*

I wonder how many times I have prayed and not really believed that anything was going to happen, and it didn't. Then I blamed God because he didn't answer. Speaking and believing are really not the same. The word says He is a rewarder of those who diligently seek Him. Believe it or not He really cares for each of us and has our best interest at heart. Sometimes the answer is not instantaneous, but it will come if we wait in faith.

So today maybe we need to touch the hem of His garment. The closer we walk, the closer we are to His hem. I really want to reach that place where I can touch the hem of His garment and look up into His face. That will be life changing. I am hoping it happens before I stand face to face with Him.

"Turn your eyes upon Jesus. Look full in His wonderful face. And the things of earth will grow strangely dim in the light of His glory and grace."

DAY 249

While Jesus was still speaking, someone came from the house of Jairus, the synagogue leader. "Your daughter is dead," he said. "Don't bother the teacher anymore." Hearing this, Jesus said to Jairus, "Don't be afraid; just believe, and she will be healed." When he arrived at the house of Jairus, he did not let anyone go in with him except Peter, John and James, and the child's father and mother. Meanwhile, all the people were wailing and mourning for her. "Stop wailing," Jesus said. "She is not dead but asleep." They laughed at him, knowing that she was dead. But he took her by the hand and said, "My child, get up!" Her spirit returned, and at once she stood up. Then Jesus told them to give her something to eat. Her parents were astonished, but he ordered them not to tell anyone what had happened. (Luke 8:49-56, Matthew 9:23-26 and Mark 5:35-43)

Jesus had stopped on His way to Jairus' house to heal the woman with the issue of blood. He is never in a hurry. Then He heard all the negative reports. The people laughed when He said, "*She is not dead but asleep*." This place was full of unbelief. No wonder He only took those with Him who would believe. Even the parents were astonished when she stood up.

It is interesting that when she stood up, Jesus told them to give her something to eat. This reminds me of the disciples on the seashore after Jesus was resurrected and Jesus was fixing breakfast. This was total proof that a miracle had happened. She was dead but now alive. Jesus is the Lord of the living, not the dead.

Again, He told the parents not to tell anyone. Have you ever noticed when you share a miracle most people do not believe what you are saying? They attribute it to anyone but God. Why?

Again, Jesus said, "*Do not be afraid. Just believe*." Now faith comes by hearing and hearing by the Word of God. So many times, we need "Now faith". Is Jesus who He says He is? Will He do what He says He will do? Will we believe before we see? We need more "Now faith!"

DAY 250

As Jesus went on from there, two blind men followed him, calling out, "Have mercy on us, Son of David!" When he had gone indoors, the blind men came to him, and he asked them, "Do you believe that I am able to do this?" "Yes Lord," they replied. Then he touched their eyes and said, "According to your faith let it be done to you;" and their sight was restored. Jesus warned them sternly, "See that no one knows about this." But they went out and spread the news about him all over the region. (Matthew 9:27-31)

What stands out to me is not that they pursued Jesus, which they did. But His question to them, *"Do you believe that I am able to do this?"* This is the first recorded time that Jesus healed a blind person. So, they did not have a lot of previous knowledge to go on. We know that prior to this Jesus had healed many sick and oppressed. (Matthew 8:16-17) but we are not sure what their problems were.

Many times, I have heard people say, "I believe Jesus is able, but I am not sure He will heal me." Evidently these men were totally convinced that Jesus not only could but would heal them. They had followed Him. They pursued Him. They believed Him. Then Jesus said, *"According to your faith, let it be done to you."*

I remember reading a Watchman Nee book where he was praying for a desk, chair, and a bicycle. He had complete faith that Jesus would answer him. When he didn't get what he had requested, Watchman asked why? There is nothing wrong with asking "why?" The Lord asked what kind of chair? What kind of desk? What kind of bicycle? Sometimes we are too generic. These men knew what they wanted and believed that Jesus would answer their request and He did!

Jesus said, *"See that no one knows this."* It is kind of like keeping a secret. Don't tell anyone but we can't resist. We tell just one person and pretty soon the whole world knows. I wonder if this was Jesus' motive. I guess we will have to wait until we see him to find out. Remember believing is receiving!

DAY 251

While they were going out, a man who was demon-possessed and could not talk was brought to Jesus. And when the demon was driven out, the man who had been mute spoke. The crowd was amazed and said, "Nothing like this has ever been seen in Israel." But the Pharisees said, "It is by the prince of demons that he drives out demons." (Matthew 9:32-33)

What amazes me about human nature is that we can always find a reason for things that happen miraculously excluding Jesus. Have you ever noticed when you share a miracle that has happened in your life people will say "but"? Nothing in life happens apart from Jesus' knowledge of it.

In this particular miracle, the Pharisees said, *"It is by the prince of demons that he drives out demons"* Just think about that for moment. Why would a demon drive out a demon? That doesn't even make sense.

It is time we begin to give Jesus credit for all of the marvelous things that He does in our lives. Thinking back over the years, I realize how many times He has saved me from disaster. How many times He has healed me? How many times He has guided me in an important decision. The list goes on and on. The question is not what He has done, but how I have responded to His mercy in my life? Have I taken the time to acknowledge His goodness, or have I shrugged it off to fate or my own ability?

Let's take time to reflect on the goodness of God. Let's take time to recall all the things He has done for us. Let's give Him credit where credit is due which is in everything.

Rejoice always, pray continually, give thanks in all circumstances; for this is God's will for you in Christ Jesus. (1 Thessalonians 5:17-18)

Don't be a Pharisee but be a believer. Believe He is able to do abundantly above all you ask or think.

DAY 252

Pool of Bethesda – *Here a great number of disabled people used to lie-the blind, the lame, the paralyzed. One who was there had been an invalid for thirty-eight years. When Jesus saw him lying there and learned that he had been in this condition for a long time, he asked him, "Do you want to get well?" "Sir," the invalid replied, "I have no one to help me into the pool when the water stirred. While I am trying to get in, someone else goes down ahead of me." Then Jesus said to him, "Get up! Pick up your mat and walk." At once the man was cured; he picked up his mat and walked...Later Jesus found him at the temple and said to him, "See, you are well again. Stop sinning or something worse may happen to you."* (John 5:1-15) Interestingly, this is the only place this miracle is recorded.

What stands out to you as you read this? The first thing I noticed was Jesus' question. *"Do you want to get well?"* On first reading we would all say, "Of course we want to get well." But let's think about it for a minute. For 38 years this man has done nothing but sit by the pool and feel sorry for himself for he says, *"I have no one to help me into the pool."* Now he will have to get a job and be a responsible citizen. What is he qualified to do after 38 years? How old is he? It does not say he was born paralyzed. This is really a profound question. *"Do you want to get well?"*

I think the same thing could be asked to many of us. We enjoy our misery even though we are miserable. I hate being in a group where the total discussion is aches and pains. This is one reason I hate Covid. We cannot turn on the TV without being accosted by negative reports. I wonder how quickly all of this would end if we did not feed into it?

There is no fear in love. But perfect love drives out fear because fear has to do with punishment. The one who fears is not made perfect in love. (1 John 4:18)

At the moment, most of us are living in fear. The question is, "Do we want to be healed or do we want to wallow in fear?" I want to go on with my life. Let's live in faith!

DAY 253

Jesus said to Philip, "Where are we to buy bread, so that these people may eat?"
He said this to test him for he himself knew what he would do. Philip answered
him, "Two hundred denarii worth of bread would not be enough for each of them
to get a little." (A denarius was a day's wages for a laborer) One of his disciples,
Andrew, Simon Peter's brother, said to him, "There is a boy here who has five
barley loaves and two fish, but what are they for so many?" Jesus said, "Have the
people sit down" …So the men sat down, about five thousand in number. (plus,
women & children) Jesus then took the loaves, and when he had given thanks,
he distributed them to those who were seated. So also, the fish, as much as they
wanted. And when they had eaten their fill, he told his disciples, "Gather up the
left-over fragments, that nothing may be lost." So, they gathered them up and
filled twelve baskets with fragments from the five barley loaves left by those who
had eaten. **(John 6:1-15, Matthew 14:13-21 and Luke 9:10-17)**

Jesus takes the impossible and makes it possible. But in the process, He has a lesson for each of us to learn. Nothing is too small for Jesus to multiply, and He is
not wasteful. He will use whatever or whoever to accomplish His purpose. One
little boy with 5 barley loaves and 2 fish fed 5,000 plus. I would like to think the
little boy came up to Jesus with his lunch pail and offered to share. Think how this
changed his life. His small offering. Sometimes I think we look at what we have to
give and minimize our gift. Jesus is not looking for the largest offering or the most
expensive. He is looking for a willing heart.

Jesus said, *"Gather up the left-over fragments, that nothing may be lost."* He uses
every gift we are willing to give Him to the fullest. He treasures our offering and,
in the process, we are filled to overflowing. Never think you have nothing to offer
because we all do. It may be a word of encouragement, a batch of cookies, a listening ear, a ride to the doctor, a hug. You fill in the blank_____.

Today, ***if you hear his voice, do not harden your hearts.*** **(Psalm 95:7-8)** Pick up
your lunch box and head toward the throne room. Jesus is waiting.

DAY 254

When evening came, he was there alone, but the boat by this time was a long way from the land, beaten by the waves, for the wind was against them. And in the fourth watch of the night, he came to them walking on the sea. (between 3 and 6 a.m.) But when the disciples saw him walking on the sea, they were terrified, and said, "It is a ghost!" and they cried out in fear. But immediately Jesus spoke to them, saying, "Take heart; it is I. Do not be afraid." And Peter answered him, "Lord, if it is you, command me to come to you on the water." He said, "Come." So, Peter got out of the boat and walked on the water and came to Jesus. But when he saw the wind, he was afraid, and beginning to sink he cried out, "Lord, save me." Jesus immediately reached out his hand and took hold of him saying to him, "O you of little faith, why did you doubt?" And when they got into the boat, the wind ceased. (Matthew 14:22-32, Mark 6:45-52 and John 6:16-21)

This story made a profound difference in my life. I was teetering between belief and unbelief. I realized that I could not have one foot in the boat and one foot dangling in the water. I needed to step out of the boat in faith. Jesus said to me, "O you of little faith, why did you doubt?" Many times, I think Jesus is saying this to all of us. "Trust me! Step out into the deep. Keep your eyes on me or you will sink." It is always when the wind is blowing the hardest and the waves are the highest that our faith is tested.

Jesus had prefaced this story with, *"Go to the other side."* If He had not thought they could get there. He would not have told them to go. When Jesus tells us to do something, He also offers the means for us to do it.

Peter walked on the water to Jesus. He didn't just take one step, but he began to walk. It was only when he looked down that he began to sink.

If you have faith like a grain of mustard seed, you will say to this mountain, "Move from here to there," and it will move, and nothing will be impossible to you. (Matthew 17:20-21) Let's step out of the boat and walk with Jesus.

DAY 255

A Canaanite woman from that vicinity came to him, crying out, "Lord, Son of David, have mercy on me! My daughter is demon-possessed and suffering terribly." Jesus did not answer a word. So, his disciples came to him and urged him, "Send her away, for she keeps crying out after us." He answered, "I was sent only to the lost sheep of Israel." The woman came and knelt before him. "Lord, help me!" she said. He replied, "It is not right to take the children's bread and toss it to the dogs." "Yes, it is, Lord," she said. "Even the dogs eat the crumbs that fall from their master's table." Then Jesus said to her, "Woman, you have great faith! Your request is granted." And her daughter was healed at that moment. (Matthew 15:22-28 & Mark 7:24-30)

The woman called Him Lord, Son of David. She knew and believed who He was and that He was merciful. She bowed down before Him. She humbled herself. She cried out for help. She was persistent. She had great faith. These are all qualities that Jesus is looking for in His believers.

Demon possessed people suffer terribly. We see this every time Jesus stops to deliver one. Why anyone would choose Satan over Jesus is beyond my comprehension. There are only two choices in this world. There is no middle ground. Either we worship God, or we worship Satan. *Every good and every perfect gift is from the Father of lights and with Him there is no variation.* (James 1:17) He is good. He desires good for His people.

The fact that Jesus came for the Jews does not diminish the fact that He is for everyone who calls upon His name. This is proven in the scriptures over and over.

I love her analogy. Even the dogs eat the crumbs that fall from their master's table. Even one crumb that falls to the ground is enough to heal her daughter. Her faith puts me to shame. How often have I fallen to my knees and humbled myself before the Lord? How often have I been persistent in prayer?

Lord, forgive me!

DAY 256

There some people brought to him a man who was deaf and could hardly talk, and they begged Jesus to place his hand on him. After he took him aside, away from the crowd, Jesus put his fingers into the man's ears. Then he spit and touched the man's tongue. He looked up to heaven and with a deep sigh said to him, "Ephphatha" (which means Be opened!) At this, the man's ears were opened, his tongue was loosened, and he began to speak plainly. (Mark 7:31-35)

Have you noticed that Jesus did not always heal the same way? He also did not command people to do the same things after their healing. It would seem to me that at one time this man could hear and speak because he began to speak plainly.

After he took him aside, away from the crowd. Often, we notice this. "Why?" I believe when we are praying for people and there are some in the group who do not believe that Jesus will answer our prayers, it become difficult to pray. Look at Jairus. Jesus made everyone stay out of the room but the parents and Peter, James, and John. Outside were all the scoffers. I wonder if part of our unanswered prayers are due to unbelief in the room? What do you think?

Some people brought to him a man. How often do we bring people to Jesus? I am particularly awed by the man that was let down through the roof by his friends. Many scriptures are prefaced with "brought by".

Who introduced you to Jesus? Did one person pursue you? Were you in a group of friends? I was introduced to Jesus by a woman that I did not even like. She was like the hound dog of heaven and never gave up. She came day after day to my home and shared the love of Christ until I finally realized how much love the Father had for me. She didn't give up on me and never did He. I am so thankful to her and to Him! Yes, we are great friends today! Stop and reflect on your salvation. Was another person involved? Take a moment right now to pray for the messenger who brought you to Christ.

DAY 257

During those days, another large crowd gathered. Since they had nothing to eat, Jesus called his disciples to him and said, "I have compassion for these people; they have already been with me three days and have nothing to eat. If I send them home hungry, they will collapse on the way, because some of them have come a long distance." His disciples answered, "But where in this remote place can anyone get enough bread to feed them?" "How many loaves do you have?" Jesus asked. "Seven," they replied. He told the crowd to sit down on the ground. When he had taken the seven loaves and given thanks, he broke them and gave them to his disciples to distribute to the people, and they did so. They had a few small fish as well; he gave thanks for them also and told the disciples to distribute them. The people ate and were satisfied. Afterward the disciples picked up seven basketfuls of broken pieces that were left over. About four thousand were present. **(Mark 8:1-9 and Matthew 15:32-39)**

Jesus always has compassion on His people. These people had been with Him three days. Do you suppose they had slept on the ground? Had He shared with them the whole time they had been there? Did they have porta potties? Just think of the logistics of this gathering. The people were physically and spiritually hungry.

Now we see His faithful disciples, *"But where in this remote place can anyone get enough bread to feed them?"* They and we are slow learners. He had just fed 5,000 plus women and children. Is anything too hard for God?

Jesus said, *"How many loaves do you have?"* "Seven and some small fish." How many did they have the 1st time Jesus fed the 5,000 plus? Five loaves and two fish. He even had more to work with. O ye of little faith. Jesus always takes what is at hand and multiplies it. This time they had seven basketfuls of broken pieces left.

How many times do we have to experience the goodness of God before we put our faith in Him? I ask myself, "What must I see before I will truly believe He is able?" Lord help my unbelief.

DAY 258

They came to Bethsaida, and some people brought a blind man and begged Jesus to touch him. He took the blind man by the hand and led him outside the village. When he had spit on the man's eyes and put his hands on him, Jesus asked, "Do you see anything?" He looked up and said, "I see people; they look like trees walking around." Once more Jesus put his hands on the man's eyes. Then his eyes were opened, his sight was restored, and he saw everything clearly. Jesus sent him home, saying, "Don't even go into the village." (Mark 8:22-26)

Once again, people brought the needy to Jesus. We each have a part in bringing people to Jesus. There are no lone rangers in the Kingdom of God. We are all part of the body and function as a unit.

Once again, He took the blind man outside the village. He is separating belief from unbelief. Remember what He had said in Nazareth, *"I cannot do many miracles here because of your unbelief."*

It is interesting that the man was not completely healed the first time. I sometimes wonder if we give up in prayer too quickly. Was this one way Jesus was showing us to keep on keeping on? We need to sometimes persevere in prayer. Just because it didn't happen immediately, doesn't mean it won't.

The second time Jesus laid hands on the man; he was healed. The man must have had sight at one time because he knew what people looked like. Also, Jesus did not reprimand him like He had several who were healed. This speaks loudly to me that all sickness is not caused by sin. *There is therefore no condemnation to those who are in Christ Jesus!* (Romans 8:1)

Jesus sent him home, saying *"Don't even go into the village."* Again, I wonder why? If I had just been part of this miracle, would I have wanted the whole world to know? I am sure I would! Jesus is still in the healing business. Let's not grow weary in well doing.

DAY 259

As he went along, he saw a man blind from birth. His disciples asked him, "Rabbi, who sinned, this man or his parents, that he was born blind?" "Neither this man nor his parents sinned," said Jesus, "but this happened so that the works of God might be displayed in him. As long as it is day, we must do the works of him who sent me. Night is coming when no one can work. While I am in the world, I am the light of the world." After saying this, he spit on the ground, made some mud with the saliva, and put it on the man's eyes. "Go" he told him, "wash in the pool of Siloam" (this word means "sent"). So, the man went and washed, and came home seeing. (John 9:1-7)

First Jesus emphasized that this man did not sin, nor his parents. If you are fighting with an illness or handicap do not let others condemn you. Only you and God know the reason and maybe only God does. Maybe the works of God are still going to be displayed in you.

Then Jesus says something that does not seem to fit in this passage but is totally true. He is the light of the world. It seems night has come. If I were one of the disciples I would have said, "Huh?" But Jesus never uttered a word without a reason.

Then He put mud on the man's eyes and told him to go. Remember this man is still blind. Again, he must have had friends or family that guided him to the pool of Siloam.

I think the most important part of this scripture is his belief. He was still blind. He had never seen Jesus but obviously he had heard about Him. *"So, I went and washed, and then I could see."* The miracle happened after he obeyed Jesus. I wondered if I would have gone or waited for the miracle and then gone? If I had waited, I do not believe there would have been a miracle. First, we obey and then we see the results. I love the old song, "Trust and obey for there's no other way".

Let's commit to having faith in our hearts and expectation!

DAY 260

When they came to the crowd, a man approached Jesus and knelt before him. "Lord, have mercy on my son," he said. "He often falls into the fire or into the water. I brought him to your disciples, but they could not heal him." "You unbelieving and perverse generation," Jesus replied, "how long shall I stay with you? How long shall I put up with you? Bring the boy here to me." Jesus rebuked the demon, and it came out of the boy, and he was healed at that moment. Then the disciples came to Jesus in private and asked, "Why couldn't we drive it out?" He replied, "Because you have so little faith. Truly I tell you, if you have faith as small as a mustard seed, you can say to this mountain, Move from here to there, and it will move. Nothing will be impossible for you." (Matt. 17:14, Mark 9:14, Luke 9:37)

Jesus had given the disciples power to heal the sick and cast out demons. Now He was seeing if they really believed. The point here isn't so much the healing, which was marvelous, but the unbelief. Jesus said, *"How long shall I put up with you?"*

Mark 16:17 he says, *"And these signs will accompany those who believe: In my name they will drive out demons."*

If we are believers, then we should be able to drive out demons in His name. I guess first we must establish the fact that there are demons on this earth, and they are on the attack. Remember Satan is the god of this world and will be until Jesus comes back.

What is the key here? *"Because you have so little faith."* How do we get this kind of faith? *Now Faith comes by hearing and hearing by the word of God.* I am convinced that faith is progressive. As we believe for little things our faith increases. It is hard to pray for cancer when we can't believe that God will heal a common cold.

If you have faith as small as a mustard seed, you can say to this mountain, "Move from here to there" and it will move. A mustard seed is very small but produces a huge plant. Mustard seed faith will bring the impossible to pass. "Only believe!"

DAY 261

After Jesus and his disciples arrived in Capernaum, the collectors of the two-drachma temple tax came to Peter and asked, "Doesn't your teacher pay the temple tax?" "Yes, he does," he replied. When Peter came into the house, Jesus was the first to speak. "What do you think, Simon?" he asked. "From whom do the kings of the earth collect duty and taxes – from their own children or from others?" "From others," Peter answered. "Then the children are exempt," Jesus said to him. "But so that we may not cause offense, go to the lake and throw out your line. Take the first fish you catch; open its mouth and you will find a four-drachma coin. Take it and give it to them for my tax and yours." (Matthew 17:24-27)

At first glance we say, "Jesus can even get money from a fish." But there is so much more to this passage. Yes, Jesus can provide for our physical needs. He has promised us this.

My God will meet all your needs according to the riches of his glory in Christ Jesus. (Philippians 4:19-20) We can all quote this scripture.

Let's look a little deeper. Jesus knew what Peter was going to ask even before he asked it. He also knows what we need before we ask. But because He wants to fellowship with us, He waits for us to make our request.

Then Jesus said, *"But so that we may not cause offense, go to the lake and throw out your line." (V27)*

"So, give back to Caesar what is Caesar's and to God what is God's." (Matthew 22:21)

Jesus did not rebel against the government. He came to establish the Kingdom of God. I am going to put my foot in my mouth but…I do not think Jesus is about worldly governments. He is totally concerned with drawing all men unto Himself. He in no way tried to overturn the government at that time but submitted to its rules as long as they did not go against God's rules. Have we taken our eyes off our calling and become consumed with the world? God knows what He is doing!

DAY 262

Jesus was driving out a demon that was mute. When the demon left, the man who had been mute spoke, and the crowd was amazed. But some of them said, "By Beelzebul, the prince of demons, he is driving out demons" Others tested him by asking for a sign from heaven. (Luke 22:14-16 and Matthew 12:22-23)

Why would Satan drive out a demon which had control of a man? Satan had the man. That makes no sense if we really think about it. Satan wants to control mankind. He is the god of this world and doesn't want to give up any of his power. But his time is short! Alleluia!

The crowd was amazed but they questioned where the power came from. I believe we are still doing that today. Nothing happens apart from God. When we give credit where credit isn't due, we are refusing to worship the creator of every good and perfect gift.

Satan when tempting Jesus said, *"If you really are the Son of God."* He is still using this phrase today. He is bringing doubt and unbelief into the lives of as many Christians as he can. *"Did God really say?"* Somehow this has got to stop. Either God is God, or He isn't. There is no middle ground. A Christian's life is full of confusion until he or she decides who God really is and what He has done for each of us. He loves us and wants the very best for us. But He wants us to trust and obey. He wants the credit for the things that He does.

Others tested him by asking for a sign from heaven. **In (Galatians 3:3)** he called the people foolish, *"Are you so foolish? After beginning by means of the Spirit, are you now trying to finish by means of the flesh?"*

Why do we always need another sign? We see God do something marvelous in our lives or others and then we say, "Did God really do this or was it" … you fill in the blank. We begin in prayer and end up giving the credit to another. Let's try to give more praise to God and less praise to man. It will make all the difference in the world in our walk.

DAY 263

On a Sabbath Jesus was teaching in one of the synagogues, and a woman was there who had been crippled by a spirit for eighteen years. She was bent over and could not straighten up at all. When Jesus saw her, he called her forward and said to her, "Woman, you are set free from your infirmity." Then he put his hands on her, and immediately she straightened up and praised God. Indignant because Jesus had healed on the Sabbath, the synagogue leader said to the people, "There are six days for work. So come and be healed on those days, not on the Sabbath." The Lord answered him, "You hypocrites! Doesn't each of you on the Sabbath untie your ox or donkey from the stall and lead it out to give it water? Then should not this woman, a daughter of Abraham, who Satan has kept bound for eighteen long years, be set free on the Sabbath day from what bound her?" (Luke 13:10-16)

For eighteen years this woman had been bound by Satan. I wonder why? It is interesting that the woman didn't ask for healing. Jesus saw her and called her out. Sometimes healing is nothing but a Jesus miracle. It has nothing to do with you or me. It is just the mercy of God being manifest in our midst.

First, He told her she was set free from her infirmity and then He laid hands on her, and she was healed. Do you suppose she had to do a little repenting and believing between being told she was healed and actually being healed?

The most important thing in this story is that she believed and praised God. She knew He was the source of her healing.

Now comes the mob! Jesus can and will heal any day of the week. We just need to ask and believe, but the thief always comes to kill, steal, and destroy. This day it was the synagogue leader trying to squash what Jesus had just done. Jesus called him and those who agreed with him hypocrites. They were humiliated, which they should have been, but the people were delighted with all the wonderful things He had done. I look in the mirror and wonder how many times I have condemned something God was doing because it didn't fit into my neat little box of dos and don'ts? Lord help me to be open to whatever You are doing and praise You for it!

DAY 264

One Sabbath, when Jesus went to eat in the house of a prominent Pharisee, he was being carefully watched. There in front of him was a man suffering from abnormal swelling of his body. Jesus asked the Pharisees and experts in the law, "Is it lawful to heal on the Sabbath or not?" But they remained silent. So, taking hold of the man, he healed him and sent him on his way. Then he asked them, "If one of you has a child or an ox that falls into a well on the Sabbath day, will you not immediately pull it out?" And they had nothing to say. (Luke 14:1-6)

Jesus performed two miracles one after the other that spoke of hypocrisy. The Pharisees wanted to find fault in Him, but they had just been humiliated by the miracle of the woman crippled for 18 years. So, they were not too anxious to fall into that trap again. Their silence spoke volumes.

Have you ever wondered why Jesus spent so much time around the Pharisees? He knew that almost all of them would not change their minds. They were definitely set in their ways.

I remember when I first began to really walk with the Lord, I was introduced to many things that I was unfamiliar with. It was a real struggle to contemplate and accept new ideas and theology. I had always been taught a certain way and I didn't know anything else. I will never forget when the Lord spoke to me and said, "Don't kick against the goad!" Besides being awed by hearing His voice, I knew I needed to change instantly. That was a life altering moment. Paul was on the road to Damascus when God spoke this to him. You might want to look it up.

How many times have we all said, "But I have always done it this way." The older we get the more set in our ways we become. It is my way or the highway. I have had to learn to let God be God. Sometimes I have really struggled with things I have read in His Word. Were they only meant for the early church, or can we still believe, "*God is the same, yesterday, today and forever*" I am still in the process of learning and hope I never stop until I stand before the Lord? His Word never changes. So, the changes must be in me!

DAY 265

As he was going into a village, ten men who had leprosy met him. They stood at a distance and called out in a loud voice, "Jesus, Master, have pity on us!" When he saw them, he said, "Go show yourselves to the priests." And as they went, they were cleansed. One of them, when he saw he was healed, came back, praising God in a loud voice. He threw himself at Jesus' feet and thanked him-and he was a Samaritan. Jesus asked, "Were not all ten cleansed? Where are the other nine? Has no one returned to give praise to God except this foreigner?" Then he said to him, "Rise and go; your faith has made you whole." (Luke 17:11-19)

They called from a distance. Jesus healed them from a distance. Our prayers are calling from a distance, but Jesus is still here to heal us. As they went, they were cleansed. This is so important. The healing did not take place until they acted upon it. I believe as they turned to go, they were acting in faith. Then the miracle happened.

As the song goes, "One leper turned and said, "Thank You!" Not only did he thank Jesus, but he threw himself at Jesus' feet. In other words, he bowed down before the Son of God in total thanksgiving and submission. He was a Samaritan. How do you think his life changed? I can only imagine.

Jesus said, *"Were not all ten cleansed? Where are the other nine?"* How often do we receive something from Jesus and just take it for granted, especially little things? Lord, I pray for a heart of praise and thanksgiving!

Recently I lost one of my good earrings. I was in class and so I said to the kids, "Let's pray I find my earring." And we did. A few minutes later, one of the students in another class brought it in. We praised the Lord. Not only was I thankful he had found my earring, but I realized what a great lesson this was for all the students. His praise should be continually in our mouths. (Big or little things) Finally, I don't know but I believe this man was made whole. There is a difference between being healed and being made whole. Today let's praise the Lord!

DAY 266

Now a man named Lazarus was sick…So the sisters sent word to Jesus, "Lord, the one you love is sick." When he heard this, Jesus said, "This sickness will not end in death. No, it is for God's glory so that God's Son may be glorified"…he stayed where he was two more days…"Our friend Lazarus has fallen asleep; but I am going there to wake him up."…Lazarus is dead, and for your sake I am glad I was not there, so that you may believe…On his arrival, Jesus found that Lazarus had already been in the tomb for four days…"Lord," Martha said to Jesus, "if you had been here, my brother would not have died. But I know that even now God will give you whatever you ask." …Jesus said to her, "I am the resurrection and the life. The one who believes in me will live even though they die; and whoever lives by believing in me will never die. Do you believe this? Did I not tell you that if you believe, you will see the glory of God?"…Jesus called out in a loud voice, "Lazarus, come out!" The dead man came out, his hands and feet wrapped with strips of linen, and a cloth around his face. Jesus said to them, "Take off the grave clothes and let him go." (John 11:1-44)

Jesus declared what was going to happen and then it happened to glorify God and his Son, Jesus. Lazarus was dead. He had been in the grave for four days. Jesus wanted them and us to believe that He is the resurrection and the life! If we believe we will not see death even though we die. He asks us also, "Do you believe this?"

Again, believing is the key to receiving. *"If you believe, you will see the glory of God."* Jesus called out in a loud voice, *"Lazarus come out!"* Jesus did not have to shout but I believe He wanted to make a statement to the people. This was a very important miracle. He was showing them and us that after death there is life eternal.

Then Jesus said, *"Take off the grave clothes and let him go."* All those things that cling to us that are not of God will be removed when we stand before Him. Our grave clothes will be no more as sin will be no more. Alleluia!

DAY 267

As Jesus and his disciples, together with a large crowd, were leaving the city, a blind man, Bartimaeus was sitting by the roadside begging. When he heard that it was Jesus of Nazareth, he began to shout, "Jesus, Son of David, have mercy on me!" Many rebuked him and told him to be quiet, but he shouted even more, "Son of David, have mercy on me!" Jesus stopped and said, "Call him." So, they called to the blind man, "Cheer up! On your feet! He's calling you." Throwing his cloak aside, he jumped to his feet and came to Jesus. "What do you want me to do for you?" Jesus asked him. The blind man said, "Rabbi, I want to see." "Go", said Jesus, "your faith has healed you." Immediately he received his sight and followed Jesus along the road. (**Mark 10:46-52, Matthew 20:29-34 and Luke 18:35-43**)

Bartimaeus knew that Jesus was the Son of David and that He was the Rabbi, the Teacher. The beginning to answered prayer is knowing who Jesus is and believing in Him. Then it is knowing that Jesus is merciful and cares for all of us deeply.

Bartimaeus was persistent. He kept calling out to Jesus even when many rebuked him and told him to be quiet. Persistence is another key to answered prayer. Keep on keeping on. Don't let others dissuade you. When Jesus calls come!

It is interesting that he threw off his cloak before he came to Jesus. Could the cloak represent those things that need to go before we approach the throne?

Then Jesus said, *"What do you want Me to do for you?"* Jesus knew he was blind so what was He really asking? I think He wanted to know what Bartimaeus really wanted. Sometimes we ask one thing but really want another or we are double minded. Bartimaeus really wanted to see.

"Go," **said Jesus,** *"your faith has healed you."* Again, Jesus is emphasizing faith. Believing is receiving.

Immediately he received his sight and followed Jesus along the road. After we witness a miracle is our walk stronger? Do we follow Jesus more intensely? We should. Today think back to times Jesus has done something special for you.

DAY 268

Early in the morning, as Jesus was on his way back to the city, he was hungry. Seeing a fig tree by the road, he went up to it but found nothing on it except leaves. Then he said to it, "May you never bear fruit again!" Immediately the tree withered. When the disciples saw this, they were amazed. "How did the fig tree wither so quickly?" they asked. Jesus replied, "Truly I tell you, if you have faith and do not doubt, not only can you do what was done to the fig tree, but also you can say to this mountain, Go throw yourself into the sea, and it will be done. If you believe, you will receive whatever you ask in prayer." (Matthew 21-18-22, Mark 11)

In Mark the scripture says, *He found nothing but leaves, because it was not the season for figs.*

I have never been able to understand why He cursed a tree for not having fruit when it was not in season. But I understand what He is trying to teach His disciples.

The whole point in this lesson is to teach them and us the importance of faith. Without faith it is impossible to please God. If we have faith we can say to a mountain, move over and it will happen. Nothing is impossible if we believe.

I am still trying to figure out how to have mountain moving faith. I know faith comes by hearing and hearing by the Word of God. But it must be more than reading the Word.

We see Jesus acting on His faith. So, I am wondering if one part of faith is action on our part? Could another part be totally trusting in the One who gives us faith in the first place? Finally, could part be finding out the will of God before we begin to pray?

Jesus says, *If you believe, you will receive whatever you ask in prayer.* Like Thomas I say, "I believe. Help my unbelief." I am asking the Lord to stretch my faith so that I can be part of the answer, not the problem. Will you join me?

DAY 269

When Jesus' followers saw what was going to happen, they said, "Lord should we strike with our swords?" And one of them struck the servant of the high priest, cutting off his right ear. But Jesus answered, "No more of this!" And he touched the man's ear and healed him. (Luke 22:49-51)

There is so much we can learn from this today. *No more of this!* It is time for us to say the same. We are not to fight the battle with swords and spears but with love and compassion, prayer, and healing. We were not called to divide but to unite in the unity of peace. As disciples of Christ, we are called to be Christ-like. Never did Jesus shake His fist or violently attack in word or deed. He came to bring peace. He is the Prince of Peace! He tells us to go and do likewise. In other words, "Stop it!" We as Christians are dividing our church and our Nation. If we truly believe God is sovereign and in control, then let Him be. Love our neighbors as ourselves. Do unto others as we would have them do unto us. Love covers a multitude of sins, etc....

Now back to the servant. His right ear had just been detached from his body. Before it could become another problem, Jesus touched the man's ear and healed him. This was a moment of truth for all that were witnessing the compassion of Christ. Jesus was loving his enemy. Do you suppose any of those standing there had second thoughts about who Jesus was? Did the servant's life change after this miracle? Did the disciples learn an important lesson on forgiveness? Do we see anything in this scripture that will change our attitudes or actions?

Jesus' greatest sacrifice was just about to happen. He was going to the cross for you and me. He was giving so that we could have eternal life. His attitude was an attitude of gratitude, not anger. He said, *"Father, forgive them for they know not what they do."* Can we do any less?

Can we become part of the healing process in our Nation? The choice is up to each one of us as individuals. Love You All!

DAY 270

Early in the morning, Jesus stood on the shore, but the disciples did not realize that it was Jesus. He called out to them "Friends, haven't you any fish?" "No" they answered. He said, "Throw your net on the right side of the boat and you will find some." When they did, they were unable to haul the net in because of the large number of fish...Jesus said to them, "Come and have breakfast." None of the disciples dared ask him, "Who are you?" They knew it was the Lord. Jesus came, took the bread, and gave it to them, and did the same with the fish. This was now the third time Jesus appeared to his disciples after he was raised from the dead. **(John 21:4-14)** ...I left out some scripture.

They did not recognize Him until they saw the miracle of the fish. I wonder how many times we have not recognized Jesus in our lives. I am sure in most big miracles we do, but what about the small ones? What about the bread and fish on our tables? There are so many people around the world who would love to have what we throw away.

Every good and perfect gift is from above, coming down from the Father of lights, who does not change like shifting shadows. **(James 1:17)** Thank you Lord!

Jesus said, **"*Throw your net on the right side of the boat.*"** I wonder why he said the right side of the boat. Jesus is seated at the right hand of the Father. I wonder if we are seated next to him. If so, that would be the right side? Just a thought.

Matthew 4:18 says, *Come, follow me and I will send you out to fish for people.* It is interesting that His last miracle recorded is about catching fish. When He called the disciples, they were to leave their nets and follow Him.

Today He is calling us to leave our nets, whatever things are holding us back, and follow Him. He is desiring that we bring in the lost by the boat load. We will have different lures or worms, but He is wanting none to perish. So, let's get out our fishing poles and dip them in the water expecting a huge catch.

DAY 271

When evening came, many who were demon-possessed were brought to him, and he drove out the spirits with a word and healed all the sick. This was to fulfill what was spoken through the prophet Isaiah: "He took up our infirmities and bore our diseases." (Matthew 8:16-17, Mark 1:32-34, Luke 4:40-41)

People brought all their sick to him and begged him to let the sick just touch the edge of his cloak, and all who touched it were healed. (Matthew 14:34-36 and Mark 6:53-56)

Isaiah 53:5 says, *But he was pierced for our transgressions, he was crushed for our iniquities; the punishment that brought us peace was on him, and by his wounds we are healed.*

1 Peter 2:24 says, *He himself bore our sins in his body on the cross, so that we might die to sins and live for righteousness, by his wounds you have been healed.*

Note in Isaiah He says *by his wounds we are healed.* And in 1 Peter He says, *by his wounds you have been healed.* It has already happened.

Things I have noticed in the study of Jesus Miracles:

1st Many times a miracle requires our faith.

2nd Many times we need to act before the miracle happens.

3rd Sometimes we have unconfessed sin in our lives.

4th Many times we must make the first move.

5th As with the leper we need to turn and say, "Thank you!"

6th Sometimes Jesus just heals because of His great love for us.

7th There is no formula to healing. It is all in His hands.

Ask and keep on asking. Seek and keep on seeking. Knock and keep on knocking!

THEY THAT WAIT UPON THE LORD

DAY 272

They that wait upon the Lord will renew their strength. They will soar on wings like eagles; they will run and not grow weary; they will walk and not faith. (**Isaiah 40:31**)

What does it mean to wait? The dictionary says, "Stay where one is or delay action until a particular time or until something else happens." So, what does it mean to wait on the Lord? We are going to spend a little time looking at people who had to wait to see their promise fulfilled. The last thing in the world we like to do is wait. We are in a rush society, hurry here and hurry there. It is hard for us to contemplate waiting on anything or anyone. But the Word of God is full of people who had to wait. Some never did see the fulfillment of their promise. It is fitting that this follows miracles because it takes a miracle to wait.

Genesis 3:15 says, *I will put enmity between you and the woman, and between your offspring and her offspring; he shall bruise your head, and you shall bruise his heel.*

Who do you think God was speaking to? I believe it was Satan, Adam, and Eve. God had only requested one thing of this couple. *You are free to eat from any tree in the garden; but you must not eat from the tree of the knowledge of good and evil, for when you eat from it you will certainly die.* (**Genesis 2:16-17**) And they died and so do you and I.

In response to the serpent's deception and Adam and Eve's disobedience, God pronounced a curse on them as well as on every generation to follow. But there was hope even in this curse and our reason for waiting. Satan damaged Christ on the cross but the ultimate victory wasn't Satan's but Christ. He rose from the dead and became eternal life for each of us, which is why we wait on the promise.

Whoever believes in the Son has eternal life, but whoever rejects the Son will not see life, for God's wrath remains on them. (**John 3:36**)

"They that wait upon the Lord will enew their strength!"

DAY 273

They that wait upon the Lord will renew their strength. They will soar on wings like eagles; they will run and not grow weary; they will walk and not faint. **(Isaiah 40:31)**

God told Noah to build an ark. Now we do not know for sure how long it took to build, but it was a while. We do know approximately how long Noah and his family were on the Ark.

The word tells us they waited in the ark for seven days before anything happened. Then it rained for 40 days. So, we add 7 to 40. Then we add the time it took for the water to recede. It is thought that they were in the ark 378 days. Now we don't know this for sure, but it is a pretty good guess.

Think about waiting when you have no idea what is going on around you. You can hear the rain on the roof, but you haven't seen rain. So, your imagination goes wild. The animals are restless. The noise is unbearable. The smell is unbelievable. Your wife and kids are more than restless. They are inconsolable. The future is unpredictable. Add a few more…

When God finally opened the door and Noah glanced out; what do you think he saw? I imagine his wife said, "It would have been better if we had died in the wilderness."

I love this verse. **But God remembered Noah and all the wild animals and the livestock that were with him in the ark, and he sent a wind over the earth, and the waters receded. (Genesis 8:1)** Whew, what a relief to Noah. What a relief to us. God does not forget us or our requests, but sometimes we must wait.

Psalm 5:3 says, *In the morning, Lord, you hear my voice; in the morning I lay my requests before you and wait expectantly.*

"They that wait upon the Lord will renew their strength!"

DAY 274

They that wait upon the Lord will renew their strength. They will soar on wings like eagles; they will run and not grow weary; they will walk and not faint. (Isaiah 40:31)

Now we are going to take a look at Job. His waiting was a contest between God and Satan and of course God knew his heart.

James 5:11 says, *As you know, we count as blessed those who persevered. You have heard of Job's perseverance and have seen what the Lord finally brought about. The Lord is full of compassion and mercy.*

The Bible does not tell us exactly how long Job suffered. We know it began with the death of his servant and the loss of his livestock and got worse and worse as time went on. He lost his children. He lost his possessions. He lost his health. But not his wife. What a wife. Finally, his friends gave him bad advice. He had nowhere to turn but to God and he wasn't too happy with God at the moment. Some say this may have taken 42 months, as a whisper of the Great Tribulation. Only God knows for sure. We do know he was waiting for answers and deliverance. He felt God had deserted him and this brought him the most pain. Have you ever felt that way?

God never did explain to Job why all these calamities had fallen on him. But when God was ready, He revealed more and more of Himself to Job. Job said, *My ears had heard of you but now my eyes have seen you. Therefore, I despise myself and repent in dust and ashes.* (Job 42:5-6)

Is it worth waiting on the Lord in order to know Him better, even if it means heartache and pain? That is a question that each of us must answer for ourselves.

Psalm 27:14 says, *Wait for the Lord; be strong and take heart and wait for the Lord.*

> *"They that wait upon the Lord shall renew their strength!"*

DAY 275

They that wait on the Lord will renew their strength. They will soar on wings like eagles; they will run and not grow weary; they will walk and not faint. (Psalm 40:31)

The Lord said to Abram,

Leave your country, your people and your father's household and go to the land I will show you. I will make you into a great nation and I will bless you; I will make your name great, and you will be a blessing. (Genesis 12:1-2)

They did not have GPS in those days and Abram had no map to show him where he was going. The only thing he did have was a promise from God that as he went, he would be shown. He could not prepare ahead of time provisions to take because he had no idea how long the trip would take. It was well over 600 miles from Haran to Canaan.

Just for a minute picture this group of nomads carrying all their personal belongs in the middle of nowhere. At most they could walk 20 miles a day and that is a stretch. They needed to find food and water for both themselves and their livestock. The weather wasn't always cool and sunny. The terrain changed constantly.

Compounding all of this was the fact that Abram began this journey when he was 75 years old. Now think about that for a moment. Today many people are in nursing homes at 75. Retirement pensions begin at 65. But God had promised Abram that He would make him into a great nation.

God also promised Abram a son and 15 years later He assured him it would happen. Then 10 years later Sarah gave birth to Isaac. We think we wait a long time for some things to happen in our lives but just figure this out. From the first promise to the answer was 25 years. During this time, he was also wandering, waiting to see where God was sending him.

We wait in hope for the Lord; he is our help and our shield. (Psalm 33:20)

"They that wait upon the Lord shall renew their strength!"

DAY 276

It is interesting to note that after Eve, the next woman mentioned by name is Sarah, the wife of Abraham. Now a lot of things had taken place between Eve and Sarah. The first time she is mentioned in the Bible is in **(Genesis 11:30) where it says,** *The name of Abram's wife was Sarai...Now Sarai was childless because she was not able to conceive.*

Her name meant "my lady" or "my princess". God renamed her "Sarah" meaning "lady", "princess" or "noblewoman." We know that her beauty caused Abraham to sin as he introduced her as his sister not once but twice. I would have felt totally betrayed. But that is not the point here. We are talking about "waiting" and Sarah was the queen of waiting.

Sarah was 90 years old when Isaac was finally born. Some of you had children late in life and some of you have wanted children but never had them. You can understand waiting, expecting and disappointment. God had promised Abraham that he would be the father of many nations. Well, you can't be a father if you don't have children. They both knew this, and they waited. When God finally told Sarah that she was going to conceive she laughed. Now none of you are 90 but we all know the possibility of this is less than slim.

Sarah had waited and waited and waited until she was way past childbearing. When God finally spoke, Abraham had said, *Shall a child be born to a man who is a hundred years old? Shall Sarah who is ninety years old bear a child?* (**Genesis 17:17**) After laughing she named her son Isaac which means 'laughter".

Nothing is impossible with God.

Sarah lived to be 127. She was able to enjoy Isaac for 37 years. *God is able to bless you abundantly, so that in all things at all times, having all that you need; you will abound in every good work.* (**2 Corinthians 9:8-9**)

Psalm 119:84 says, *How long must your servant wait?* Sarah waited 90 years. How long are we willing to wait to see the salvation of God in our lives?

> *"They that wait upon the Lord shall renew their strength!"*

DAY 277

They that wait upon the Lord shall renew their strength. They will soar on wings like eagles; they will run and not grow weary; they will walk and not faint. **(Isaiah 40:31)**

Abraham said, "Go to my father's family and to my own clan and get a wife for my son...The servant said, "See, I am standing beside this spring. If a young woman comes out to draw water and I say to her, Please let me drink a little water from your jar, and if she says to me, Drink, and I'll draw water for your camels too, let her be the one the Lord has chosen for my master's son." **(Genesis 24)**

What a huge responsibility this servant had. He was to go and get the right wife for Isaac. He had no clue who it would be or where he would find her. Rebekah had no idea what she was getting into, but she went with the servant trusting God.

Isaac was 40 years old when he married Rebecca. We really don't know how old Rebekah was, but I assume she was young. Twenty years went by, and they were still childless. They both prayed continually that God would give them a child and eventually God answered their prayers and Rebekah gave birth to twin boys, Esau, and Jacob.

Now remember the promise God had given Abraham. I will make you the father of many nations. So far it doesn't look too promising. He and Sarah only had one child and now Isaac had two. This was a very slow start to a nation. But God!

It seems to me God is more interested in our faith than the amount of time it takes for Him to fulfill a promise. The longer we wait believing, the stronger our faith becomes. Waiting is probably one of the hardest things we can do but one of the most pleasing to God.

Be still before the Lord and wait patiently for him; do not fret when people succeed in their ways. **(Psalm 37:7)** The quickest way we can lose a promise is to listen to others. Waiting is a personal choice.

"They that wait upon the Lord shall renew their strength!"

DAY 278

They who wait for the Lord shall renew their strength; they shall mount up with wings like eagles; they shall run and not be weary; they shall walk and not faint. **(Isaiah 40:31)**

Jacob had deceived his brother Esau and stolen his birthright. He had run away from his family to his uncle's home. We know that what goes around, comes around.

Genesis 29:10-11 says, *When Jacob saw Rachel, daughter of his uncle Laban, and Laban's sheep, he went over and rolled the stone away from the mouth of the well and watered his uncle's sheep. Then Jacob kissed Rachel and began to weep aloud.*

This was love at first sight. Jacob was willing to do anything to get the hand of Rachel. In the process he worked seven years for Laban and was deceived into marrying Leah.

Galatians 6:7 says, *Do not be deceived: God cannot be mocked. A man reaps what he sows'*

Jacob was in love with Rachel and said, "I'll work for you seven years in return for your younger daughter Rachel." (V18)

We know what happened. On the wedding night it was not Rachel but Leah who married Jacob. After the bridal week was over Laban gave Rachel to Jacob but he had to work seven more years. This was a total of fourteen years that Jacob waited to be free and even then he had to deceive Laban in order to leave. Deception was in their blood line.

Was the wait worth it? In many ways yes, but there was always strife in his family. Rachel was jealous of Leah because it was easy for her to get pregnant. Leah was sad because Jacob did not love her. The fourteen-year wait may have helped Jacob learn that love is more than physical. Waiting can be a blessing!

"They that wait upon the Lord shall renew their strength!"

DAY 279

But they who wait for the Lord shall renew their strength; they shall mount up with wings like eagles; they shall run and not be weary; they shall walk and not faint. (Isaiah 40:31)

Do pride and jealousy go hand in hand? I am beginning to think so. Joseph was 17 when he brought his father a bad report about his brothers. Tattletale. The brothers already did not like him because he was his father's favorite. Remember the coat of many colors that his father had given him. One way of flaunting. Then he had two dreams in which his brothers bowed down to him. Eventually his brothers sold him for 20 shekels of silver. He ended up in Egypt with Potiphar one of Pharaoh's officials. Potiphar's wife tried to seduce him.

Joseph said, *"My master has withheld nothing from me except you, because you are his wife. How then could I do such a wicked thing and sin against God?"* (**Genesis 39:9**) He ended up in prison. Then we see the cupbearer and the baker. They both had dreams. Joseph interpreted them correctly. Two years later Pharaoh had two dreams and Joseph was brought before Pharaoh because he heard he could interpret dreams.

Joseph said, *"I cannot do it, but God will give Pharaoh the answer he desires."* (**Genesis 47:16**) He had learned to depend upon God.

Joseph was 17 when he was sold into Egypt. He was 30 when he was made overseer. He was 39 when his brothers first came to Egypt and probably 41 when they came the second time. Twenty-four years passed from the time Joseph was first taken out of the well until he was finally reunited with his family. Why?

God sent me ahead of you to preserve for you a remnant on earth and to save your lives by a great deliverance. (**Genesis 45:7**)

Sometimes there is a very important reason to wait. During the interim we don't know what God has in mind, but he does. Read Lamentations 3:25-26

"They that wait upon the Lord shall renew their strength!"

DAY 280

But they who wait for the Lord shall renew their strength; they shall mount up with wings like eagles; they shall run and not be weary; they shall walk and not faint. (Isaiah 40:31)

Waiting is one of the hardest things to do. Waiting on a report from the doctor; waiting for a loved one who is missing; waiting for a spouse who has left to return; even waiting in line at the grocery store. Waiting is an act of worship.

Moses learned the act of waiting on the Lord. As we know he grew up as a prince in Egypt, but he was a Jew, and he knew it because his real mother was his nanny. He must have felt the call on his life from a very young age. He was to deliver his people from bondage. But he did what so many of us do, and that is to take matters into his own hands. He had to flee Egypt and I am sure he could not understand the turn of events.

This act forced him into the wilderness, the desert of Midian where he lived for 40 years. Moses went from being a prince to a nobody. How many times in the word was a person driven into the wilderness for a time of learning who God really is? If we want to know God, we also will have dry spells in our lives where the only thing we can do is trust. But during this time, He is preparing us and was preparing Moses for his real calling. Forty years in the desert prepared him for forty years in the desert.

After forty years had passed, an angel appeared to Moses in the flames of a burning bush in the desert near Mt. Sinai..." I am the God of your fathers, the God of Abraham, Isaac and Jacob...Take off your sandals, for the place where you are standing is holy ground." (Acts 7:30-33) It took forty years for him to hear from God. How long are we willing to wait?

I wait for your salvation, Lord, and I follow your commands. I obey your statutes, for I love them greatly. I obey your precepts and your statutes, for all my ways are known to you. (Psalm 119:166-168)

"They that wait upon the Lord shall renew their strength!"

DAY 281

But they who wait for the Lord shall renew their strength; they shall mount up with wings like eagles; they shall run and not be weary; they shall walk and not faint. **(Isaiah 40:31)**

After the death of Moses, the servant of the Lord, the Lord said to Joshua...Moses my servant is dead. Now then, you and all these people get ready to cross the Jordan River into the land I am about to give to them...I will give you everyplace where you set your foot, as I promised Moses. **(Joshua 1:1-3)**

Joshua was 40 years old when he and the 11 others went to spy out the land. It was 45 years later when he led the Israelites into the promised land. During that time, he was a student under Moses.

Deuteronomy 3:28 the Lord says, *"Commission Joshua, and encourage and strengthen him, for he will lead this people across and will cause them to inherit the land that you will see."* Moses only saw the land, but Joshua inherited it.

Deuteronomy 34:9 says, *Now Joshua, son of Nun was filled with the spirit of wisdom because Moses had laid his hand on him. So, the Israelites listened to him and did what the Lord had commanded Moses.*

The Lord said, *"As I was with Moses, so I will be with you; I will never leave you nor forsake you. Be strong and courageous, because you will lead these people to inherit the land, I swore to their ancestors to give them."* **(Joshua 14)**

Joshua had known for 45 years his calling but had to wait upon the Lord's timing. During that time, he was learning what it takes to be a leader. He saw the good, the bad and the ugly in the people. He watched his mentor and gleaned from him. Then for the next 25 years he led Israel. So, what does it take to be a leader?

The Lord would speak to Moses face to face, as one speaks to a friend. Then Moses would return to the camp, but his young aide Joshua son of Nun did not leave the tent. **(Exodus 33:1)**

"They that wait upon the Lord shall renew their strength!

DAY 282

But they who wait for the Lord shall renew their strength; they shall mount up with wings like eagles; they shall run and not be weary; they shall walk and not faint. (Isaiah 40:31)

Saul waited seven days, the time set by Samuel; but Samuel did not come to Gilgal, and Saul's men began to scatter. So, he said, "Bring me the burnt offering and the fellowship offerings." And Saul offered up the burnt offering. Just as he finished making the offering, Samuel arrived, and Saul went out to greet him. "What have you done?" ask Samuel. (I Samuel 13:7-11)

Saul was the king the people begged for so that they could be like other nations. God knew what was in Saul's heart and He knew Saul would not be a good king, but because the people insisted, He let them have their way. You know sometimes God will do this in each of our lives. He knows what is best for us but when we keep insisting, He allows us to fall.

Saul did not instantly lose his kingdom, but he lost the Spirit of the Living God in his life. Samuel had told him to wait seven days. His waiting was nothing like those who had come before him or would come after him. Was impatience worth it? I think not.

Saul was mortally wounded by the Philistines and his sons were killed in the battle. Saul not able to even wait on death committed suicide by falling on his own sword.

Proverbs 3:5-7 says, *Trust in the Lord with all your heart and lean not on your own understanding; in all your ways submit to him, and he will make your paths straight. Do not be wise in your own eyes.*

Great peace have those who love your law, and nothing can make them stumble. I wait for your salvation, Lord, and I follow your commands. I obey your statutes for I love them greatly. I obey your precepts and your statutes for all my ways are known to you. (Psalm 119:165-168) If Saul had waiting?

"They that wait upon the Lord shall renew their strength!"

DAY 283

But they who wait for the Lord shall renew their strength; they shall mount up with wings like eagles; they shall run and not be weary; they shall walk and not faint. **(Isaiah 40:31)**

The Lord said to Samuel, "How long will you mourn for Saul, since I have rejected him as king over Israel? Fill your horn with oil and be on your way; I am sending you to Jesse of Bethlehem. I have chosen one of his sons to be king." (1 Samuel 16:1)

We know the story. Each son was presented to Samuel and each time the Lord said, "No". Finally, there was only one son left and he was tending the sheep. Isn't it fitting that David would write the 23rd Psalm? The Lord is my shepherd. He understood sheep and being a shepherd. God always uses who we are to make us into who He is.

David was the youngest of Jesse's eight sons. How do you think they felt when the anointing was given to David? *People look at the outward appearance, but the Lord looks at the heart.* **(1 Samuel 16:7)**

David was anointed but now the wait began. He faced Goliath, was banished by Saul, hid in the desert, lived on the run, forced out of the nation and fought many battles. Did God really say? The devil was at it again with the age-old question.

David was a teenager when he was anointed, probably 13 or 14 and he became King when he was 30. Looking at his bio, it seems he had a lot to learn between the anointing and the actual kingship. Do you think David ever doubted? Was he human?

What I appreciate most about David was his ability to worship the Lord regardless of his circumstances. We are so blessed to have his praise in writing.

David said, *"Lord, I wait for you; you will answer, Lord my God. For I said, Do not let them gloat or exalt themselves over me when my feet slip." (Psalm 38:15)*

"They that wait upon the Lord shall renew their strength!"

DAY 284

But they who wait for the Lord shall renew their strength; they shall mount up with wings like eagles; they shall run and not be weary; they shall walk and not faint. (Isaiah 40:31)

The word of the Lord came to Jonah son of Amittai; "Go to the great city of Nineveh and preach against it, because its wickedness has come up before me." (Jonah 1:1)

And Jonah ran…We know the story. Eventually he was swallowed by a huge fish and was in the belly of the fish three days and nights. Finally considering his future he agreed to obey the Lord. Believe it or not God had not changed his mind. *"Go to Nineveh and proclaim to it the message I give you."*

His waiting period wasn't very long. Three days in the belly of the fish and three days to go through Nineveh proclaiming, *"Forty more days and Nineveh will be overthrown."* (Jonah 3:4)

The people repented and Jonah was very angry. *He prayed to the Lord, '" Isn't this what I said, Lord, when I was still at home? That is what I tried to forestall by fleeing to Tarshish. I knew that you are a gracious and compassionate God, slow to anger and abounding in love, a God who relents from sending calamity. Now, Lord, take away my life, for it is better for me to die than to live."* (Jonah 4:3-4)

God's grace is beyond our understanding and sometimes I think we are like Jonah. "Not that person, Lord. He doesn't deserve your forgiveness." Oh really, what about you, my child?

I love God's object lesson to Jonah. Jonah had gone outside the city to wait and see what God would do, as if he didn't know. The Lord provided a leafy plant to give Jonah shade for his head to ease his discomfort. The next day God provided a worm, which chewed up the plant so that it withered. Again, Jonah was angry. Even though God's concern was for the people of Nineveh, He was also concerned about Jonah's well-being. I wonder what Jonah learned from this.

"They that wait upon the Lord shall renew their strength!"

DAY 285

But those who wait for the Lord shall renew their strength; they will mount up with wings like eagles; they shall run and not be weary; they shall walk and not faint. (Isaiah 40:31)

We live in an instant society. The microwave has taken place of the oven. Texting has taken place of talking on the phone. The car has taken place of the horse and buggy. Computers have taken place of the classroom. You name it. We have very little personal communication with each other. Our ability to wait has lessened which means we have also forgotten how to wait on the Lord.

And I heard the voice of the Lord saying, "Whom shall I send, and who will go for us?" Then I said, "Here I am! Send me." And he said, "Go, and say to this people: Keep on hearing, but do not perceive. Make the heart of this people dull, and their ears heavy, and blind their eyes; lest they see with their eyes and hear with their ears, and understand with their hearts, and turn and be healed." Then I said, "How long, O Lord?" (Isaiah 6:8-11)

Isaiah's problem wasn't waiting on his call but waiting for the call to be fulfilled. It is believed that he prophesied for about 64 years. He is known as the prophet who predicted the coming of Jesus even though he lived 700 years before the prophecy actually happened.

The theme of most of his prophecy was the judgement of God's people and their ultimate salvation which we see in Jesus. Even his name meant his calling which was "God is salvation".

Deuteronomy 18:22 says, *When a prophet speaks in the name of the Lord, if the word does not come to pass or come true, that is a word that the Lord has not spoken; the prophet has spoken it presumptuously. You need to be afraid of him.*

How would you have like to have Isaiah's calling? Well, we do! *He said to them, "Go into all the world and preach the gospel to all creation."* (**Mark 16:15**) He is still waiting on each of us to fulfill our calling.

"They that wait on the Lord shall renew their strength!"

DAY 286

But they who wait for the Lord shall renew their strength; they shall mount up with wings like eagles; they shall run and not be weary; they shall walk and not faint. (Isaiah 40:31)

For 21 days Daniel fasted and prayed. He was waiting on an answer from God. Each day he expected to hear but nothing happened…Then on the 21st day, *Behold, a hand touched me and set me trembling on my hands and knees. And he said to me, "O Daniel, man greatly loved, understand the words that I speak to you and stand upright, for now I have been sent to you." And when he spoke this word to me, I stood trembling. Then he said to me, "Fear not, Daniel, for from the first day that you set your heart to understand and humbled yourself before God, your words have been heard, and I have come because of your words. The prince of the kingdom of Persia withstood me twenty-one days, but Michael, one of the chief princes, came to help me, for I was left there with the kings of Persia, and came to make you understand what is to happen to your people in the latter days. For the vision is for days yet to come."* (Daniel 10:10-14)

Daniel knew that the 70 years of exile were almost over. But he did not know what was going to happen in the end times. His prophecies are still being fulfilled today.

Blessed is the one who waits for and reaches the end of the 1,335 days. As for you, go your way till the end. You will rest, and then at the end of days you will rise to receive your allotted inheritance. (Daniel 12:12-13)

Things we can learn from this passage. 1st Daniel prayed and he fasted. 2nd God heard his prayer on the first day and answered it. 3rd Sometimes the answer is delayed. 4th Persistence pays off. 5th God cares about all of us and says we are greatly loved.

You too, be patient and stand firm, because the Lord's coming is near. (James 5:7)

"They that wait upon the Lord shall renew their strength!"

DAY 287

But they who wait for the Lord shall renew their strength; they shall mount up with wings like eagles; they shall run and not be weary; they shall walk and not faint. **(Isaiah 40:31)**

And the angel said to her, "Do not be afraid, Mary, for you have found favor with God. And behold, you will conceive in your womb and bear a son, and you shall call his name Jesus. He will be great and will be called the Son of the Most High. And the Lord God will give to him the throne of his father David, and he will reign over the house of Jacob forever, and of his kingdom there will be no end." **(Luke 1:30-33)**

At first glance we think Mary had to wait nine months before this promise was fulfilled. Let's consider that nine months. She was not married. She was young. People were sure to talk. She probably spent six months with Elizabeth. There is no mention that Joseph was with her, but the word does tell us after the angel came to him, he married her. Jesus was born in a manger and then they had to flee. What a beginning to a marriage and a family.

But that was just the beginning for Mary. She watched as His ministry took off and feared constantly for His life. She knew He was special, but do you really think she understood the full impact of His life?

She stood by as He was crucified and wondered with everyone else. "Was this the end?" Hearing and knowing are not the same. She had listened to Him preach and heard the promises of eternal life, but it took His resurrection for her to really begin to realize who He was and then she had questions.

She watched His ascension and heard Him say, ***"But you will receive power when the Holy Spirit comes on you; and you will be my witnesses in Jerusalem, and in all Judea and Samaria, and to the ends of the earth."*** **(Acts1:8)** and then He was gone.

She waited in the upper room not knowing what was going to happen. But she waited and was filled with the Holy Spirit. She is still waiting. Are you?

"They that wait upon the Lord shall renew their strength!"

DAY 288

But they who wait for the Lord shall renew their strength; they shall mount up with wings like eagles; they shall run and not be weary; they shall walk and not faint. (Isaiah 40:31)

Let's look for a moment at the people who Jesus healed that had waited years for their healing.

1st The man born blind in John 9:1

2nd The man at the pool of Bethesda who had been an invalid for thirty-eight years. John 5:2

3rd The crippled woman who for eighteen years had been bent over. Luke 13:11

4th The woman who had been subject to bleeding for twelve years. Matthew 9:20

5th Lazarus in the tomb for four days. John 11:17

*"Lord', Martha said to Jesus, "if you had been here my brother would not have died." (*John 11:21)

Where was Jesus while all these people waited? Where is He today? Believe it or not He is here, and He listens, and He answers our prayers. But sometimes He says, "wait". Do we understand? "No" but there is a reason. Maybe we will not understand until we meet Him face to face, but we must keep on keeping on.

His promise is, *They who wait for the Lord shall renew their strength; they shall mount up with wings like eagles; they shall run and not grow weary; they shall walk and not faint.*

He has promised to give us strength in the waiting. He has promised us endurance and that we can walk regardless of the situation. So, if you are waiting and we all are on one thing or another, believe that He cares and wants the very best for us.

"They that wait upon the Lord shall renew their strength!"

DAY 289

But they who wait for the Lord shall renew their strength; they shall mount up with wings like eagles; they shall run and not be weary; they shall walk and not faint. **(Isaiah 40:31)**

Not only did those who needed something from Christ wait for him, but we too wait on the Lord.

Micah 7:7 says, *But as for me, I watch in hope for the Lord, I wait for God my Savior; my God will hear me.*

Psalm 130:5-6 says, *I wait for the Lord, my whole being waits, and in his word, I put my hope. I wait for the Lord more than watchmen wait for the morning, more than watchmen wait for the morning.*

My question is, "Why are we waiting? What are we waiting for? Who are we waiting for? Are we waiting?

I Thessalonians 5:10 says, *He died for us so that, whether we are awake or asleep, we may live together with him. Therefore encourage one another and build each other up, just as in fact you are doing.*

We are waiting for the return of Christ. We are waiting for a new Garden of Eden. We are waiting to see Him face to face. We are waiting for new bodies and hearts that will praise him continually.

Hebrews 9:28 says, *So Christ was sacrificed once to take away the sins of many; and he will appear a second time, not to bear sin, but to bring salvation to those who are waiting for him.*

James 5:7 says, *Be patient, then brothers and sisters, until the Lord's coming. See how the farmer waits for the land to yield its valuable crop, patiently waiting for the autumn and spring rains. You too, be patient and stand firm, because the Lord's coming is near.*

"But they that wait upon the Lord shall renew their strength!"

DAY 290

But they who wait for the Lord shall renew their strength; they shall mount up with wings like eagles; they shall run and not be weary; they shall walk and not faint. (Isaiah 40:31)

Not only are we waiting but have you ever thought that maybe the Lord is waiting too? From the time He walked with Adam and Eve in the cool of the evening and fellowshipped with them, He has been waiting for a bride without spot or wrinkle. The engagement is almost over and soon the wedding will begin.

He says in John 14:2-3, *"I go to prepare a place for you...I will come again and will take you to myself, so that where I am, there you may be also."*

But here is the clincher. **Matthew 24:36,** *But about that day or hour no one knows, not even the angels in heaven, nor the Son, but only the Father.* Then He tells us a parable about five foolish and five wise virgins. We know the foolish virgins did not take any oil with them and the bridegroom was a long time coming. "Give me oil in my lamp keep me burning, burning, burning."

For as lightning that comes from the east is visible even in the west, so will be the coming of the Son of Man. (Matthew 24:27)

Look, I am coming soon! My reward is with me, and I will give to each person according to what they have done. I am the Alpha and the Omega, the First and the Last, the Beginning and the End. (Revelation 22:12)

The Spirit and the bride say, "Come!" And let the one who hears say, "Come!" Let the one who is thirsty come; and let the one who wishes take the free gift of the water of life. (Revelation 22:17)

He brought me to His banqueting table and His banner over me is love. The Lord is still waiting for His bride, but it won't be long until He comes to claim her. He is waiting and so should we.

I wait for the Lord more than watchmen wait for the morning. (Psalm 130:6)

"They that wait upon the Lord shall renew their strength!"

DAY 291

But they who wait for the Lord shall renew their strength; they shall mount up with wings like eagles; they shall run and not be weary; they shall walk and not faint. (Isaiah 40:31)

So, Joshua said to the Israelites: "How long will you wait before you begin to take possession of the land that the Lord, the God of your ancestors, has given you?" (Joshua 18:3)

The Lord is still asking us the same question. How long will you wait before you begin to take possession of the land? How long will you straddle the fence? How long will you waver between what is right and what seems good in your own eyes? How long will you be double-minded? How long?

It seems to me today we are straddling the fence so much of the time. If this were not true, we would begin to see the greatest revival this country has ever known. We would begin to see lives changed; churches growing; miracles of all kinds being manifest. We ask the question, "Why are we not seeing God move?" And He is saying, "How long will you wait before you begin to take possession of the land?" It is not a question of God moving, but of us moving. How long?

Abraham did not waver through unbelief regarding the promise of God but was strengthened in his faith and gave glory to God, being fully persuaded that God had power to do what he had promised. (Romans 4:20)

Elijah said, *"How long will you waver between two opinions? If the Lord is God follow him; but if Baal is God, follow him."* (1 Kings 18:21)

Joshua said, *"Choose for yourselves this day whom you will serve, whether the gods your ancestors served…But as for me and my household, we will serve the Lord."* (Joshua 24:15) How long?

"But they who wait for the Lord shall renew their strength!"

DAY 292

"Aleph"

Blessed are those whose way is blameless, who walk in the law of the Lord!... Oh, that my ways may be steadfast in keeping your statutes! **(Psalm 119:1 & 5)**

There are 22 letters to the Hebrew alphabet, and they all have a special meaning. Looking into the deeper meaning of the letters can lead us into a deeper walk with the Lord. Nothing is happenstance in the Word of God.

Aleph is the first letter of the Hebrew alphabet and signifies the number one. Aleph indicates the Oneness and Unity of the Creator and that He is the source of everything. Aleph represents the creation of something from nothing. It is perfection beyond human comprehension.

Blessed are those who keep his testimonies, who seek him with their whole heart. **(V 2)**

Lord our desire is to seek you with our whole heart. But what does that mean? *Verse 3 says, who do no wrong but walk in his ways! Verse 4 says, You have commanded your precepts to be kept diligently.* In other words, we are to read His word and strive to live by it with love as our main motivator.

I will praise you with an upright heart when I learn your righteous rules. **(V 7)** In order to praise Him with an upright heart, I must understand what is required of me.

He has told you, O man, what is good; and what does the Lord require of you but to do justice, and to love kindness, and to walk humbly with your God? **(Micah 6:8)**

I will keep your statutes; do not utterly forsake me! **(V 8) But we have nothing to fear for He has said,** *I will never leave you nor forsake you!* **(Hebrews 13:5)**

"Aleph!"

Psalm 119 and You

DAY 293

"Beth"

Beth is the 2nd letter of the Hebrew alphabet. The created world is meant to house within it the spiritual. The physical world is meant to be a place for the Creator's glory to manifest. This is what Beth means.

With my whole heart I seek you; let me not wander from your commandments! (V 10)

Wandering seems to be a way of life. We travel from place to place. Even in our minds we do a lot of wandering. Trying to be still and know God has caused me to realize how hard it is to center on the Lord or anything else for any period of time. I am still meditating on how to be silent for 30 minutes in heaven.

I have stored up your word in my heart, that I might not sin against you. (V 11)

Meditating on this verse I began to realize the way I receive a check in my spirit is by knowing what God has to say and then obeying.

Blessed are you, O Lord; teach me your statutes! With my lips I declare all the rules of your mouth. (V 12-13)

It is said if you repeat something 7 times, you will not forget it. If you speak it out loud it will even be more meaningful. If you tell it to someone else, it will become a permanent truth in your heart. Do we do this with God's word?

In the ways of your testimonies, I delight as much as in all riches. I will meditate on your precepts and fix my eyes on your ways. I will delight in your statutes; I will not forget your word. (V 14-16)

"Beth" – The physical world is meant to be a place for the Creator's glory to manifest. Are we filling our physical world with the things of God or are we listening to the world? Our outlook on life will be determined by what fills our hearts.

"Beth!"

DAY 294

"Gimel"

Gimel means a dynamic balance between opposing powers. Gimel includes the opposites of both giving and receiving, reward and punishment, creating balance and motion between these opposites.

Deal bountifully with your servant, that I may live and keep your word. Open my eyes, that I may behold wondrous things out of your law. (**V 17-18**) Give me an open mind and receptive heart. Teach me to listen.

My soul is consumed with longing for your rules at all times. (**V 20**)

If this were really true in my life, I would be constantly in the Word. I am guilty of being lazy and not spending the time in God's word that I should. Convict me Lord!

You rebuke the insolent, accursed who wander from your commandments. Take away from me scorn and contempt, for I have kept your testimonies. (**V 21-22**)

So, I find it to be a law that when I want to do right, evil lies close at hand. For I delight in the law of God, in my inner being, but I see in my members another law waging war against the law of my mind and making me captive to the law of sin that dwells in my members. Wretched man that I am! Who will deliver me from this body of death? Thanks be to God through Jesus Christ our Lord! (**Romans 7:23**)

Even though princes sit plotting against me, your servant will meditate on your statutes. Your testimonies are my delight; they are my counselors. (**V 23-24**)

Today spend a few minutes delighting in the Lord. Bring to mind things you are thankful for and prepare your heart to enjoy tomorrow wherever you are and whatever you are doing. This is the day that the Lord has made. I will rejoice and be glad in it.

"Gime!"

DAY 295

"Daleth"

Daleth is the word for door, gate and indicates resistance and the state of selfless-ness and humility needed to pass through it.

My soul clings to the dust; give me life according to your word! (V 25)

Then the Lord God formed the man of dust from the ground and breathed into his nostrils the breath of life, and the man became a living creature. (Genesis 2:7)

The God who formed us is more than able to take care of us. But so many of us are not willing to humble ourselves and allow Him to be God. Today we live in a state of selfishness not selflessness. "I'll do it my way." "Whatever pleases me." "My way or the highway." You know the standard phrases. Humility and selflessness are a thing of the past or maybe they have never existed.

Make me understand the way of your precepts, and I will meditate on your won-drous works. My soul melts away for sorrow; strengthen me according to your word! (V 27 & 28)

I am sure we have all been in a place with the Lord when we truly did not under-stand either something in His word or something He was doing in our lives. Sorrow seems to shroud us and unbelief tries to step in. That is the time we need to ask for His wisdom.

Put false ways far from me and graciously teach me your law! I have chosen the way of faithfulness; I set your rules before me. I cling to your testimonies, O Lord; let me not be put to shame! I will run in the way of your commandments when you enlarge my heart! (V 29-32)

I am praying that the Lord will enlarge my heart. Help me be the door or the gate through which others can find you. May I be selfless and truly humble before you and others.

"Daleth!"

DAY 296

"He"

He is the 5th letter of the Hebrew alphabet. It represents divine revelation, the breath of the Creator. *By the word of the Lord the heavens were made, and by the breath of his mouth all their host.* **(Psalm 33:6)**

Teach me, O Lord, the way of your statutes; and I will keep it to the end. Give me understanding, that I may keep your law and observe it with my whole heart. Lead me in the path of your commandments, for I delight in it. Incline my heart to your testimonies, and not to selfish gain! **(V 33-36)**

David loved the word of the Lord. He meditated on it day and night. It gave him insight and wisdom to be the king he needed to be for his people. The word gave him direction and guidance for everyday living. These things seem to be needed today as much as they were then. Teach me, O Lord!

Turn my eyes from looking at worthless things; and give me life in your ways. **(V 37)**

What a powerful verse. Turn my eyes from looking at worthless things. How many times in a day do I say or do something that is totally worthless? How many things have I desired that eventually went to Goodwill? How much worthless stuff do I possess? Lord, turn my eyes toward things of Godly worth.

Confirm to your servant your promise, that you may be feared. Turn away the reproach that I dread, for your rules are good. Behold, I long for your precepts; in your righteousness give me life! **(V 38-40)**

In other words, give me divine revelation. Teach me to speak your words with power. Help me to realize that *Death and life are in the power of the tongue.* **(Proverbs 18:21)** Teach me to speak life.

Let the words of my mouth and the meditation of my heart be acceptable in your sight, O Lord, my rock, and my redeemer. **(Psalm 19:14)**

"He!"

DAY 297

"Waw"

"Waw" is the 6th letter of the Hebrew alphabet. Waw is the power to unite everything that is separated in creation. It has the power to connect heaven and earth. It also represents the 6 days of creation.

Let your steadfast love come to me, O Lord, your salvation according to your promise; then shall I have an answer for him who taunts me, for I trust in your word. (V 42-42)

This speaks to me of those who are unsaved. God is wanting to unite the saved and the unsaved into one people given entire to Him. He would have none perish but, the but is where the rub comes in. So many do not see a need for a savior.

And take not the word of truth utterly out of my mouth, for my hope is in your rules. I will keep your law continually, forever, and ever, and I shall walk in a wide place, for I have sought your precepts. (V 43-45)

We continually come back to knowing the Word and walking in it. The Word has power, not my word but the Word.

I will also speak of your testimonies before kings and shall not be put to shame, for I find my delight in your commandments, which I love. (V 46-47)

There is a huge difference between I have to, and I love to. When I have to read the Word or pray, then it becomes rote. I am not honoring God and I am truly wasting my time and His.

I will lift up my hands toward your commandments, which I love, and I will meditate on your statutes. (V 48)

You shall love the Lord your God with all your heart and with all your soul and with all your might. (Deuteronomy 6:5) Love has the power to unite!

"Waw!"

DAY 298

"Zayin"

Zaylin is the 7th letter of the Hebrew alphabet. It is the symbol of spirit, sustenance, and struggle. It represents the struggle between opposites, the struggle for existence, the struggle for sustenance but also the day of rest.

Remember your word to your servant, in which you have made me hope. This is my comfort in my affliction, that your promise gives me life. **(V 49-50)**

I want to share a minor affliction with you in hopes that you too will see the goodness of God even in the midst of adversity. We could hardly wait to see our family Thanksgiving. Several days before we were to go, I felt I needed to pray, "Lord, If there is any reason, we should not go please show me." Within 30 minutes of this prayer the phone rang with news that one of the people in my pod at school had covid. I was devastated not only for this person but for the fact that we could not go. We struggled with our decision to go anyway, but as my husband was praying, he felt to go was to disobey God. I had also felt this way. But it had been 5 months since we had seen any of our family. The minute we determined to obey God we both felt peace. The question is what might have happened if we had disobeyed? His promise gave us life. P.S. this person with covid is doing fine.

When I think of your rules from of old, I take comfort, O Lord. **(V 52)** Does the Lord ever tell us to do something or give us a command that is not for our best interest?

Your statutes have been my songs in the house of my sojourning. **(V 54)** I love this verse because most of the scriptures I remember are from when we use to open our Bibles and sing scriptures.

I remember your name in the night, O Lord, and keep your law. This blessing has fallen to me, that I have kept your precepts. **(V 56)** It is truly a blessing to obey the Lord even when we want to do the opposite. Father knows best!

"Zaylin!"

DAY 299

"Heth"

The 8th letter of the Hebrew alphabet is "heth". It represents infinite possibilities. It represents the power of choice and the ability to go above and beyond limitations.

The Lord is my portion; I promise to keep your words. I entreat your favor with all my heart; be gracious to me according to your promise. (V 57-58)

Portion means my destiny, lot, fate, fortune, heritage. So, I say the Lord is my destiny. I am a sojourner on this earth. My final destiny is not here but in heaven with the Lord. I am His child just waiting to return home. While I wait, I ask for His favor in my life. I ask for His direction, guidance, and protection.

When I think on my ways, I turn my feet to your testimonies; I hasten and do not delay to keep your commandments. (V 59-60)

With this said I live with infinite possibilities to be and do the things that are in God's word. He has said, ***I can do all things through Christ who strengthens me.*** As I not only quote this scripture but put it into practice my abilities go above and beyond limitations. But the secret is keeping His commandments.

Though the cords of the wicked ensnare me, I do not forget your law. At midnight I rise to praise you, because of your righteous rules. (V 61-62)

At midnight I can be found praying and praising the Lord. Most mechanical things that we purchase have an instruction manual. Without the manual the object is worthless because we do not know how to put it together or use it. In the same way without reading God's manual, we do not know how or what to do. His word is our instruction. It represents infinite possibilities.

I am a companion of all who fear you, of those who keep your precepts. The earth, O Lord, is full of your steadfast love; teach me your statutes! (V 63-64)

"Heth!"

DAY 300

"Teth"

"Teth" has a literal meaning of basket or nest and is the symbol of the good in all creation. Even within the bad things that happen there is hidden good. It teaches us to distinguish between good and bad and to choose good.

You have dealt well with your servant, O Lord, according to your word. Teach me good judgment and knowledge, for I believe in your commandments. (V 65-66)

Praise the Lord we have the Holy Spirit dwelling in us leading and guiding us into all truth. He is our check and balance. We can trust His small nudges. But we need to follow those nudges and not blame Him when we fail to obey.

Before I was afflicted, I went astray, but now I keep your word. You are good and do good; teach me your statutes. (V 67-68)

How do we learn? *I will instruct you and teach you in the way you should go; I will counsel you with my eye upon you. (Psalm 32:8)* We have the counselor living in us. Now we must learn to listen.

The insolent smear me with lies, but with my whole heart I keep your precepts; their heart is unfeeling like fat, but I delight in your law. (V 69-70)

When God tells us something, instantly the enemy comes in to cause confusion. "Did God really say?" We are no different than Eve. If we begin to reason and doubt what we have heard, we have lost the battle. The first voice is God. The second voice is the enemy trying to deceive us and he does a pretty good job. So, stand fast and see the salvation of God.

It is good for me that I was afflicted, that I might learn your statutes. The law of your mouth is better to me than thousands of gold and silver pieces. (V. 71-72)

What do we learn in affliction and suffering? It all depends upon us. I know for a fact that I have learned more in the valley than on the mountain top. Selah!

"Teth!"

DAY 301

"Yodh"

"Yodh" represents the Creator, the single point from which all creation emerges, and the Unity within. It is the hidden Divine spark which causes everything to be. Many grains of sand are used to make one pot, many pages make up one book, many drops of water make up the ocean. There are many occurrences in the world, but they all stem from One God, perfect and indivisible.

Your hands have made and fashioned me; give me understanding that I may learn your commandments. (V 73)

We are His creation. We are not self-made men and women even though sometimes we think we are.

Those who fear you shall see me and rejoice because I have hoped in your word. I know, O Lord, that your rules are righteous, and that in faithfulness you have afflicted me. (V 74-75)

Psalm 34:19 says, **Many** *are the afflictions of the righteous, but the Lord delivers him out of them.* **Praise God!**

Let your steadfast love comfort me according to your promise to your servant. Let your mercy come to me, that I may live; for your law is my delight. (V 76-77)

David's joy and pleasure came from his delight in the Lord and His Word. He could rejoice when things were good and when things were not so good.

Let those who fear you turn to me, that they may know your testimonies. May my heart be blameless in your statutes, that I may not be put to shame! (V 79-80)

Lord, give us a blameless heart. Help us to keep our eyes on you and not on the things of this world. Help us to understand that we are but one grain of sand among many. But nevertheless, You know every hair on our head. Everything begins and ends with You!

"Yodh!"

DAY 302

"Kaph"

"Kaph" teaches us to bend and govern our tendencies, and to shape our character. It teaches us humility, that we must bend our ego and the resistances in our character. It teaches us molding, sorting, comparing.

My soul longs for your salvation; I hope in your word. My eyes long for your promise; I ask, "When will you comfort me? How long must your servant endure?" (V 81-82 & 84)

Sometimes we all ask, "How Long?" But maybe the length of time depends upon how fast we learn whatever the Lord is trying to teach us. Are we bending to His will or ours?

The insolent have dug pitfalls for me; they do not live according to your law. (V 85) The Lord says they are not your problem. Let me handle others. You handle you. Ouch!

All your commandments are sure; they persecute me with falsehood; "help me!" They have almost made an end of me on earth, but I have not forsaken your precepts. (V 87)

Is the world dragging us down? Are we allowing it? Are all our present trials causing us to turn toward the Lord or are we grumbling and complaining? I am afraid I am doing a little of both. Forgive me Lord! What have I learned so far during this pandemic? Have I become more patient? Have I felt the needs of those in need? Have my eyes been opened to the things of God or my own creature comforts? Am I molding into your image? I hope so!

In your steadfast love give me life, that I may keep the testimonies of your mouth. (V 88)

Make me; mold me; fill me; use me!

"Kaph!"

DAY 303

"Lamedh"

The 12th letter of the Hebrew alphabet is "Lamedh" and is the symbol of learning and also staff or goad. Learning is mostly done with the heart and soul, not just the mind. Learn from everything in life and align with the will of the Creator.

Forever, O Lord, your word is firmly fixed in the heavens. **(V 89)**

Have you ever considered God's word will still be active in heaven? His word never changes. It is the sure footing on which we will always stand. Even in heaven we will meditate on His precepts. However, we will also have the Lord, Himself as our teacher. When we have a question, He will be there to answer and right now I have a few.

Your faithfulness endures to all generations; you have established the earth, and it stands fast. By your appointment they stand this day, for all things are your servants. **(V 90-91)** What is His is mine. That is mind boggling.

If your law had not been my delight, I would have perished in my affliction. I will never forget your precepts, for by them you have given me life. **(V 92-93)**

Memorizing has always been my short suit. I can still remember having to memorize the Gettysburg Address. It was shear torture. But I can remember God's word. He has promised to give us just the right words to say when we need them, and He does!

I am yours; save me, for I have sought your precepts. The wicked lie in wait to destroy me, but I consider your testimonies. I have seen a limit to all perfection, but your commandment is exceedingly broad. **(V 94-96)**

The only time I have audibly heard the voice of God was one evening when I was coming home from an Aglow meeting and questioning God on something I had seen, and audibly He said, "Don't kick against the goad." I had no idea what a goad was, but I found out instantly. I quickly aligned with the word of God.

"Lamedh!"

DAY 304

"Mem"

"Mem" is the 13ᵗʰ letter of the Hebrew alphabet. It means the waters of wisdom and knowledge. It dives deep into wisdom. It teaches us about balanced emotions and humility.

Oh, how I love your law! It is my meditation all the day. Your commandment makes me wiser than my enemies, for it is ever with me. **(V 97-98)**

For the word of God is living and active, sharper than any two-edged sword, piercing to the division of soul and of spirit, of joints and of marrow, and discerning the thoughts and intentions of the heart. **(Hebrews 4:12)**

One anointed word spoken is enough to change any circumstance; to bring life!

I have more understanding than all my teachers, for your testimonies are my meditation. I understand more than the aged, for I keep your precepts. **(V 99-100)**

Age may bring experience, but it does not necessarily bring wisdom. Wisdom comes from meditating on God's word and acting upon it. To read the word is one thing, but to live it is another. Help me Lord!

I hold back my feet from every evil way, in order to keep your word. I do not turn aside from your rules, for you have taught me. **(V 101-102)**

God's word is not a smorgasbord where we pick and choose what we want to believe. I am afraid we have molded the Word to fit our lifestyle. No wonder we are powerless.

How sweet are your words to my taste, sweeter than honey to my mouth! Through your precepts I get understanding; therefore, I hate every false way. **(V 103-104)**

The Old Testament is full of admonitions to read the Word.

DAY 305

"Nun"

"Nun" is the symbol of faithfulness. It stands for humility. Nun shows that to be bound to the Creator's will, not our own personal egoistic way, we must bend above and below. It represents the fish. (Interesting this was the symbol the 1st Christians used)

Your word is a lamp to my feet and a light to my path. I have sworn an oath and confirmed it, to keep your righteous rules. **(V 105-106)**

When God speaks His word to us, we can be assured we are on the right path. I remember a time when we thought we could pray and then open the Bible randomly and find the answer. Dangerous concept. *Judas went out and hung himself. Go and do likewise.* Not!

I am severely afflicted; give me life, O Lord, according to your word! Accept my freewill offering of praise, O Lord, and teach me your rules. **(V 107-108)**

He has promised He will lead us and guide us in all truth. So many times, I need His guidance and direction in my life.

I hold my life in my hand continually, but I do not forget your law. The wicked have laid a snare for me, but I do not stray from your precepts. **(V 109-110)**

I hold my life in my hands is true so often. Rather than allowing the Lord to be Lord, I think I can do it myself and only ask His help when I fail. Not to smart!

Your testimonies are my heritage forever, for they are the joy of my heart. I incline my heart to perform your statutes forever, to the end. **(V 111-112)**

Am I a fish swimming against the stream or am I in the heavenly flow? Am I bending toward His will or am I unbendable in my own beliefs? Is it my way or the highway? Teach me to be pliable in Your hands, O Lord!

"Nun!"

DAY 306

"Samekh"

"Samekh" is the symbol of support, protection, and memory. It means to lean upon, support, uphold. The Samekh teaches us that to know our Creator, we have to get out of our limited selves. We must empty ourselves in order to be filled.

I hate the double-minded, but I love your law. You are my hiding place and my shield; I hope in your word. (V 113-114)

I love the thought that the Lord is my hiding place. He is the place that I can run to when I feel alone. He is my shield. He is my hope.

Depart from me, you evildoers, that I may keep the commandments of my God. Uphold me according to your promise, that I may live, and let me not be put to shame in my hope! (V 115-116)

Usually, we think of an evildoer as someone who does bad things. But the evildoer could be a person with negative responses who is always trying to bring us down. When you need a shot of hope, find the person you know who is most positive and spend some time together. Dwell on the good things in life. There are many!

Hold me up, that I may be safe and have regard for your statutes continually! You spurn all who go astray from your statutes, for their cunning is in vain. All the wicked of the earth you discard like dross, therefore I love your testimonies. My flesh trembles for fear of you, and I am afraid of your judgments. (V 117-120)

The fear of the Lord is the beginning of knowledge; fools despise wisdom and instruction. (Proverbs 1:7)

Sometimes I feel I need a good dose of the "fear of the Lord" because I have become too lackadaisical. Either I think I have plenty of time or I think He really didn't mean what He has said. In either case Lord help me fear You in awe.

"Samekh!"

DAY 307

"Ayin"

"Ayin" is the 16th letter of the Hebrew alphabet. It has to do with vision and bringing forth lights that are hidden. It teaches us to understand the cause and effect in our lives; how past actions lead to future outcomes, and how to think for the future. To break through the walls of limitations in order to see what is not yet visible to us.

I have done what is just and right; do not leave me to my oppressors. Give your servant a pledge of good; let not the insolent oppress me. (V 121-122)

I pray that as I stand before the Lord, He will say, "Well done thou good and faithful servant."

My eyes long for your salvation and for the fulfillment of your righteous promise. Deal with your servant according to your steadfast love and teach me your statutes. I am your servant; give me understanding, that I may know your testimonies. (V 123-125)

Give me understanding. There are so many things that I do not understand both in the natural and in the supernatural. Help me to see what I need to see and have faith for the things that I don't need to see yet.

It is time for the Lord to act, for your law has been broken. (V 126)

I keep wondering how long the Lord will put up with our disobedience. How long will He keep watching the evil that is going on in the world? How long?

Therefore, I love your commandments above gold, above fine gold. Therefore, I consider all your precepts to be right; I hate every false way. (V 127-128)

"Ayin" implores us to open our eyes, to see beyond today. Open our eyes to the Spirit of the Living God. Live beyond today and dream of tomorrow.

"Ayin!"

DAY 308

"Pe"

The Hebrew "Pe" means mouth and refers to the power of speech. What one speaks has the power to become. We should view our words as precious as gold and not be spilling them haphazardly. *Life and death are in the power of the tongue.* **(Proverbs 18:21)**

Your testimonies are wonderful; therefore, my soul keeps them. The unfolding of your words gives light; it imparts understanding to the simple. **(V 129-130)**

God's word gives us power to live. Through His word we have life. His word brings salvation and healing. His word brings direction and comfort.

I open my mouth and pant because I long for your commandments. Turn to me and be gracious to me, as is your way with those who love your name. Keep steady my steps according to your promise, and let no iniquity get dominion over me. **(V 131-133)**

When my dog is hungry, which is all the time, she pants. I wish I were as desperate for God's word as my dog is for food. When Jesus was being tempted by Satan, He used the Word to stop Satan in his tracks. That word is still available to us today if we will only use it and believe it.

Redeem me from man's oppression, that I may keep your precepts. **(V 134)**

There is a difference between knowing the Word and keeping it. The Pharisee's knew the Word. They wrote it on their foreheads and around the bottom of their robes. They had it on their doorpost. But...

Make your face shine upon your servant and teach me your statutes. My eyes shed streams of tears because people do not keep your law. **(V 135-136)**

David wrote 176 verses about knowing and walking in God's word and God said he was a man after His own heart. I am guessing the Word is still important today.

"Pe!"

DAY 309

"Tsadhe"

"Tsadhe" is the 18th letter of the Hebrew Alphabet. The Tsadhe strives to be true, loving justice and fairness, straight and fully honest with their conscience. They are people who are hidden because they appear as ordinary people, despite their great spiritual stature. The literal meaning is a fishing hook.

Righteous are you O Lord, and right are your rules. You have appointed your testimonies in righteousness and in all faithfulness. (V 137-138)

Peace will only come in our lives when we truly believe that God is righteous and faithful to us. He knows what is best for each of us. Our job is to trust Him.

My zeal consumes me, because my foes forget your words. Your promise is well tried, and your servant loves it. (V 139 - 140)

I remember the song, "The Zeal of God has consumed me." This is my prayer today, that the zeal of God will consume each of us.

I am small and despised, yet I do not forget your precepts. Your righteousness is righteous forever, and your law is true. Trouble and anguish have found me out, but your commandments are my delight. (V 141-143)

I picture myself as a grain of sand and am awed that the God of the Universe knows my name and delights in me.

Your testimonies are righteous forever; give me understanding that I may live. (V 144)

When I don't know what to pray, He is there. When I need direction, He is there. When I am feeling lonely, He is there. When I have a need, He is there. When I am sick or hungry, He is there.

Though he slays me, I will hope in him. (Job 13:14)

"Tsadhe!"

DAY 310

"Qoph"

The "Qoph" has to do with the requirement of removing the husk of the superficial to reveal the holiness within.

With my whole heart I cry; answer me, O Lord! I will keep your statutes. I call to you; save me, that I may observe your testimonies. **(V 145-146)**

With my whole heart I cry out to the Lord. There have been times in my life when I have truly cried out to the Lord. But I must admit, there are more times when I have not. There have been times when I trusted Him completely and times when I doubted, He even knew I existed. Have you found yourself in the same place?

I rise before dawn and cry for help; I hope in your words. My eyes are awake before the watches of the night, that I may meditate on your promise. **(V 147-148)**

Age has a way of changing our prayer patterns. I can truly say I am praying before dawn and waiting on the Lord.

Hear my voice according to your steadfast love; O Lord, according to your justice give me life. They draw near who persecute me with evil purpose; they are far from your law. **(V 149-150)**

Who or what causes you to stumble? I notice so often it is those who are the closest. When I should be a witness, I am drawn into conflict. Can you relate?

But you are near, O Lord, and all your commandments are true. Long have I known your testimonies that you have founded them forever. **(V 151-152)**

The Lord is asking us to remove the husk so that we may display what is true. It is so hard to be vulnerable. We are so afraid of what others will think. It is so difficult to reveal the God in us to those who want nothing to do with Him. Help us Lord to be a reflection of you.

"Qoph!"

DAY 311

"Resh"

The 20th letter of the Hebrew alphabet is "Resh". It means to head, leader and beginning. It is the symbol of choosing between greatness and degradation. The qualities of being a leader, not a follower.

Look on my affliction and deliver me, for I do not forget your law. Plead my cause and redeem me; give me life according to your promise! **(V 153-154)**

What is life? Have you ever really thought about it? My thinking so often of life is the here and now. But true life is abundant and full of the Living God. It is breathing in His goodness moment by moment. It is a choice.

Salvation is far from the wicked, for they do not seek your statutes. Great is your mercy, O Lord; give me life according to you rules. **(V 155 – 156)**

Give me life according to your rules. What are his rules? Love the Lord your God with all your heart and your neighbor as yourself. That is it. His rules are a love relationship with Him and with others.

Many are my persecutors and my adversaries, but I do not swerve from your testimonies. I look at the faithless with disgust because they do not keep your commands. **(V 157-158)**

My prayer so often is how Lord? How will they come to know You? How will they come to believe? How will they experience Your love? Show them Lord! And He said, *"I have."*

Consider how I love your precepts! Give me life according to your steadfast love. The sum of your word is truth, and every one of your righteous rules endures forever. **(V 159-160)**

Help me Lord to be a leader, not a follower. Keep me passionately humble.

"Resh!"

DAY 312

"Sin & Shin"

"Sin & Shin" is the letter of fire and transformation. Shin is the whole process of transformation, healing, breaking, and restoring.

Princes persecute me without cause, but my heart stands in awe of your words. I rejoice at your word like one who finds great spoil. **(V 161 – 162)**

Have you ever been reading the Word and all of a sudden something jumps out at you or you find the answer to something you have been seeking the Lord on. Those are such precious moments. Those are moments of transformation.

I hate and abhor falsehood, but I love your law. Seven times a day I praise you for your righteous rules. **(V 163 – 164)**

Is your prayer life a steady stream or is it a once-a-day habit? Do you stop to praise the Lord intermittently? Do you dwell on His goodness? Is He really a part of your daily life or an afterthought? I confess both.

Great peace have those who love your law; nothing can make them stumble. I hope for your salvation, O Lord, and I do your commandments. **(V 165 – 166)**

Peace comes with obedience and obedience comes with faithfulness.

My soul keeps your testimonies; I love them exceedingly. I keep your precepts and testimonies, for all my ways are before you. **(V 167 – 168)**

Healing, breaking, restoring. It seems like all of life follows this pattern. In order to be transformed into the image of Christ we must go through the fire. Now this will mean different things to different people. But I know we can all attest to going through the fire. The question then becomes, "Did we come out as gold, or did we come out of the fire bitter?" Bitter or better? The Father does not give up on us. So, if we have failed a time or two there is still hope. He loves us and wants the very best for us. Allow the fire to burn away your dross.

"Sin & Shin!"

DAY 313

"Taw"

"Taw" is the last letter of the Hebrew alphabet. It means mark, sign, omen, or seal. It is the symbol of truth, perfection, and completion. It is the idea that the Creator set in motion all of existence in order to reach a final state of perfection. However, as soon as the Taw is reached, we begin again immediately by going back to the Aleph, the one source of everything. The end is never really the end, but the beginning of something new. (The alpha and omega, the beginning, and the end)

Let my cry come before you, O Lord; give me understanding according to your word! Let my plea come before you; deliver me according to your word. (V 169-170) This is his final cry for deliverance in this Psalm.

My lips will pour forth praise, for you teach me your statutes. My tongue will sing of your words, for all your commandments are right. (V 171-172)

David trusted God. He believed God's word. He knew how to praise. He was a man after God's own heart.

Let your hand be ready to help me, for I have chosen your precepts. I long for your salvation, O Lord, and your law is my delight. (V 173-174)

We are told to choose this day who we will serve. I say as for me and my house we will serve the Lord!

Let my soul live and praise you, and let your rules help me. I have gone astray like a lost sheep; seek your servant, for I do not forget your commandments. (V 175-176)

What have I learned from this Psalm? First, I now know part of the meaning of the Hebrew alphabet. I know that David's secret was found in loving God and loving His word. I know David knew God's mercy. I know David was willing to admit his short comings. I know that David was a prayer warrior and a worshipper. Lord, I pray to do the same. Selah!

"Taw!"

WATER FROM THE ROCK

DAY 314

I will stand there before you by the rock at Horeb. Strike the rock, and water will come out of it for the people to drink. (**Exodus 17:6**)

It is interesting, the Israelites were at a place called Massah or Meribah. Massah means testing and Meribah means quarreling. The people had said, *Is the Lord among us or not?* (**Exodus 17:7**)

The Lord had caused plagues to fall on the Egyptians. He had sent His people away with the Egyptians bounty. They had crossed the Red Sea without a drop of water on their clothes. The Egyptians had followed and drowned. God did all these things for the Israelites. Surely this was enough to show God was with them.

When the Israelites saw the mighty hand of the Lord displayed against the Egyptians, the people feared the Lord and put their trust in him and in Moses his servant. Then Moses and the Israelites sang this song to the Lord: I will sing to the Lord for he is highly exalted. Both the horse and driver he has hurled into the sea. (**Exodus 14:31 – 15:1**)

We sing when we are happy, but do we sing when we are not? Sometimes, we are more like the Israelites then we think. The Lord said, ***"Strike the rock!"*** What happened? Water came out of the rock, enough for all the six hundred thousand men, plus women and children. That is a lot of water! We add one more miracle to what they had already experienced. How much does it take for us to believe that God is, and that He is a rewarder of those who diligently seek Him?

Our youngest daughter was five years old when she was diagnosed with a fatal liver disease. For one year we took her to the K.U. Medical Center for treatment. She was having a biopsy and the doctor asked what I thought. I said, *"I believe she is healed and will not have to come back."* The doctors were amazed, but she was healed and did not go back. Did I become a super Christian immediately? No

"There is no rock like our God!"

DAY 315

Then the Lord said, "There is a place near me where you may stand on a rock. When my glory passes by, I will put you in a cleft in the rock and cover you with my hand until I have passed by. Then I will remove my hand and you will see my back; but my face must not be seen." (Exodus 33:21-22)

When our desire is to see the Lord, what are we really asking for? The Lord said, **"You cannot see my face, for no one may see me and live." (Exodus 33:20)** Have you ever thought about that? My question then is, "Who have people really seen when they claim to have seen God?" May I make a wild guess? I think they have seen Jesus. After Jesus rose from the dead, He was seen by his disciples. He was seen by the women who went to the tomb and others. He is the visible form of the Godhead.

Acts 1:3 says, He (Jesus) appeared to them over a period of forty days and spoke about the kingdom of God.

Then Moses said, "Now show me your glory." And the Lord said, "I will cause all my goodness to pass in front of you, and I will proclaim my name, the Lord in your presence. I will have mercy on whom I will have mercy, and I will have compassion on whom I will have compassion." (Exodus 33:19)

The Lord showed Moses all His goodness and mercy. Can you even begin to fathom that? Later Moses would remind God of His goodness and mercy as he pleaded for the fallen Israelites.

Before we begin to plead to see God, maybe we had better count the cost. Seeing Him might destroy us.

There was a time when many were claiming to have seen angels. My oldest son came in one day and said, "Mom, I think I just saw an angel in the sky. I watched while he disappeared behind a cloud and then I saw him on the other side."

"There is no rock like our God!"

DAY 316

He and Aaron gathered the assembly together in front of the rock and Moses said to them, "Listen, you rebels, must we bring you water out of this rock?" Then Moses raised his arm and struck the rock twice with his staff. Water gushed out, and the community and their livestock drank. But the Lord said to Moses and Aaron, "Because you did not trust in me enough to honor me as holy in the sight of the Israelites, you will not bring this community into the land I give them." **(Numbers 20:10-12)**

The Lord had told Moses to speak to the rock. God honored Moses' request by giving the people water, but He was displeased with Moses and Aaron.

Moses had seen God's glory. He had spent 40 days with Him on Mount Sinai. I would say he knew God much better than most of us do. But Moses did not follow God's instructions. God said, *"Speak to the rock."* I am wondering if a little self or frustration got in Moses's way. He said, *"Listen, you rebels, must we bring you water out of this rock?"* Moses was angry. Can any of us bring water out of a rock just by hitting it? Moses took matters into his own hands, and it cost him the promised land.

Just because we have seen God move one way does not mean He will do the same thing again. I have learned this lesson the hard way.

I have always believed that healing is for today, and that we should be able to lay hands on people and see them recover. But, believing and seeing it happen are two different things. When my oldest son was in high school, he broke his foot playing football. The referee said, "Son put your shoe on." His shoe was on. I sat by his bed in the hospital praying in the Spirit. The doctor came in and said, "In the morning we will do surgery." I believed that surgery would not be necessary, and it wasn't. In six weeks, he was playing on the basketball team. Other times I have prayed, and nothing happened. It is up to God, not us!

"There is no rock like our God!"

DAY 317

He is the Rock, his works are perfect, and all his ways are just. **(Deuteronomy 32:4)**

One definition of a rock is something solid, stable, and grounded. It represents strength and resiliency. A tradition current among the Jews affirms that this rock followed the people in their travels and gave forth a living stream for their supply. This sounds like a few of God's many attributes.

The Lord is my rock, my fortress and my deliverer, my God is my rock, in whom I take refuge, my shield and the horn of my salvation, my stronghold. **(Psalm 18:2)**

I know I would rather stand on a rock than on sinking sand. I would rather stand on God and His Word than trust in man. As I pray for my family I often say, "Lord be a fortress around them. Be a shield to protect them. Be their stronghold."

As the Israelites drank water from the rock, we can drink living water from the well that never runs dry.

John 7:37-38 says, *Let everyone who is thirsty come to me and drink. Whoever believes in me, as Scripture has said, rivers of living water will flow from within them.*

Remember when we used to have pet rocks and carried them around in our pockets? We would decorate them and give them names. Kids can think up some of the craziest things.

But we have a Rock that is not just another fad. His name is Jesus. He is solid, stable, full of strength, and able to supply all our needs. We don't need to strike Him. We just need to call upon His name. His works are perfect, and all His ways are just.

"There is no rock like our God!"

DAY 318

Your dwelling place is secure, your nest is set in a rock. **(Numbers 24:21)**

What a neat scripture. I would never have seen it if I weren't looking for places the word "rock" is found in the Bible. Your nest is set in a rock. When I think of a nest, I picture a bird taking care of her young. She has found a worm and is dropping it into the baby's mouth.

Isn't this so like our Lord? He has us securely in His nest, set in a rock. We are totally protected and cared for by Him.

Psalm 84:3 says, *Even the sparrow has found a home, and the swallow a nest for herself, where she may have her young – a place near your altar, Lord Almighty, my King, and my God.*

Matthew 6:26-27 says, *Look at the birds of the air; they do not sow or reap or store away in barns, and yet your heavenly Father feeds them. Are you not much more valuable than they?*

Not only are we secure in His nest, but we are set in a rock. If we are in a rock, we are protected on three sides and the Word tells us He is our rear guard. We have nothing to fear.

Our oldest daughter had just left the courtroom. Her divorce was final. She had just opened a gift shop, thinking that with both of their incomes, they could make it. Now she was alone. The only recourse was bankruptcy. She closed the shop, packed all her belongings, and headed home. This was not the way she had envisioned her life as she walked down the aisle. She had two choices: to give up or to shake the dust off her sandals and begin again. She has a very strong walk with the Lord. He opened doors for her, and her life went on. It was not the way she had planned it. But she was hidden in the Rock!

"There is no rock like our God!"

DAY 319

They abandoned the God who made them and rejected the Rock their Savior. They made him jealous with their foreign gods and angered him with their detestable idols. (**Deuteronomy 32:15**)

Did you know that God is a jealous God? *Do not worship any other god, for the Lord, whose name is Jealous, is a jealous God.* (**Exodus 34:14**)

One of the things that really angers God is our idol worship. He has told us to have no other gods before Him. We don't have statues in our homes. We don't bow down to idols. We have not rejected the Rock our Savior.

Let's think about this for a moment. How many things do we put before God? How many possessions are more important to us than God? How many activities do we engage in instead of attending church? Help me out! I confess, I sometimes reject the Rock of My Salvation. I would not call it rejecting, but I have things to do that are more important at the moment.

For whom is God besides the Lord? And who is the Rock except our God? It is God who arms me with strength and keeps my way secure. (**Psalm 18:31-32**)

The Lord lives! Praise be to my Rock! Exalted be God my Savior! (**Psalm 18:46**)

When Covid hit, we all stayed home from church. Most of us found a TV evangelist that we liked and began to watch our Sunday morning service online. We became comfortable sitting at home. We could drink our coffee. Get up and check on the laundry and still listen. We got in the habit. Now many of us are used to staying at home. We have traded the pew for the easy chair. We have traded fellowship for convenience. But the Father desires that we fellowship, not only with Him but with each other. Has the easy chair become an idol?

"There is no rock like our God!"

DAY 320

Then Hannah prayed and said, "My heart rejoices in the Lord; in the Lord my horn is lifted high. My mouth boasts over my enemies, for I delight in your deliverance. There is no one holy like the Lord; there is no one besides you; there is no Rock like our God." (1 Samuel 2:1-2)

Hannah desperately wanted a child. She had prayed and prayed. She promised that if the Lord would give her a son, she would give him back to the Lord. Eli the priest thought she was drunk. Have you ever prayed so fervently that you appeared drunk? God will listen to desperation prayers. When Eli finally realized that she was fervently praying he said, *"Go in peace, and may the God of Israel grant you what you asked of him." (1 Samuel 1:17)*

God answered her prayer. She bore a son and named him Samuel. Here is where her story differs so much from most of ours. She had promised to give this child back to the Lord and she did. If we were Christians when we had our first born, I would imagine we made lots of promises to the Lord. Have we kept them?

Hannah said to Eli, *"I prayed for this child, and the Lord has granted me what I asked of him. So now I give him to the Lord. For his whole life he will be given over to the Lord." And he worshiped the Lord there. (1 Samuel 1:27)*

Here was a woman who wanted a child. The moment he was weaned she literally gave him to God. Once a year she visited him. What a sacrifice! She said, *"There is no Rock like our God."*

My first child was born breech. I was clueless about raising a child. I didn't know the first thing about diapers, feeding, crying, etc. I was like Junie B. Jones. I wanted to give this thing back. My reasons were not like Hannah's. Today I am so blessed to have my first-born daughter. She is such a special person. She has a heart for the Lord. She is a giver, and she is a keeper!

"There is no rock like our God!"

DAY 321

David sang to the Lord the words of this song when the Lord delivered him from the hand of all his enemies and from the hand of Saul. He said: "The Lord is my rock, my fortress and my deliverer; my God is my rock, in whom I take refuge, my shield and the horn of my salvation." (2 Samuel 22:2-3)

David knew who was behind his deliverance in all situations. He understood that man may have the muscle, but God has the final say. He knew that the Lord was his rear guard.

Isaiah 52:12 says, *But you will not leave in haste or go in flight; for the Lord will go before you, the God of Israel will be your rear guard.*

Isaiah 58:8 says, *Then your light will break forth like the dawn, and your healing will quickly appear; then your righteousness will go before you, and the glory of the Lord will be your rear guard.*

When we truly begin to realize who is watching over us, and the extent of His love, we are on our way to victory! The Lord is our rock, our fortress, and our deliverer. We can take refuge in Him! We can hide under the shadow of His wings!

Romans 9:33 says, *See, I lay in Zion a stone that causes people to stumble and a rock that makes them fall, and the one who believes in him will never be put to shame.*

We are either on the Rock or under it. When we believe that Jesus is the Christ, the Son of the Living God, we are on the Rock. We have a firm foundation. We cannot be shaken. But those under the Rock are still struggling to be set free. They are trapped and cannot find their way out. But God!

I am so thankful I am saved, sanctified, and set free by the Blood of Jesus. Aren't you?

"There is no rock like our God!"

DAY 322

Exalted be my God, the Rock, my Savior! He is the God who avenges me, who put the nations under me, who sets me free from my enemies. **(2 Samuel 22:47-48)**

There is nothing worse than being around a bully or being bullied, except being the bully. Girls don't seem to be tagged bullies, but they are, even though they may not use fists. They get in little cliques and talk about other girls. They exclude people from their group. They face chat about girls they don't like at the moment. They can be catty! We usually think of a bully as someone bigger and tougher than the rest of the kids. But this is not necessarily so.

We have a Savior in Christ Jesus. He is our avenger. He sets us free from our enemies. He is like a rock, ready to attack those who attack us. He has our back.

Psalm 27:5 says, *For in the day of trouble he will keep me safe in his dwelling; he will hide me in the shelter of his sacred tent and set me high upon a rock.*

No problem Mr. Bully. The Lord is my rear guard. You cannot sneak up on me from behind. I am protected on all sides. My bodyguard never slumbers nor sleeps. He keeps watch over me at all times.

For their rock is not like our Rock, as even our enemies concede. **(Deuteronomy 32:31)**

Our oldest son was a sleepwalker. One evening he spent the night at a friend's who lived about five houses away from us. In the middle of the night, we heard a loud knock at a door we never used. We both got up and went to the door prepared for battle. There stood our son. He had no idea how he had gotten there. He was in his pajamas with no shoes on and a bewildered look on his face.

Aren't you glad we are under the shelter of His wings?

"There is no rock like our God!"

DAY 323

And who is the Rock except our God? It is God who arms me with strength and keeps my way secure. He makes my feet like the feet of a deer; he causes me to stand on the heights. He trains my hands for battle. **(2 Samuel 22:32-35)**

About the time I think I can do it in my own strength, I stumble and fall. My way is not always the right way. Sometimes I need to take a detour and regroup. I need to rethink where I am going and the way I am getting there. There is a difference between a stop sign and a caution sign. Thank goodness we have a God who not only tells us to stop, but always nudges us with caution.

The fascinating thing about a deer is that its back feet always go in the imprint of its front feet. When the front feet feel safety, the back feet follow. Therefore, the deer is less likely to stumble and fall. If our feet are following the imprint of the Master hiker, we will not fall either.

He says He will train our hands for battle.

Ephesians 6:13-17 tells us how we are being trained. *Therefore, put on the full armor of God, so that when the day of evil comes, you may be able to stand your ground, and after you have done everything, to stand. Stand firm then, with the belt of truth buckled around your waist, with the breastplate of righteousness in place, and with your feet fitted with the readiness that comes from the gospel of peace. In addition to all this take up the shield of faith, with which you can extinguish all the flaming arrows of the evil one. Take the helmet of salvation and the sword of the Spirit, which is the word of God. And pray in the Spirit on all occasions with all kinds of prayers and requests.*

Need I say anything else. We have every weapon we need to win the battle, but we must put on the full armor, not just one piece. I can have a sword but if I do not have a shield, I will be vulnerable. Today we need to stand equipped.

"There is no rock like our God!"

DAY 324

The God of Israel spoke, the Rock of Israel said to me: "When one rules over people in righteousness, when he rules in the fear of God, he is like the light of morning at sunrise on a cloudless morning, like the brightness after rain that brings grass from the earth." (2 Samuel 23:3-4)

Christians, it is time we quit quarreling over who is right and who is wrong, who should be in office and who shouldn't. It is what it is! Let's move on. We are told to pray for those in authority. We are to respect them. We are to hold up the feeble hands that hang down. Jesus never raised up arms against those who ruled over Him. He gave to Caesar what was Caesar's and to God what was God's. I fail to see Christ in much of what I am seeing on TV and hearing from many.

I don't know the heart of any other person, but I know the Lord has admonished us to pray for one another. He has never told us to raise up arms, to bad mouth, or to undercut another. Those in authority are there because God has put them there, even if we don't believe it. God is still on His throne!

"Whose image is this? And whose inscription?" "Caesar's," they replied. Then he said to them, "So give back to Caesar what is Caesar's, and to God what is God's." When they heard this, they were amazed. So, they left him and went away. (Matthew 22:21-22)

I am hoping they went away to pray for those in authority.

For our struggle is not against flesh and blood, but against the rulers, against the authorities, against the powers of this dark world and against the spiritual forces of evil in the heavenly realms. (Ephesians 6:12)

I am not the least bit interested in politics. I am interested in being obedient to Christ first and foremost. My allegiance is to Him and Him alone. I will give unto Caesar the things that are Caesar's BUT, I will give to God my whole heart!

"There is no rock like our God!"

DAY 325

In their hunger you gave them bread from heaven and in their thirst, you brought them water from the rock; you told them to go in and take possession of the land you had sworn with uplifted hand to give them. (Nehemiah 9:15)

For forty years the Lord sustained the Israelites in the wilderness. They did not lack for anything. It is interesting that their clothes did not wear out nor did their feet become swollen. Now why would the Lord even consider swollen feet? I think he was trying to show them and us that he cares about every little detail in our lives. When I sit too long my feet become swollen. My ankles lose their shape, and I am a bit miserable. This didn't happen in the wilderness.

Then he told them to possess the land. I understand what it meant for them, but does it have meaning for us today? I think so. Ever since we lost the right to pray in school, our Christianity has been slowly taken away from us. We are like a frog in a pot of water. The frog does not even realize that the heat has been turned up slowly, until he is no more. We need to begin taking back our land. But how can we do that?

Remember how the Lord your God led you all the way in the wilderness these forty years, to humble and test you in order to know what was in your heart, whether or not you would keep his commands? (Deuteronomy 8:2)

I think the key is knowing what is in our hearts. So many times, I am double minded. I truly want the things of God, but I also want the things of this world. I like nice clothes, a nice home, a nice car, etc. I would be lying if I said I didn't. How do I walk in the world and not be of the world? I think the answer lies in being open handed. By this I mean being willing at any moment to stop what I am doing and direct my attention toward the Lord. "Yes Lord!" should constantly be on my lips.

"There is no rock like our God!"

DAY 326

To You, Lord I call; you are my Rock, do not turn a deaf ear to me. For if you remain silent, I will be like those who go down to the pit. (Psalm 28:1)

I sometimes wonder if I understand what silence is. Even when my mouth is still, my mind is still going 100 miles a minute. How do I learn to truly be silent in a world that is rushing so fast that I can hardly take a breath? Is this just me or do you have the same problem? I cannot imagine being alone in the wilderness for 40 days.

David isn't speaking of his silence, but of God's. I am wondering if they are one and the same. If I am not silent, I will not hear God. If God is not speaking, maybe I need to just sit and wait.

Be silent, Israel and listen! You have now become the people of the Lord your God. Obey the Lord your God and follow his commands and decrees that I give you today. (Deuteronomy 27:9-10)

The Lord commanded the Israelites to be silent and listen. They must have had the same problem that we have, itchy ears that did not listen to the right voice.

Then David says, *"If you remain silent, I will be like those who go down to the pit."*

I can totally relate to David. So many times, I want a word from the Lord and either don't listen or miss it. That is a "pit!" We use that word a lot to describe negative things. When we have missed the awesome word of the Lord because we didn't listen, we are in a pit.

Life is a series of ups and downs. Sometimes we are on the mountain top and other times we have gone down to the pit. I ask myself, "Why?" I know the answer, but I do not follow it. *May the God of hope fill you with all joy and peace as you trust in him.* (Romans 15:13) "Trust"

"There is no rock like our God!"

DAY 327

Since you are my rock and my fortress, for the sake of your name lead and guide me. (Psalm 31:3)

Sometimes I think it is all about me. I have tunnel vision. I pray "give me" prayers and ask "give me" requests. I want what seems right in my own eyes. I won't admit it, but I feel entitled. I am sure I am not alone in this. Every now and then I check my prayer list to see if I have any praise on it. He gives and He gives, and I take, and I take, but where is appreciation?

David says, *"For the sake of your name lead and guide me."* It is not all about me. It is for His name's sake that we were placed on planet earth. We are His possession not the other way around. We were created for His good pleasure.

His pleasure is not in the strength of the horse, nor his delight in the legs of the warrior; the Lord delights in those who fear him, who put their hope in his unfailing love. (Psalm 147:10-11)

Have you ever heard or said, "Well, my daddy is bigger than yours!" Small children delight in bragging about their fathers. It is a natural response for a young child to see his father as someone big and strong and able to handle any problem the child has. Where do you think children got this idea? I believe it is heaven sent. Our Heavenly Father wants us to look up to Him as big and strong and able to handle any problem that we have.

It is for His name's sake that we were created in the first place. It is for His delight that we were born. He is our proud Father. He looks down and says, "Those are My kids!" Today let's grab onto His hand and look into His eyes and tell Him how much we love Him; how much He means to us. Let's crawl up on His lap and give Him a big hug. You know we can, and He loves it when we do.

"There is no rock like our God!"

DAY 328

Trust in the Lord forever, for the Lord, the Lord himself, is the Rock eternal. **(Isaiah 26:4)**

Trust is the firm belief in the reliability or strength of someone or something. It is confidence, faith in, certainty and assurance. Every one of these definitions describes our Father. He is trustworthy. He is reliable and His word will stand for ever. He is the Rock on which our faith is established.

Salvation is found in no one else, for there is no other name under heaven given to mankind by which we must be saved. **(Acts 4:12)**

There are all sorts of religions out there. There are all sorts of holy men. There are all sorts of doctrines floating around. But there is only One that is true and reliable. There is only One that we can put our whole trust in, and His name is Jesus. All others are wood, hay and stubble.

There is a statue of Buddha on the front counter of the nail salon that I go to. I look at that statue and shake my head. How personal is a statue? Can a statue give us comfort in time of need? Can a statue guide and direct us when we are lost? Can a statue give us eternal life?

They exchanged the truth about God for a lie and worshiped and served created things rather than the Creator - who is forever praised. Amen. **(Romans 1:25)**

A statue may seem silly to you, but I wonder how many other idols we worship? I wonder how many things get in the way of true worship.

What agreement is there between the temple of God and idols? For we are the temple of the living God. As God has said: "I will live with them and walk among them, and I will be their God and they will be my people." **(2 Corinthians 6:16)**

"There is no rock like our God!"

DAY 329

See, a king will reign in righteousness and rulers will rule with justice. Each one will be like a shelter from the wind and a refuge from the storm, like streams of water in the desert and the shadow of a great rock in a thirsty land. (Isaiah 32:2)

I love Isaiah analogy, *like streams of water in the desert and the shadow of a great rock in a thirsty land.* Can't you just picture being in a desert, hot and dry, with sand in your mouth, struggling to take your next step? Suddenly you spy an oasis. Thinking that it is just a mirage, you slowly approach and find there truly is water to drink and not only water, but a rock to provide shade from the heat.

This is one of the many pictures of God's provision for His people. *And my God will meet all your needs according to the riches of his glory in Christ Jesus.* **(Philippians 4:19)**

He is our oasis in the wilderness. He is the Rock we can stand on. He is our sure word of deliverance. He provides water for the thirsty and shade for the weary. There is nothing too hard for Him.

To you, Lord I call; you are my Rock, do not turn a deaf ear to me. For if you remain silent, I will be like those who go down to the pit. (Psalm 28:1)

We have nothing to fear. Our God is as near as we will allow Him to be. The closer we come, the easier it is to hear His voice and to obey Him. He will keep us under the shelter of His wings.

Whoever dwells in the shelter of the Most High will rest in the shadow of the Almighty. I will say of the Lord, "He is my refuge and my fortress, my God, in whom I trust." (Psalm 91:1-2)

He provides streams of water in a dry and thirsty land, and a rock to shelter us both day and night.

"There is no rock like our God!"

DAY 330

Do not tremble, do not be afraid. Did I not proclaim this and foretell it long ago? You are my witnesses. Is there any God besides me? No, there is no other Rock; I know not one. (Isaiah 44:8)

What a fitting scripture for today. The world is turning upside down. The economy is questionable. Climate change is on everyone's mind. Morals are decaying. People do not know who they are. And the Lord says, *"Did I not proclaim this and foretell it long ago?"*

We are living in the most exciting age since the birth of Christ. We are experiencing end times. Now I do not profess to know a date or a time, but I know we are getting closer to seeing the Lord in the air. I hope I am here to experience it. Don't you?

But about that day or hour no one knows, not even the angels in heaven, nor the Son, but only the Father. (Matthew 24:36)

If the Son of God does not know what is in the Father's mind on this, then I ask, "How can we know?" But the word says we will know the season.

Two men will be in the field; one will be taken and the other left. Two women will be grinding with a hand mill; one will be taken and the other left. (Matthew 24:40)

Then Jesus begins to speak about Noah and the ark. We are going full circle. Noah warned the people over and over, but they would not listen. Finally, the Lord told Noah and his family to get into the ark and God himself shut the door. All the screaming the people did was to no avail. The door was shut. The flood came and took them all away.

Is there any God besides me? No, there is no other Rock; I know not one.

"There is no rock like our God!"

DAY 331

On that day when all the nations of the earth are gathered against her, I will make Jerusalem an immovable rock for all the nations. All who try to move it will injure themselves...On that day I will set out to destroy all the nations that attack Jerusalem. (**Zechariah 12:3 & 9**)

Have you ever wondered why the Jewish people are just like the energizer bunny? They just keep coming back. I have been thinking about all the horrible things that have happened to them over the years, and still, they remain and are even stronger than ever. One might ask the question, "Why?"

The people of Jerusalem are strong because the Lord Almighty is their God. (**Zechariah 12:5**) However, most of the Jewish people do not believe that Jesus is the Christ, the Son of the Living God. How can they still find favor with the Lord? Their eyes have been blinded until the time the Lord chooses to open them.

And I will pour out on the house of David and the inhabitants of Jerusalem a spirit of grace and supplication. They will look on me, the one they have pierced, and they will mourn for him as one mourns for an only child and grieve bitterly for him as one cries for a firstborn son. (**Zachariah 12:10**)

The Jewish people have always been God's chosen. But by the grace of God, we have been grafted in.

If some of the branches have been broken off, and you, though a wild olive shoot, have been grafted in among the others and now share in the nourishing sap from the olive root, do not consider yourself to be superior to those other branches. (**Romans 11:17-18**)

We are told to pray for the peace of Jerusalem in Psalm 122:6. Jerusalem is an immovable rock for all the nations. Watch Jerusalem and see how God is moving.

"There is no rock like our God!"

DAY 332

Therefore, everyone who hears these words of mine and puts them into practice is like a wise man who built his house on the rock. The rain came down, the streams rose, and the winds blew and beat against that house; yet it did not fall because it had its foundation on the rock. (Matthew 7:24-25)

One of my favorite songs is the one that says, "My faith is built on nothing less than Jesus' blood and righteousness."

If our faith is in anyone or anything other than Jesus, we are like *the foolish man who built his house on sand. The rain came down, the streams rose, and the winds blew and beat against that house, and it fell with a great crash.* (Matthew 7:26-27)

We are living in a fallen world. All around us are idols of wealth, prestige, fame, etc. Our goals usually include success, popularity, recognition, and acclaim. Where is our Rock in all of this? We have built our homes on sand. Our families have been infiltrated by sand. Our schools and our churches are full of sand. What has happened to the Rock of our salvation?

But there is hope! Our young people are beginning to rise up and take back the land. Revival is beginning among our youth. Our youngest granddaughter is so on fire for the Lord. She is dancing and singing His praises continually.

It has been 50 years since we truly had a revival in our country. I would like to say it is the older folk who are sparking this fire and fanning the flames. But most of us have gotten comfortable in our easy chairs and allowed the world to take over. Father forgive us!

It is time to rebuild our spiritual houses on the Rock! It is time to get back into the Word of God. It is time for us to begin to act like the early church. It is time for the fire of the Holy Spirit to again invade our lives and our families. It is time!

"There is no rock like our God!"

DAY 333

"But what about you?" he asked. "Who do you say I am?" Simon Peter answered, "You are the Messiah, the Son of the living God." Jesus replied, "Blessed are you, Simon son of Jonah, for this was not revealed to you by flesh and blood, but by my Father in heaven. And I tell you that you are Peter, and on this rock, I will build my church, and the gates of Hades will not overcome it." (Matthew 16:15-18)

I think some people are confused by the rock in this passage. Jesus was not telling Peter He was going to build His church on Peter. He was telling Peter the church would be built on his confession. What was his confession? *You are the Messiah, the Son of the living God.*

The church is built on Jesus Christ.

The stone the builders rejected has become the cornerstone. (Psalm 118:22)

See, I lay a stone in Zion, a tested stone, precious cornerstone for a sure foundation; the one who relies on it will never be stricken with panic. (Isaiah 28:16)

From Judah will come the cornerstone. (Zechariah 10:4) **and finally,** *Jesus is the stone you builders rejected, which has become the cornerstone.* (Acts 4:11)

There is only one rock on which we can build a solid foundation and that is Jesus Christ, the Messiah, the Son of the Living God, the Author and Finisher of our faith, the First Born from the dead, the Prince of Peace, the Lamb of God, Emmanuel, the Good Shepherd, the Light of the World, the Morningstar, the Bread of Life, the Chief Cornerstone. We could go on and on. He is our All in All!

"There is no rock like our God!"

DAY 334

See I lay in Zion a stone that causes people to stumble and a rock that makes them fall, and the one who believes in him will never be put to shame. (Romans 9:33)

Is Jesus a stumbling block to you? Does He cramp your style? Are you uncomfortable when the Spirit of God begins to move? Is Jesus a name to you or a real live person who you can communicate with? These may seem like silly questions, but I am guilty so often of taking Jesus for granted. I want Him in my life, but I also want my life. Does this make sense to you?

I wonder how many times I have been with people who were not Christians and I have joined right along with them in their worldly pleasures? How many times have I denied Christ by not acknowledging Him? No one said it was easy to be a Christian. It is not. But in the long run, the benefits are worth far more than the short-term pleasures.

Anyone who loves their father or mother more than me is not worthy of me; anyone who loves their son or daughter more than me is not worthy of me. Whoever does not take up their cross and follow me is not worthy of me. Whoever finds their life will lose it, and whoever loses their life for my sake will find it. (Matthew 10:37-39)

Is this what Jesus meant when he said that He would lay in Zion a stone that would cause people to stumble and a rock that would make them fall? I am beginning to think so. But shouldn't we honor our father and mother? Shouldn't we love our brother and sister? Yes, the key words are *"more than me"*. Jesus should be first in each of our lives, and then everything and everybody else will fall into place.

"There is no rock like our God!"

DAY 335

Now to you who believe, this stone is precious. But to those who do not believe, the stone the builders rejected has become the cornerstone, and a stone that causes people to stumble and a rock that makes them fall. **(1 Peter 2:7-8)**

Now here comes a statement that totally confuses me. *They stumble because they disobey the message – which is also what they were destined for.* **(V 8)** If the Lord would have all of us saved. If He wishes that none should perish. If He commands us to go into all the world and preach the gospel. Then are some people destined for hell even before they are born? It is hard for me to believe a loving God would put a stamp of disapproval on some before they even have an opportunity to turn to Him or away from Him. This is definitely one of the questions I am going to ask when I get to heaven. I am sure there is a loving explanation.

But you are a chosen people, a royal priesthood, a holy nation, God's special possession, that you may declare the praises of him who called you out of darkness into his wonderful light. Once you were not a people, but now you are the people of God; once you had not received mercy but now you have received mercy. **(V 9)**

When the Holy Spirit nudges us to follow Jesus, we should jump for joy. We should run to Him with open arms. We should embrace Him and hold on tight. We are His chosen people. We have been grafted into His kingdom. We are blessed beyond measure.

I would love to hear what you think on this. I pray daily that my family will harken to His voice. I pray that they would come with open arms into the Kingdom of God.

"There is no rock like our God!"

DAY 336

Our ancestors were all under the cloud and they all passed through the sea. They were all baptized into Moses in the cloud and in the sea. They all ate the same spiritual food and drank the same spiritual drink; for they drank from the spiritual rock that accompanied them, and that rock was Christ. **(1 Corinthians 10:1-4)**

This scripture reaffirms that Jesus Christ is, was and always will be. He came from the Father, and He returned to the Father. He will come again and receive those who are His. The word tells us that, *Jesus Christ is the same yesterday and today and forever.* **(Hebrews 13:8)**

John 1:1 & 14 says, *In the beginning was the Word, and the Word was with God, and the Word was God...The Word became flesh and made his dwelling among us. We have seen his glory, the glory of the one and only Son, who came from the Father, full of grace and truth.*

Genesis 1 says, *In the beginning God...and the Spirit of God was hovering over the waters...God said, "Let there be..."*

From the very first words spoken in the Word, the Trinity was visible to all who have eyes to see. The Trinity has always been and always will be. I picture the Father as the Mastermind, Jesus as the spoken Word, and the Spirit overseeing and ready to intervene in human lives.

I also picture the Father as the beginning, the Son as the middle and the Holy Spirit as the finale. Have you ever thought about it?

They drank from the same spiritual rock that accompanied them and that rock was Jesus.

Isn't it fun to speculate? Won't it be interesting when we get to heaven to see what was true and what was just wood, hay and stubble?

"There is no rock like our God!"

DAY 337

May these words of my mouth and this meditation of my heart be pleasing in your sight, Lord, my Rock, and my Redeemer. **Psalm, 19:14**

This is the cry of my heart. Words express who a person is, and what that person believes. Words speak much louder than we often give them credit for. A word spoken in secret becomes an announcement from the roof top. If you have ever played the gossip game where one person whispers to the next, and it goes around the circle until the last person saying what he thought he heard, then you have proof that what begins as one thing can very easily end as another.

A word spoken can bring hope or it can crush the spirit. Sometimes I think we have oral diarrhea. We talk just to talk, or we think what we say is more important than a listening heart.

Ephesians 5:4 says, *Nor should there be obscenity, foolish talk, or coarse joking, which are out of place, but rather thanksgiving.*

I have a real problem with emails that glorify God and in the same moment express smut. That is talking out of both sides of your mouth. This should not be!

Lord help us to choose our words carefully, knowing that we will have to give an account for every word that comes out of our mouth.

May these words of my mouth and this meditation of my heart be pleasing in your sight, Lord, my Rock, and my Redeemer.

"There is no rock like our God!"

DAY 338

I waited patiently for the Lord; he turned to me and heard my cry. He lifted me out of the slim pit, out of the mud and mire; he set my feet on a rock and gave me a firm place to stand. He put a new song in my mouth, a hymn of praise to our God. Many will see and fear the Lord and put their trust in him. **(Psalm 40:1-3)**

When we are standing firmly on the Rock, many will see and fear the Lord and put their trust in Him. The solid Christian is a true witness to the world. A solid Christian does not waver in his beliefs. A solid Christian stands on the Word of God even when everyone else is doubting. A solid Christian knows his Lord intimately and is not afraid to share his beliefs with others.

The world is watching and waiting for Christians to fall. But God has given us a firm place to stand and that is in His Son, Jesus Christ. He will never leave us nor forsake us. He is the Rock! Never doubt this. It is time we come out of the woodwork and begin to stand for what we say we believe. It is time to be bold. It is time to put the old adage into practice. "He said it. I believe it. That settles it."

When we pray we are not responsible for the results. Our only responsibility is to pray believing. It is God who gives the increase. We cannot change a single hair on our head. We are not expected to produce results but only believe. It sounds easy, but take my word for it, it is not. Faith is an exercise in belief. Hope is a desire, but faith is a firm resolution. They are not the same.

When we believe and trust in the Word of God, He sets our feet on a rock and gives us a firm place to stand. He puts a new song in our mouth, a hymn of praise to our God. Most importantly, many will see and fear the Lord and put their trust in Him. Be solid as a rock today and watch God work in and through you.

"There is no rock like our God!"

DAY 339

From the ends of the earth, I call to you, I call as my heart grows faint; lead me to the rock that is higher than I. (Psalm 61:2)

Lead me to the rock that is higher than I. Sometimes I forget that it is not all about me. In my busyness, I forget that I am not the only one on Planet Earth. I forget to go to the source of everything. I forget to go to the One who brought water from the rock. Lord, I am thirsty. Fill my cup.

Let them give thanks to the Lord for his unfailing love and his wonderful deeds for mankind, for he satisfies the thirsty and fills the hungry with good things. (Psalm 107:8-9) He is our Rock!

See, a king will reign in righteousness and rulers will rule with justice. Each one will be like a shelter from the wind and a refuge from the storm, like streams of water in the desert and the shadow of a great rock in a thirsty land. (Isaiah 32:1-2)

We live under the shadow of a great Rock. He is solid. He does not bend. He is a shelter from the storms of life. He is a stream of water in the desert.

He says, *"Whoever drinks the water I give them will never thirst. Indeed, the water I give them will become in them a spring of water welling up to eternal life." (John 4:14)*

And I echo the woman at the well, *"Sir, give me this water so that I won't get thirsty and have to keep coming here to draw water." (V 15)*

My question is, "What well are we drawing water from?" Are we tapping into the water of Life or into a muddy well of stale and stagnant man-made water?

"There is no rock like our God!"

THE JOY OF THE LORD IS MY STRENGTH

DAY 340

This day is holy to our Lord. Do not grieve, for the joy of the Lord is your strength. (Nehemiah 8:10)

In this time of aloneness, uncertainty, depression, fear, etc. we need to find strength. The Word tells us there is One who gives us strength even in the worst of times and that is the Lord.

What is joy? It is a feeling of great pleasure and happiness. It is delight, jubilation, triumph, exultation, rejoicing, happiness, exuberance, rapture, radiance, etc. Have you noticed how much better you feel when you have a really good belly laugh? I love to be around people who find humor in life. It is so rare these days. That is one of the reasons I love holidays. We play games and laugh and laugh. I always realize how revived I am after one of these evenings.

The Lord knew what He was saying when He admonished us to find joy in life. He says **in Psalm 5:11-12 But** *let all who take refuge in you be glad; let them ever sing for joy. Spread your protection over them, that those who love your name may rejoice in you.*

An attitude of gratitude is better than any medicine we can take. It is better than a visit to the doctor. It is better than a dump session. Believe me, it is time for us to begin finding joy in living. A quick glance at the mountains on a sunny day brings joy. A small child's hug brings joy. An unexpected phone call with an uplifting message brings joy. A plate of homemade cookies brings joy. You fill in the blank. What brings you joy? When you have made a list then respond to your list by doing unto others as you would have them do unto you.

I remember hearing about a man that was dying in the hospital, who decided to find ways to laugh. He got lots of old silly movies and began to watch them and laugh. Believe it or not he was healed.

"The Joy of the Lord was his strength!"

DAY 341

This day is holy to our Lord. Do not grieve, for the joy of the Lord is your strength. (**Nehemiah 8:10**)

The Book of Nehemiah was written to remind the people how God had brought them back to their land and had rebuilt the city and walls of Jerusalem. He had restored them, and their nation and they were rejoicing. Captivity was over and life would begin again. There was joy in the city.

Nehemiah and the Levites had read the whole book of the Law to the people. It says, *Ezra praised the Lord, the great God; and all the people lifted their hands and responded, "Amen! Amen"! Then they bowed down and worshiped the Lord with their faces to the ground.* (**V 6**)

V 11, *Then all the people went away to eat and drink, to send portions of food and to celebrate with great joy, because they now understood the words that had been made known to them.*

From the days of Joshua's son of Nun until that day, the Israelites had not celebrated it like this. And their joy was very great. (**V 17**)

I noticed two very important things in these passages. First, they were excited when the Word of God was read. They listened and they responded by lifting their hands, praising God and bowing down with their faces to the ground. The Word of God caused them to worship. Secondly, they shared their bounty with others. Both of these things gave them cause to be joyful. *And their joy was very great.*

The time in my life when I felt the most joy in the Lord was in the 1960's & 70's. The Spirit of God truly descended upon His people. Our praise and worship lifted the roof right off the place in which we were worshiping. As we sang in the Spirit heaven seemed to join us as a universal choir. I long for that to happen again!

"The Joy of the Lord was his strength!"

DAY 342

This day is holy to our Lord. Do not grieve, for the joy of the Lord is your strength. **(Nehemiah 8:10)**

In the Book of Esther there was also a time of great joy. Remember Haman and his plot to kill all the Jewish people, "but Esther". She had become King Xerxes wife. The most famous line in her life was, *And who knows but that you have come to your royal position for such a time as this…I will go to the king, even though it is against the law. And if I perish, I perish.* **(Esther 4:14 & 16)** We know what happened. Her people were spared.

For the Jews it was a time of happiness and joy, gladness, and honor. In every province and in every city to which the edict of the king came, there was joy and gladness among the Jews, with feasting and celebrating. **(Esther 8:16-17)**

Purim was established which was two days of feasting and celebrating, *When the Jews got relief from their enemies, and as the month when their sorrow was turned into joy and their mourning into a day of celebration.* **(Esther 9:22)**

On these days they were to feast and have joy. They were to give presents of food to one another and gifts to the poor. What better way to have joy then to give to one another.

And whatever you do, whether in word or deed, do it all in the name of the Lord Jesus, giving thanks to God the Father through him. **(Colossians 3:17)**

Whatever we do, do it with an open hand, expecting nothing in return.

Christmas has always been exciting to me. It was more fun when my grandkids were little because all they want now is money. But way back when, buying presents and wrapping them gave me great joy. Watching them unwrap gifts and their excitement, was more rewarding than anything given to me. There is great joy in giving.

"The Joy of the Lord is Our Strength!"

DAY 343

This day is holy to our Lord. Do not grieve, for the joy of the Lord is your strength. **(Nehemiah 8:10)**

The central theme of Chronicles is God's covenant with David as the basis of Israel's life and hope. We really don't know who wrote the Chronicles, but whoever it was knew God intimately. Traditionally he was thought to either be a priest or Levite in the temple.

Splendor and majesty are before him; strength and joy are in his dwelling place. Ascribe to the Lord, all you families of nations ascribe to the Lord glory and strength. **(1 Chronicles 16:27-28)**

Let the trees of the forest sing, let them sing for joy before the Lord, for he comes to judge the earth. Give thanks to the Lord, for he is good; his love endures forever. **(1 Chronicles 8:33-34)**

The people had celebrated the goodness of God for seven days, and they still could not get enough of His presence. So, they celebrated for seven more days. It says in **2 Chronicles 30:26-27**, *There was great joy in Jerusalem, for since the days of Solomon, son of King David of Israel there had been nothing like this in Jerusalem. The priests and the Levites stood to bless the people, and God heard them, for their prayer reached heaven, his holy dwelling place.*

Could this happen again today? Could it happen in our church? What if we spent seven days collectively praising God? When was the last time we really worshipped? When was the last time we submitted to God whole heartedly? Adversity either brings bitterness or betterness. Where are we?

We used to have women dancing in church, carrying banners that expressed who God is. We would watch them for a while and then begin to worship. It was beautiful. Our services were a constant reminder of the joy of the Lord.

"The Joy of the Lord was Our Strength!"

DAY 344

This day is holy to our Lord. Do not grieve, for the joy of the Lord is your strength. (**Nehemiah 8:10**)

The Lord was using Job to show Satan that a man of God can remain faithful even in times of extreme trial, trouble, and sorrow. God had confidence in Job and knew that in the end, Job would not waver.

Job 8:12 says, *He will yet fill your mouth with laughter and your lips with shouts of joy.* This was Bildad the Shuhite telling Job to get a grip on it, laugh it off. Don't you hate people like that. It isn't their problem, and they are not experiencing the pain. So, they give advice on things they haven't gone through.

Then there was Elihu who said, *Then that person can pray to God and find favor with him, they will see God's face and shout for joy; he will restore them to full well-being.* (**Job 33:26**)

We have all heard of Job's friends and said, "No thank you!" I agree but I am not sure their advice was that far off. It was just the wrong time and the wrong place. We need discernment to know when God is dealing with a person and when a person is having a pity party. They are two totally different things.

Job said to them, *Turn away from me so I can have a moment's joy.* (**Job 10:20**) His friends were dragging him down. But after God spoke Job understood and he finally said, *Surely, I spoke of things I did not understand, things too wonderful for me to know…My ears had heard of you but now my eyes have seen you.* (**Job 42:3 & 5**)

A woman came up to me in a meeting and said, "I have never liked you. Will you forgive me?" I honestly did not know why she didn't like me. Now I was in a position to forgive something I knew nothing about. So, I said yes. But I was left with a deep pain. Job said, *Turn away from me so I can have a moment's joy.*

"The Joy of the Lord was My Strength!"

DAY 345

This day is holy to our Lord. Do not grieve, for the joy of the Lord is your strength. **(Nehemiah 8:10)**

David was a man after God's own heart. Knowing David's history, he seemed to always be on the run. His enemies were pursuing him. He made some bad choices. For years he lived in the wilderness. Where did David find all this joy?

But let all who take refuge in you be glad; let them ever sing for joy. Spread your protection over them, that those who love your name may rejoice in you. **(Psalm 5:11)**

Joy is a choice. David learned this early while tending the sheep. He was surrounded by solitude and instead of feeling sorry for himself, he picked up his lyre and began to praise the Lord. This was a lifestyle for David.

You make known to me the path of life; you will fill me with joy in your presence, with eternal pleasures at your right hand. **(Psalm 16:11)**

He says You Lord fill me with joy. You Lord fill me with Your presence. You make known to me the path of life. David knew the Lord intimately. This is my desire!

Then David goes on to say, *The precepts of the Lord are right, giving joy to the heart. The commands of the Lord are radiant, giving light to the eyes. The fear of the Lord is pure, enduring forever.* **(Psalm 19:8-9)**

In this day and age, the one thing most of us are missing is the fear of the Lord. Do we even understand reverence?

Our youngest son is a man after God's own heart. He desires to walk close to the Lord and be obedient to His word. He spends time in the word and in prayer. He listens for the still small voice of God. His desire is to do the will of the Father. I wish there were more young men like him and I am grateful he is our son!

"The Joy of the Lord is Our Strength!"

DAY 346

This day is holy to our Lord. Do not grieve, for the joy of the Lord is your strength. **(Nehemiah 8:10)**

The Psalms are so rich with the goodness of God. Joy seems to be one of the main themes. There has got to be a reason for this. I believe the Lord wants us to be filled with joy as a means of surviving these times of trial and worry.

David says, *May we shout for joy over your victory and lift up our banners in the name of our God.* **(Psalm 20:5)** What is our victory? His name is Jesus. He has conquered death and hell. He is seated at the right hand of the Father making intercession for us. Now that is a reason to shout for joy!

Psalm 21:1 says, *The king rejoices in your strength, Lord. How great is his joy in the victories you give!* How great is his joy when we walk in it? Joy is another example of our faith in him. David says, *I will sacrifice with shouts of joy. I will sing and make music to the Lord.* **(Psalm 27:6)** When I think of a sacrifice, I think of something I do, not out of my plenty but out of my lack. I shout for joy when I don't feel like it. I shout for joy when I am sad. I shout for joy when I am lost. I shout for joy when I am hungry. You fill in the blank.........

The Lord is my strength and my shield; my heart trusts in him, and he helps me. My heart leaps for joy, and with my song I praise him. **(Psalm 28:7)** He says, *"You turn my wailing into dancing; you removed my sackcloth and clothed me with joy, that my heart may sing your praises and not be silent. Lord my God, I will praise you forever."* **(Psalm 30:11-12)**

Our oldest grandson stayed with us for a while when he was little. I still remember him in the bathroom singing at the top of his lungs, "How Great Thou Art! How Great Thou Art!" That was fine but we were in a restaurant, and he had to use the restroom. We could hear him clear in the dining area singing, "How Great Thou Art! How Great Thou Art!" Today he is a musician in L.A.

"The Joy of the Lord is Our Strength!"

DAY 347

This day is holy to our Lord. Do not grieve, for the joy of the Lord is your strength. **(Nehemiah 8:10)**

These things I remember as I pour out my soul; how I used to go to the house of God under the protection of the Mighty One with shouts of joy and praise! **(Psalm 42:4)**

I can really relate to this scripture. I used to go to the house of God. It seems like we have gotten use to watching sermons on T.V. and so comfortable in our own homes, that we have gotten out of the habit of actually going to church. I am guilty. What are we missing when we fall into this habit? "Fellowship" and we were meant to fellowship.

Then David goes on, *Why, my soul, are you downcast? Why so disturbed within me?* **(Psalm 42:5)** Could the answer be in the fact that we are not fellowshipping? "But you don't understand." Then we begin with all our reasons. Now I am not talking to you but to me. If this applies you take it to heart. Otherwise toss it out.

Then I will go to the altar of God, to God, my joy, and my delight. I will praise you with the lyre, O God, my God. **(Psalm 43:4)** Do you remember the old song, "Come home! Come home! All who are weary come home"? Do you think we need to take this to heart today?

Great is the Lord, and most worthy of praise, in the city of our God, his holy mountain. Beautiful in its loftiness, the joy of the whole earth, like the heights of Zaphon is Mount Zion, the city of the Great King. **(Psalm 48:1-2)**

I remember our oldest grandson coming out of the bathroom and using a Jim Carey line from a movie saying, "Puey! Do not go in there!" He was so funny. Do we sometimes feel the same way about going to church? We have a hundred reasons not to go and some of them are valid. But are we part of the puey or are we part of those edifying and uplifting the Body of Christ?

"The Joy of the Lord is Our Strength!"

DAY 348

This day is holy to our Lord. Do not grieve, for the joy of the Lord is your strength. **(Nehemiah 8:10)**

Create in me a pure heart, O God, and renew a steadfast spirit within me. Do not cast me from your presence or take your Holy Spirit from me. Restore to me the joy of your salvation and grant me a willing spirit, to sustain me. **(Psalm 51:10-12)**

Today Lord, I am praying that You will restore the joy of Your salvation in our hearts; that You will grant to us a willing spirit, to sustain us. Lord, we need You like never before. For many of us the well has run dry.

My lips will shout for joy when I sing praise to you - I whom you have delivered. My tongue will tell of your righteous acts all day long. **(Psalm 71:23-24)** David went from Psalm 71 to Psalm 81 before he mentioned joy again. I wonder what was going on in his life. Had he too lost his joy? But David never gave up.

Sing for joy to God our strength, shout aloud to the God of Jacob! Begin the music, strike the timbrel, play the melodious harp and lyre. **(Psalm 81:1-2)** David is back to shouts of joy. Regardless of the time or place there is always a reason to shout for joy, even if it is an act of sacrifice.

The final joy in **Psalms is 149:4-6 is *For the Lord takes delight in his people; he crowns the humble with victory. Let his faithful people rejoice in this honor and sing for joy on their beds. May the praise of God be in their mouths and a double-edged sword in their hands.***

I am feeling like my well has run dry. Maybe, I am taking too much time looking back and not enough time looking forward. The older we get it seems the more we think about what used to be. Today, Lord, help me to look forward to what lies ahead instead of the "Good Ole Days!" I wonder if they were really that good?

"The Joy of the Lord was his strength!"

DAY 349

This day is holy to our Lord. Do not grieve, for the joy of the Lord is your strength. (Nehemiah 8:10)

Solomon said, *"A wise son brings joy to his father, but a foolish son brings grief to his mother."* **(Proverbs 10:1)** I think that is an interesting statement. But the more I thought about it, the more I realized it is true. A mother will grieve for a wayward child. A father is proud of a son who carries on his name in a godly manner. There is joy in a household where children love the Lord.

Proverbs 12:20 says, *Deceit is in the hearts of those who plot evil, but those who promote peace have joy.* Have you noticed when you are angry there is no joy in your heart? But when you are a peacemaker, your heart seems to flood with joy.

Each heart knows its own bitterness, and no one else can share its joy. **(Proverbs 14:10)** Joy is a choice and there is no room for anger or bitterness in a joyful heart.

A person finds joy in giving an apt reply – and how good is a timely word! **(Proverbs 15:23)** I think I need to put this one on my refrigerator to remind me how important our words are and how uplifting it is to encourage or be encouraged by another.

Finally, *Be wise, my son (daughter), and bring joy to my heart; then I can answer anyone who treats me with contempt.* **(Proverbs 27:11)** When I feel good about myself, I can withstand all kinds of criticism. So, encourage those around you. Uplift the downtrodden. Find something good in every person and circumstance.

My mother was a joyful person. She always had something good to say about everyone and consequently, everyone liked her. She never met a stranger. Just before she breathed her last breath, she took my husband's hand and said, "You look so nice today." I wish I had been there to receive a blessing too!

"The Joy of the Lord is Our Strength!"

DAY 350

This day is holy to our Lord. Do not grieve, for the joy of the Lord is your strength. **(Nehemiah 8:10)**

The people walking in darkness have seen a great light; on those living in the land of deep darkness a light has dawned. You have enlarged the nation and increased their joy. **(Isaiah 9:3)**

David said, *You fill me with joy in your presence.* **(Acts 2:28)**

We are those who have walked in darkness but have now seen the light. We were once far from the Lord, but He has now drawn us close. We were lost, but now we have been found. We were dead in our sin, but now we have been set free by the blood of Jesus Christ. If this isn't a reason to rejoice and be filled with joy, then I don't know what is.

Isaiah 12:3 says, *With joy you will draw water from the wells of salvation.*

They will enter Zion with singing; everlasting joy will crown their heads. Gladness and joy will overtake them, and sorrow and sighing will flee away. **(Isaiah 35:10)** This verse is speaking of the redeemed. I know I have been redeemed by the blood of the Lamb. So, I too can enter Zion with singing and everlasting joy.

Shout for joy you heavens; rejoice, you earth; burst into song, you mountains! For the Lord comforts his people and will have compassion on his afflicted ones. **(Isaiah 49:13)** Let's just pretend we are at a ballgame and be as exuberant in our praise as we are sitting on a bleacher. For the joy of the Lord is our strength!

Our youngest son didn't have a lot of self-confidence when he was young. I still remember sitting in the stands at a baseball tournament. Our team was losing, and he hit a homerun. The stands went wild. That one hit gave him more confidence than anything we could have said or done. That's what joy does!

"The Joy of the Lord was his Strength!"

DAY 351

This day is holy to our Lord. Do not grieve, for the joy of the Lord is your strength.
(Nehemiah 8:10)

Then this city will bring me renown, joy, praise and honor before all nations on earth that hear of all the good things I do for it; and they will be in awe and will tremble at the abundant prosperity and peace I provide for it...there will be heard once more the sounds of joy and gladness, the voices of bride and bridegroom, and the voices of those who bring thank offerings to the house of the Lord, Give thanks to the Lord Almighty, for the Lord is good; his love endures forever. **(Jeremiah 33:9-11)** Jeremiah is known as the weeping prophet, but there is also hope in his message.

How often have we prayed, *If my people, who are called by my name, will humble themselves and pray and seek my face and turn from their wicked ways, then I will hear from heaven, and I will forgive their sin and I will heal their land.* **(2 Chronicles 7:14)**

Our nation is in desperate need of healing. We have forgotten "In God We Trust" and like the people in Jeremiah's day, turned from Him. "If it is to be, it is up to me" was on the doorway of our grade school for a long time. This has become the mindset of our country. We have failed to see the falsehood in this statement. Instead, we should declare, "If it is to be it is up to Thee oh Lord." Forgive us.

In our town we observe "Meet me at the flagpole" day. All the students gather outside around the flag, and we have a little celebration. We say the Pledge of Allegiance and sing a few American songs. We used to be so proud of our country. Today we are questioning everything we once stood for. Are all our founding fathers not what they seemed to be? Do we have any "Honest Abe's" left in our country? I hope so and I hope we still believe, "In God We Trust".

"The Joy of the Lord is Our Strength!"

DAY 352

This day is holy to our Lord. Do not grieve, for the joy of the Lord is your strength. **(Nehemiah 8:10)**

Matthew 13:20 says, *The seed falling on rocky ground refers to someone who hears the word and at once receives it with joy. But since they have no root, they last only a short time. When trouble or persecution comes because of the word, they quickly fall away.*

There are many kinds of joy, some are lasting, and others only endure for a moment. Why do some of us have joy? Let's study the seed falling on rocky ground, and I think we will have part of our answer. Since this seed has no root, it does not last. How does a plant get roots? First it is a seed. Then the farmer plants it, waters it and digs around it to keep the soil from becoming hard. The sun energizes it, and the rain nurtures it. As it grows it takes root. The deeper the root system, the more chance it has to survive. Now I am not a gardener, but I understand this principle.

Apply this to our lives and place joy as the seed. What we plant in our heart reaps a harvest. The more we meditate on good things, the stronger our root system becomes. When we turn negative into positive, we are on our way to joy!

Philippians 4:8 says, *Finally, brothers and sisters, whatever is true, whatever is noble, whatever is right, whatever is pure whatever is lovely, whatever is admirable – if anything is excellent or praiseworthy – think about such things.*

My husband loves the outdoors. He is a gardener at heart and the things he plants seem to grow. The minute spring comes, he is outside either sitting in a chair sunbathing, or working in the yard. When he was younger, he loved to hike in the mountains. He loves to sit on a log at the back of our six acres and meditate while our dog roams around. He believes the closer to nature we are, the closer to God we become. I can't argue with that.

"The Joy of the Lord is His Strength!"

DAY 353

This day is holy to our Lord. Do not grieve, for the joy of the Lord is your strength. (Nehemiah 8:10)

The kingdom of heaven is like treasure hidden in a field. When a man found it he hid it again, and then in his joy went and sold all he had and bought that field. (Matthew 13:44)

This man was sold out. He had found what he was looking for and was filled with joy. There is a principle involved in his joy. The word says, *And then in his joy went and sold all he had.* He was sold out. He was not a Sunday Christian or a holiday Christian. He was sold out. What does this mean to you? What does it mean to me?

If I go into the grocery store and they are out of milk, they are all sold out. There is nothing left. I can grumble and complain, but that will not change the situation. They are all sold out! Now put this thought into the positive. When we are all sold out to the Lord our lives definitely change. Our thoughts are centered on Him. Our actions are a reflection of who He is. Our daily activities include Him. Our workplace is a place of peace and harmony. He becomes the center of everything we do and say. We are all sold out!

But you are a chosen people, a royal priesthood, a holy nation, God's special possession, that you may declare the praises of him who called you out of darkness into his wonderful light. (1 Peter 2:9)

My youngest son desires to be sold out to the Lord, but he has a young family with lots of wants and needs. He has a big home. He has nice cars. He lives in a great neighborhood. He has everything that he wants. Yet he asks, "How can I really be sold out?" Does it require poverty to follow the Lord? I don't think so. I think it only requires an open hand.

"The Joy of the Lord is His Strength!"

DAY 354

This day is holy to our Lord. Do not grieve, for the joy of the Lord is your strength. **(Nehemiah 8:10)**

He has risen from the dead and is going ahead of you into Galilee. There you will see him. Now I have told you. So, the women hurried away from the tomb, afraid yet filled with joy, and ran to tell his disciples. Suddenly Jesus met them. **(Matthew 28:7-9)**

It is amazing that it was women who truly believed. They were the ones waiting for Him. They were the ones ministering to Him. So, it is only natural that they were filled with joy at seeing Him first.

I love the part that says, *Suddenly Jesus met them.* When we live with great expectation, we can expect to see Him.

Paul wrote in **Romans 8:18, *I consider that our present sufferings are not worth comparing with the glory that will be revealed in us. For the creation waits in eager expectation for the children of God to be revealed.***

Everything in nature is waiting with eager expectation for Jesus to be revealed in us. Not only can we experience joy, but so does everything in creation. Can't you just see the angels standing by the Father cheering us on? They want us to succeed just as much as the Father does. It gives Him and them great joy when one of the lost is found.

Though you have not seen him, you love him; and even though you do not see him now, you believe in him and are filled with an inexpressible and glorious joy, for you are receiving the end result of your faith, the salvation of your soul. **(1 Peter 1:8)**

I have always felt that women were overlooked in the church. We are good in the nursery, but not in the pulpit. Now I ask you, if we can teach the children who grow up to be the men in the church, why does our responsibility stop there?

"The Joy of the Lord is Our Strength!"

DAY 355

This day is holy to our Lord. Do not grieve, for the joy of the Lord is your strength. (Nehemiah 8:10)

Then the angel of the Lord appeared to him…" Do not be afraid, Zechariah; your prayer has been heard. Your wife Elizabeth will bear you a son, and you are to call him John. He will be a joy and delight to you, and many will rejoice because of his birth, for he will be great in the sight of the Lord." (Luke 1:13-14)

Have you ever considered the fact that some of us are forerunners? We are not the main show. We have been assigned the task of preparing a person's heart so that someone else can come in and finish the task. So many times, I have felt guilty because I was not the one to lead a person to Christ. But who can say? Maybe I was a forerunner.

John 4:37-38 says, *Thus the saying "One sows, and another reaps" is true. I sent you to reap what you have not worked for. Others have done the hard work, and you have reaped the benefits of their labor.*

All glory for another lost soul coming into the kingdom needs to go to the Lord of the Harvest. He is truly the one who plants the seed in the first place.

I love this scripture, *This is what the Lord says: "Restrain your voice from weeping and your eyes from tears, for your work will be rewarded," declares the Lord. "They will return from the land of the enemy. So, there is hope for your descendants," declares the Lord. "Your children will return to their own land."* **(Jeremiah 31:16)**

I have friends and family members who are not yet saved. I am beginning to see that without meaning to, I am being judgmental. It is "my way or the highway". The only requirement for salvation is faith in Jesus Christ. Everything else will come as we walk. My children are still recovering from some of the hell and damnation they were exposed to as children. Salvation should not come by way of fear but by love.

"The Joy of the Lord is Our Strength!"

DAY 356

This day is holy to our Lord. Do not grieve, for the joy of the Lord is your strength.
(Nehemiah 8:10)

Elizabeth said, *"As soon as the sound of your greeting reached my ears, the baby in my womb leaped for joy. Blessed is she who has believed that the Lord would fulfill his promises to her."* **(Luke 1:44)**

As we hear the word of the Lord, I wonder if we leap for joy? Is the word of God something we treasure in our hearts, or is it just a book of remembrance? Do we believe it is the living word of the living Lord?

So many times, I have had a need, picked up the Bible, and soon had my answer. The word of God speaks to us in a variety of ways, but nevertheless, it speaks if we have ears to hear. It is interesting that we can read the same passage ten different times and it will speak something different to us each time.

It is written: "Man shall not live on bread alone, but on every word that comes from the mouth of God." **(Matthew 4:4)**

When Elizabeth heard the sound of Mary's voice, the baby in her womb leaped for joy. Was the Son of God growing within Mary inspiring her to speak?

Hebrews 4:12 says, *For the word of God is alive and active. Sharper than any double-edged sword, it penetrates even to dividing soul and spirit, joints, and marrow; it judges the thoughts and attitudes of the heart.*

Never minimize what the word of God can do in your life, and as Elizabeth felt joy leap within her, so should we as we meditate on the things that God has told us and is still telling us through his word.

Our oldest son was entering rehab for the 6th or 7th time. We were on an airplane heading home from California. I was totally undone. If I had been alone, I would have totally broken down. I was at the very end of the end. A lady at the airport handed me a cross. As I grasp it the Lord said, "Let go!" and I have!

"The Joy of the Lord is His Strength!"

DAY 357

This day is holy to our Lord. Do not grieve, for the joy of the Lord is your strength. (**Nehemiah 8:10**)

Blessed are you when people hate you, when they exclude you and insult you and reject your name as evil, because of the Son of Man. Rejoice in that day and leap for joy, because great is your reward in heaven. (**Luke 6:22-23**)

Sometimes I feel like a man without a country. I feel misunderstood. I feel rejected and excluded. I am hearing the beat of a different drummer and people don't understand. Frankly, sometimes neither do I. Has this ever happened to you? I have reacted in many different ways over the years. Sometimes I have argued. Sometimes I have stopped to listen to their argument. Sometimes I have just turned and walked away. But the one thing I have learned is not to react in an offensive way because this just reinforces their views.

Have you ever had someone say, "Well if you were really a Christian you would not be doing this or that?" I am not a full-grown Christian. I am still in boot camp and there are times when I really blunder, but I am thankful for the blood of Jesus which cleanses me from all my sins.

But to you who are listening I say: Love your enemies, do good to those who hate you, bless those who curse you, pray for those who mistreat you. If someone slaps you on one cheek, turn to them the other also. If someone takes your coat, do not withhold your shirt from them. Give to everyone who asks you, and if anyone takes what belongs to you, do not demand it back. Do to others as you would have them do to you. (**Luke 6:27-31**)

Now you know why I am still in boot camp. I am so glad the Lord does not give up on us. He has been where we are and knows how difficult it is to turn the other cheek. He knows how much it hurts when we see loved ones rejecting Him. There are so many things I need to undo or unsay. I wish I could start all over. Have you ever felt like that?

"The Joy of the Lord was his strength!"

DAY 358

This day is holy to our Lord. Do not grieve, for the joy of the Lord is your strength. (**Nehemiah 8:10**)

The seventy-two returned with joy and said, "Lord, even the demons submit to us in your name" …However, do not rejoice that the spirits submit to you, but rejoice that your names are written in heaven. (**Luke 10:17 & 20**)

At times, we are so clued into what we have done in the name of the Lord, that we lose sight of the real author and finisher of our faith. It is very difficult for a popular pastor or evangelist to remain humble. Somewhere along the way self enters in and the struggle begins. People begin to look at the person rather than looking at him or her as the conduit through which the Holy Spirit operates. Satan is having a hay day. He begins to turn up the fire and look for a crack in this person's armor and usually will find one. We wonder why this or that evangelist fell, and we are critical. My question is, "Have you ever walked in that person's shoes?" Think of how many times in your life someone has given you a compliment that went straight to your head.

Be alert and of sober mind. Your enemy the devil prowls around like a roaring lion looking for someone to devour. Resist him, standing firm in the faith, because you know that the family of believers throughout the world is undergoing the same kind of sufferings. (**1 Peter 5:8**)

We should not worship the things created, but the creator who made heaven and earth and all those things in it. We need to lift up those in authority over us, but not worship them. They too are but men.

I had just given a talk on the Tabernacle to a group of women. I had spoken too long because there was so much to cover in such a short amount of time. As I put on my coat and prepared to leave, one of the women said, "There is no way we could begin to grasp all that you said. Next time make it shorter." If there were any pride in that talk it was deflated at that moment.

"The Joy of the Lord was his strength!"

DAY 359

This day is holy to our Lord. Do not grieve, for the Joy of the Lord is your strength!
(Nehemiah 8:10)

While he was blessing them, he left them and was taken up into heaven. Then they worshiped him and returned to Jerusalem with great joy. **(Luke 24:51-52)**

Jesus physical presence was leaving this earth. Those who had waited for Him watched as He ascended and were filled with joy. They would not see Him again until they joined Him in heaven. Still, they were filled with joy.

As we witness someone we love leave this earthly body and ascend to heaven, we also can be filled with joy if that person has known the Lord. We do not minimize our loss, but in the midst of our heartache, we can somehow turn our mourning into joy. What we have lost, the Father has gained.

Then he said to Thomas, "Put your finger here; see my hands. Reach out your hand and put it into my side. Stop doubting and believe." **(John 20:27)**

Jesus is trying to show Thomas what is and what is to come. We all have our moments of doubt. If we didn't, we wouldn't be human, but there comes a time in each of our lives when we have to settle the issue, "Is Jesus who he says He is, and can we trust Him with our lives?"

Then Jesus told him, **"Because you have seen me, you have believed; blessed are those who have not seen and yet believed."** (John 20:29)

We are part of the group Jesus is speaking about. Our seeing has come by faith. *And without faith it is impossible to please God because anyone who comes to him must believe that he exists and that he rewards those who earnestly seek him.* **(Hebrews 11:6)**

When my mother died, I was in church. I knew she wasn't doing very well but I honestly could not stand to watch her suffer. I have regretted that choice ever since. The Lord gave me this scripture. *Weeping may tarry for the night, but joy comes with the morning.* **(Psalm 30:5)** Still that did not excuse my absence.

"The Joy of the Lord was his strength!"

DAY 360

This day is holy to our Lord. Do not grieve, for the joy of the Lord is your strength! **(Nehemiah 8:10)**

After they (Paul and Silas) had been severely flogged, they were thrown into prison, and the jailer was commanded to guard them carefully. **(Acts 16:23)**

Can you imagine how they physically felt? They were in an inner cell and their feet were fastened in the stocks

About midnight Paul and Silas were praying and singing hymns to God, and the other prisoners were listening to them. **(V 25)**

"About midnight" the darkest time of night, deliverance came. Don't give up when it seems all is lost. Hang in there and see what God will do!

Suddenly there was such a violent earthquake that the foundations of the prison were shaken. At once all the prison doors flew open, and everyone's chains came loose. **(V 26)**

The jailer knew if he didn't kill himself the magistrates would, because all these prisoners were now free.

Paul shouted, "Don't harm yourself! We are all here!" **(V 28)** That in itself, was a miracle. I wonder if there were changes in the other prisoners that day?

Then the jailer asked, *"What must I do to be saved?" They replied, "Believe in the Lord Jesus, and you will be saved – you and your household."* **(V 30)**

He (the jailer) was filled with joy because he had come to believe. **(V 34)**

Someone is watching you. It may be one of your kids. It may be someone at school. Believe me, you are an open book. I remember a pastor lived by us. One day he was painting a wall. His daughter and I were good friends, and had just come into the house, when he cut loose with a swear word. I never forgot. Of course, I have never said a bad word in my whole life! I wish this were true.

"The Joy of the Lord is Our Strength!"

DAY 361

This day is holy to our Lord. Do not grieve, for the joy of the Lord is your strength! (Nehemiah 8:10)

For the kingdom of God is not a matter of eating and drinking, but of righteousness, peace, and joy in the Holy Spirit, because anyone who serves Christ in this way is pleasing to God and receives human approval. (Romans 14:17-18)

God is pleased when we walk in righteous, peace, and joy. But I have always skipped over the rest of the verse which says and *receives human approval.* We have a cloud of witnesses in heaven watching us, but I think this means people are also watching and approve when we walk in the Spirit.

Romans 15:13 says, *May the God of hope fill you with all joy and peace as you trust in him, so that you may overflow with hope by the power of the Holy Spirit.*

The Father wants us to be filled with joy, and peace at all times. Do you think this is possible? We know that the key to success lies in the Holy Spirit. He is here to lead us and guide us into all truth. We know that apart from the Holy Spirit, we have no power. He is our comforter, our advocate, our intercessor, etc.

It seems to me the Holy Spirit is the key to a successful Christian life.

But the fruit of the Spirit is love, joy, peace, forbearance, kindness, goodness, faithfulness, and self-control. Against such things there is no law. Those who belong to Christ Jesus have crucified the flesh with its passions and desires. Since we live by the Spirit, let us keep in step with the Spirit. (Galatians 5:22-25)

The fruit comes from the root. If we are rooted and grounded in Christ Jesus and led by the Holy Spirit, we will be filled with joy.

When I was first filled with the Holy Spirit, I was a crazy woman. I went around singing, shouting and praising God. I remember being in McDonald's one evening with my Spirit-filled friends, overflowing with joy. In our exuberance, we were obnoxious. To those around who didn't understand our joy, we were making a scene. That did not edify the Father.

"The Joy of the Lord is Our Strength!"

DAY 362

This day is holy to our Lord. Do not grieve, for the joy of the Lord is your strength! (Nehemiah 8:10)

Therefore, if you have any encouragement from being united with Christ, if any comfort from his love, if any common sharing in the Spirit, if any tenderness and compassion, then make my joy complete by being like-minded, having the same love, being one in spirit and of one mind. (**Philippians 2:1-2**)

As Paul said, *Make my joy complete by being like-minded, having the same love, being one in spirit and of one mind.*

I pray constantly for my family. I know some are still young and trying out the world and things of the world. However, I would wager to say that most of us came to a saving faith by the influence of someone other than a family member. Keep this in mind the next time you feel lost not knowing quite what to say.

This is what the Lord says: "Restrain your voice from weeping and your eyes from tears, for your work will be rewarded," declares the Lord. "They will return from the land of the enemy. So, there is hope for your descendants," declares the Lord. "Your children will return to their own land." (Jeremiah 31:16-17)

Be encouraged today. We have both a hope and a promise. *He who is the Glory of Israel does not lie or change his mind; for he is not a human being, that he should change his mind.* (**1 Samuel 15:29**)

As we pray for our family and our friends, be confident that God hears our prayers and is in the process of answering them. Even though we know there is battle going on in the heavens, we can rest assured we know the winner.

One of my granddaughters goes to Cornell. If she has any thought of becoming a Christian, that thought is in the distant future. All her friends think Christianity is silly. She is caught in the middle of this. I understand why she doesn't believe now. But I pray, without ceasing, that one day she will be surrounded by Christian friends. Do any of you have this same problem?

"The Joy of the Lord is Our Strength!"

DAY 363

This day is holy to our Lord. Do not grieve, for the joy of the Lord is your strength!
(Nehemiah 8:10)

For what is our hope, our joy, or the crown in which we will glory in the presence
of our Lord Jesus when he comes? Is it not you? Indeed, you are our glory and joy.
(1 Thessalonians 2:19-20)

Every time we either bring a person to Christ or watch as another person does, we should be filled with joy. The word says there is joy in heaven over one lost sinner coming to Christ. Our joy should equal the joy in heaven.

One of the most important assignments we have on earth is to lead others to Christ and then to mentor them. Thankfully, we each have different gifts and callings, and we have the Holy Spirit who leads us and guides us as we walk along-side another.

We wouldn't hand one of our children a manual on driving and then expect him to get in the car and drive away. We would take him out to a desolate place and instruct him. It is the same with new Christians. They not only need the manual, but they need one on one instruction and lots of love and forgiveness. Remember when you first came to Christ and some of the dumb things you did? I do!

We are instruments in the Lord's hands. There is nothing we can do to lead another to Christ, apart from the Holy Spirit. But our obedience can certainly speed up the process. When we feel a prompting from the Holy Spirit to share with another, our job is to share without delay. The Holy Spirit will give us the right words to say. We just need to be obedient.

The man was in the hospital dying. He was restrained because he kept seeing what I call hell. As I shared the gospel with him, he settled down. He opened his eyes and said, "I want to be saved." I led him in the sinner's prayer. He said, "I want to be baptized." I dumped the pitcher of water on the nightstand on his head and he was baptized in the name of the Father, the Son, and the Holy Spirit. He was filled with joy!

"The Joy of the Lord was His Strength!"

DAY 364

This day is holy to our Lord. Do not grieve, for the joy of the Lord is your strength! (**Nehemiah 8:10**)

Therefore, since we are surrounded by such a great cloud of witnesses, let us throw off everything that hinders and the sin that so easily entangles. And let us run with perseverance the race marked out for us, fixing our eyes on Jesus, the pioneer and perfecter of faith. For the joy set before him he endured the cross, scorning its shame, and sat down at the right hand of the throne of God. Consider him who endured such opposition from sinners, so that you will not grow weary and lose heart. (**Hebrews 12:1-3**)

Do you not know that in a race all the runners run, but only one gets the prize? Run in such a way as to get the prize. (**1 Corinthians 9:24**)

We are to throw off everything that hinders and the sin that so easily entangles.

It is like taking out the trash. Once it is in the container and on the side of the road, our job is done. The trash truck comes and hauls it away. As we throw off everything that is hindering us, the Holy Spirit takes those things and dumps them in the sea of forgetfulness. Hallelujah!

But one thing I do: Forgetting what is behind and straining toward what is ahead, I press on toward the goal to win the prize for which God has called me heavenward in Christ Jesus. (**Philippians 3:13-14**)

As a child I remember my grandmother saying, "God is watching you!" I don't believe this was a positive comment. But we are surrounded by a great cloud of witnesses, who are cheering us on. As long as we fix our eyes on Jesus, we will win the race. The word that stands out to me in this scripture is endure. Jesus had to endure the cross, scorning its shame. Can we expect any less in our Christian walk? As grandma said, "God is watching you!" Let's turn this into a positive statement. "God is watching you because He loves you!"

"The Joy of the Lord is Our Strength!"

DAY 365

This day is holy to our Lord. Do not grieve, for the joy of the Lord is your strength! (Nehemiah 8:10)

Though you have not seen him, you love him; and even though you do not see him now, you believe in him and are filled with an inexpressible and glorious joy, for you are receiving the end result of your faith the salvation of your souls. (1 Peter 1:8)

Praise be to the God and Father of our Lord Jesus Christ! In his great mercy he has given us new birth into a living hope through the resurrection of Jesus Christ from the dead, and into an inheritance that can never perish, spoil, or fade. (1 Peter 1:3-4)

As you come to him, the living Stone -- rejected by humans but chosen by God and precious to him – you also, like living stones, are being built into a spiritual house to be a holy priesthood, offering spiritual sacrifices acceptable to God through Jesus Christ. For in Scripture, it says: "See, I lay a stone in Zion, a chosen and precious cornerstone, and the one who trusts in him will never be put to shame." (1 Peter 2:4-8)

We have spent three hundred and sixty-five days in the Word of God. I hope you have enjoyed this study as much as I have. I pray that your faith will daily increase and that you will turn to the Lord as the author and finisher of everything that you do in life. My blessings go with you.

To him who is able to keep you from stumbling and to present you before his glorious presence without fault and with great joy – to the only God our Savior be glory, majesty, power and authority, through Jesus Christ our Lord, before all ages, now and forevermore! Amen. (Jude 24-25)

Life is short. Enjoy every moment that you can. Look up to the mountains, look out on the ocean. Look down in the valleys and see the wonders God has created just for you.

"Remember, The Joy of the Lord is Our Strength!"

Special Thanks

When Covid first confined us to our homes, I felt the Lord asking me to write a daily thought each morning and send it to family and friends as a means of encouragement. I had no intention of doing anything but putting on paper what my heart was saying and then deleting it. One year later I am ready to put it into a devotional called, "Morning's with Mom". Isn't God awesome!

This Bible Study would never have been put into print had my oldest son Mike not called, saying he felt God was asking him to take my morning thoughts and make them into a devotional. He not only encouraged me but also provided the means for this to happen. A great big thank you Mike!

I also owe a huge thank you to my dear friend Emily Fevinger who spent hours going over every page to correct all the mistakes I made. Thank you, Emily. I also want to thank everyone who prayed and encouraged me during the writing process. I never would have made it without you.

Finally, I want to thank my husband who has put up with me for the past 61 years. That in itself, is a miracle!

I will sing of your strength, in the morning I will sing of your love; for you are my fortress, my refuge in times of trouble. You are my strength, I sing praise to you; you, God are my fortress, my God on whom I can rely. (Psalm 59:16)